A LOOK AT

TENNESSEE WILLIAMS

STEEN, Mike. A look at Tennessee Williams. Hawthorn, 1969. 318p
il 70-85432. 6.95

CHOICE   NOV. '70

Speech, Theater & Dance

While occasionally interesting, this informal series of interviews con-
ducted by Steen with some friends and associates of Williams is less
rewarding than one would expect upon reading the names of those
being interviewed: Paul Bowles, Hume Cronyn, Karl Malden, Eli
Wallach, Geraldine Page, Mildred Dunnock, Estelle Parsons, and 16
others. While Steen admits to a "one-sided" look at Williams, the
reader may be surprised at the genuinely uncritical impressions presented. And ultimately, the book reveals more about the interviewer
and the interviewed than it does about Williams. The failure of this
book is not, however, the fault of the casual approach, which should,
in fact, provide many interesting and valid insights to Williams and his
work. The book fails to add substantially to our knowledge of Williams largely because of the over-anxiousness of the participants to
prove their own cordial relations with the playwright. There is
throughout the book an impressive superficiality, and only in a few
cases is there anything which could be called objectivity. The evasive-
ness and lack of honesty therefore severely limit the book's potential.
It is refreshing, however, to find people publicly saying that Williams
is still America's greatest playwright, and to find champions of two of

Continued

STEEN

CHOICE   NOV. '70

Speech, Theater & Dance

his most underrated plays, *Camino Real* (1953) and *The milk train
doesn't stop here anymore* (CHOICE, May 1965). These endorsements,
from people who have worked intimately with many of our major plays,
may signal a badly needed reevaluation of Williams.

A LOOK AT

TENNESSEE WILLIAMS

by MIKE STEEN

Hawthorn Books, Inc., Publishers
New York

A LOOK AT TENNESSEE WILLIAMS

1 2 3 4 5 6 7 8 9 10

To my sister, Dorothy

Tennessee Williams at his house in Key West, Florida. 1967. (*Photo by the author*)

Tennessee Williams. 1961.
(*Photo courtesy
Friedman-Abeles*)

PREFACE

This book is not a biography of Tennessee Williams. Several years ago Tennessee told me that he hoped no one would write his biography until after his death. Tennessee rightly wondered how anyone's life story could be written when his life was not yet completed.

This book is a one-sided look at Tennessee Williams. It is an honest look, but a far from complete look.

How does one write an informative and interesting book about a beloved friend without betraying the friendship? I can only say that Tennessee is such a multicolored personality that there is enough about him to discuss without bringing in adverse material. The contributors and I are all fond of the man. We think there are more things about him to admire and like than to criticize and dislike. It is usually the positive side of a person that makes anyone else want to spend time with him, and in this book we want you to enjoy our happier memories of Tennessee.

The contributors are all people who have known Tennessee socially or professionally or both. They are his contemporaries, who can give their firsthand insight into the brighter side of his personality and at the same time give some of their views on his work and the theatre in general. They are celebrities who themselves are interesting to hear talk about how their lives have come into contact with the fascinating life of Tennessee Williams. And as their relationships vary with Tennessee, so do my relationships vary with them. Some, like William Inge and Shelley Winters, I know well, and therefore their interviews may be more conversational. Others, like Deborah Kerr and Hume Cronyn, I met for the first time, and their interviews might come off more formal. But every person I spoke with made me feel comfortable and welcome at his home, apartment, or office. We had a mutual knowledge of and respect for Tennessee to bring us together.

All of these interviews, except the one with Hal Wallis, were made with a tape recorder and were unrehearsed. I have done as little editing as possible in order to preserve the natural, unplanned, and conversational quality of each tape.

Mike Steen
Silverlake
Los Angeles, California

Grateful acknowledgment to
    Arthur S. T. O'Keefe
    Doris Keibel
    Rupert Allan
    Madge Mahan
    Mark Fabian
    Ruth Burch
    Shirley Norman
    William S. Gray
    George Raffalovich
    Lawson E. Sanderson
    The Los Angeles Public Library
    The Academy of Motion Picture Arts and Sciences
        Library
    The Ouachita Parish Public Library, Monroe, Louisiana
And, of course, to the twenty-four artists
whose interviews made this book possible

CONTENTS

INTRODUCTION
TO AN INDIVIDUAL

by William S. Gray, Ph.D.
Professor of English, Randolph-Macon College

Meeting and knowing are two different things. I first met Thomas Lanier Williams, professionally known as Tennessee Williams, in New York at a party in the Plaza Hotel in 1948. At that casual meeting he struck me as an agreeable and pleasant person. A few years later, in 1952, when I was a graduate student at Tulane University, in New Orleans, I met him again. Quite early one Sunday morning during a rainstorm, I dashed inside a newsstand and he looked up at me and said, "Hello, what are you doing here?"

And from there we went to friendship. A great part of that friendship was due to Mike Steen, my roommate in college and afterward in New Orleans and New York. Mike had always been interested in the theatre. Because of this, and because of their mutual sensitivity to the needs of other people, I wanted Mike and Tennessee to know one another. I knew that they would respond and relate to one another, and I was not wrong. I introduced them, that summer in New Orleans, and the three of us had great fun together— early afternoons swimming at Pontchartrain Beach, late afternoons having long conversations over a cool drink on a

Tennessee Williams with the author in Key West. November, 1967.

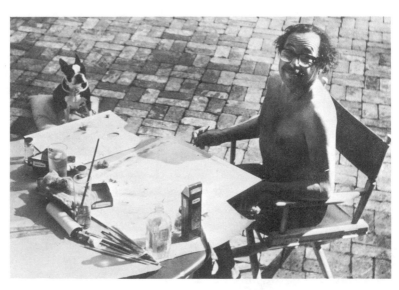

Tennessee Williams in Hermit's Glen, Hollywood, painting his dog Gigi's portrait. October, 1968. (*Photo by the author*)

patio, evenings eating at some fine French Quarter restaurant, then walking around the colorful streets of the Quarter. These are among the happiest memories of my life.

Tennessee likes to eat, especially chili, more con brio than con carne, and he eats with gusto, the way food should be eaten.

He also likes to drink—vodka in the morning, scotch in the afternoon, champagne with dinner. Drinking seems to relax him and make him just a little bit happier.

Tennessee is one of the most observant people I have known. When you think he is not watching you is when he is. I remember playing a game with him once. We were in my apartment in New York and had been discussing sensitivity to environment. I asked Tennessee to close his eyes and describe the room he was in. He did this with amazing accuracy. I then asked him to describe how I was dressed. He missed only the color of my tie.

As one would expect, Tennessee's ear is faultless. He is capable of repeating a conversation verbatim, playing all of the parts, but when he mimics, it is always in a kind way, never cruel, making the persons sound better than they actually do, the way that they truly would like to sound.

What I have enjoyed best with Tennessee is talking with him. We usually talked about what I wanted to talk about. Alas, it was I who did most of the talking—what we all like best. But when I would falter, need a thought, or even a word, he would provide it, so charmingly and so graciously that I was hardly ever aware of it. The talk was best because now, years later, it all comes back to me, just as he said it, and in his manner of speaking. There is no way that I know to describe Tennessee's voice. I have never heard anyone's voice who reminded me of his.

We read together a great deal. He read aloud from Hart Crane, Federico García Lorca, D. H. Lawrence, Anton Chekhov, and especially Charlotte Mew. We used to cry over her poem "Madeline in Church."

Tennessee, like Mike Steen, always wants and expects his friends to know and like one another. Tennessee introduced me to William Inge, Carson McCullers, Truman Capote, Gore Vidal, Anna Magnani, Tallulah Bankhead, and so very many other people who have enriched my life, just as because of Mike I have come to know and admire such people as Anaïs Nin and Christopher Isherwood.

Many plays, people, and places have come between Tennessee and me and yet I know that a firm bridge is still there.

What can I say, briefly and truthfully? Tennessee Williams is the most sensitive (*A Streetcar Named Desire*) and the most perceptive (*Camino Real*) playwright that we have ever had in this country. Tennessee has certainly confirmed his rank among the great playwrights of the world. But, of course, the history of American literature in the twentieth century has yet to be written, and Tennessee continues to write each and every day.

In addition to this, Tennessee always has remained an extraordinary personality. I should think that no friend really knows him better than Mike Steen, who consequently is able to increase our knowledge of Tennessee through conversations with celebrated people who have known him personally and professionally. I am grateful for a book like this—an insight into genius.

Ashland, Virginia
February 16, 1969

A LOOK AT
TENNESSEE WILLIAMS

KARL MALDEN

Karl Malden was the first person I interviewed for this book, which makes him the first person I ever interviewed. On my arrival at his home in Mandeville Canyon, I was slightly nervous. He greeted me politely at the front door and led me upstairs to his study. I immediately got the impression that he was a warm person, eager to be helpful. He had a sincere, boyish enthusiasm. However, I still was not completely relaxed during the first few minutes. Then the telephone rang. A friend was calling to invite him to participate in one of the Big Brother organizations, an obligation which requires the volunteer to assume the role of chum, adviser, and counselor to some young boy from a broken home. Karl Malden willingly and wholeheartedly agreed to take on the responsibility. My admiration for his attitude enabled me to feel at ease during the remainder of my visit.

Karl Malden created the role of Mitch in A Streetcar Named Desire *on Broadway. He repeated the role in the film of this prize-winning play and received an Academy Award as Best Supporting Actor.*

His performance later in Tennessee's film Baby Doll, *also directed by Elia Kazan, was equally outstanding.*

As I switched on my tape recorder, I asked him when he had last seen Tennessee.

Carroll Baker, Eli Wallach, and Karl Malden in the film *Baby Doll*. 1955.

Elia Kazan directing Karl Malden and Vivien Leigh in the movie production of *A Streetcar Named Desire*. 1951.

MALDEN: It was about six years ago, between six and seven years ago. I was on my way to London. I spent a week in New York and Kazan—Gadge—invited me to come to dinner, and when I arrived there, Tennessee was also invited for dinner and we had a wonderful dinner at the house, a lot of reminiscing. I think I hadn't seen Tennessee in at least ten years and so we did an awful lot of talking. Finally —the entertainment for the evening Kazan brought out his sixteen-millimeter print of *Baby Doll,* and he started to run it off. I hadn't seen it in a number of years. I have always enjoyed the picture. I thought it was one of Kazan's best pictures.

MIKE: Were you the only member of the cast there?

MALDEN: Yes, I was. Eli Wallach wasn't there, neither was Carroll Baker, or Lonny Chapman, or Millie Dunnock, and the thing I want to say about it is that we all sat there as though we were looking at it for the first time, laughing at it, and the one who enjoyed it more than anyone was Tennessee—he really enjoyed it! He thought it was the craziest thing he ever saw and he enjoyed it and he made comments about it.

MIKE: Giggled a lot, I bet.

MALDEN: What's that?

MIKE: That special giggle that he has.

MALDEN: That's right. "Yeeee," that little high kind of giggle that he has which is quite fascinating, and that cigarette, you know, he holds that cigarette in the holder—and he really enjoyed the evening, and then when it was over he said, "Doggone it, Gadge," he said, "I remember when you brought me down there." And he did bring him down to Mississippi, where we made the picture, to work on the ending. The ending was never kind of solved because, as you know, *Baby Doll* is two of his one-act plays, really, it's *27 Wagons Full of Cotton* and *The Unsatisfactory Supper*—it was never resolved because the characters were the same and yet—a little—Tennessee was there for, oh, I think three or four weeks, working on the last twenty pages of the script, and every day he'd come in with something new and Kazan would read it and say, "You can do better than that, Tenn," and Tenn would kind of giggle and say, "Well, you know, Gadge, I think that's good," and then he would walk off. And we would shoot during the day. Tenn would be at the hotel, and in the evening he would come back. I was fortunate, because of Kazan, to be around at that time, and Gadge would read it, and I would read it, and I would say, "Gee, that's pretty good," and Gadge would say, "Oh, I don't know," and go back to Tennessee and say, "Tennessee, stay another day and write another version, will you?" And that is the way it went on. It finally ended up where, I think, Gadge had about six different versions or six different endings and we shot a combination of six different kinds of endings to make the ending of the picture. But Tennessee did say, "You know, Gadge, you know we really never did solve the ending, did we?" He knew himself that the ending was never really solved.

MIKE: That happens in a lot of his plays.

MALDEN: That's right.

MIKE: I think, in a way, he doesn't really want them solved sometimes, as if they could continue and—and leave the audience thinking what could happen next, you know.

MALDEN: You know, I think that's true.

MIKE: Even in *Streetcar*, the ending was changed for the film from the play.

MALDEN: That's right, a little bit.

MIKE: So you weren't absolutely sure if Stella was going back inside to Stanley.

MALDEN: Or whether they were really going to take Blanche away, or whether she was just getting rid of this time of her life and going into something else.

MIKE: Yes.

MALDEN: That's true. You know, I'm guessing about this, but I wonder whether this is Tennessee's great—what's the word I'm looking for?—not *inspiration*—but great *talent* in that he always will write something—I'm guessing at this a little now—he will always write something, come to the conclusion and give it an ending, and see it end that way, and then say to himself, "What happens if it ends this other way?" Or "What happens if it ends this third way?" And as an artist I think he likes to see those different endings attached to the people that he has written up to a point.

MIKE: I think that is a perfect analysis of it. It's as if he doesn't want anything to end because he doesn't want life to end.

MALDEN: I don't think Tennessee wants to end! I think Tennessee would like to go on and on and on. And if anyone deserves to go on, I think Tennessee should, because I think—we have many great playwrights—but I think Tennessee is the most prolific and the most "honest-to-himself" playwright I've ever met.

MIKE: Yes, I think so.

MALDEN: He writes! And it's proven! I'm not just saying this, the proof is right there. Damned near every year, for

—what?—five, six, seven years, he had a play on Broadway. He had a play he had written. Some of the others write great plays, too, but then periods of three, four, five years go by before anything else comes out. And I think part of being a—I was going to say—it's a corny expression—being a professional writer, I mean a sincere writer, is to *have* to write. In my young days when I was still in school and interested in the theatre I used to read an awful lot of the playwrights. I think Maxwell Anderson, Robert Sherwood, Sidney Howard, I think damned near every year they had a play on. And these, to me, were the cream of the crop. When you say Maxwell Anderson, Robert Sherwood, Elmer Rice, Sidney Howard and S. N. Behrman, and Clifford Odets—damned near every year they had something on. And I think Tennessee belongs in that category.

MIKE: Do you think that when Tennessee saw the screening of *Baby Doll* again he felt it was a film that had been really well done of his work, that he seemed to be content and didn't have any regrets about it?

MALDEN: Well, now that you bring that up, I am beginning to recollect that evening again, and when the film was over, and we had looked at each other and we were laughing, Tennessee got up and finished his drink, he still had that cigarette, he's always got that cigarette, and he finished his drink and walked to Gadge and said, "Gadge, that was a damned good movie." I also think it was one of Gadge's best. I don't think that at the time you are doing it, and at the time it is being distributed, and at the time those six months after, when it's hot and everything is going, I don't think a person realizes art until he can look at it in perspective. I think three, four, five years, ten years later you look at a painting, you look at something, and say, "Now that is really a work of art." You have to look at it in perspective and we

were looking at it in perspective and saying, "Doggone it!"
And he, especially, said, "Gadge, that is a damned good film."

MIKE: Do you think they are going to re-release the film?
Have you ever heard anything about it?

MALDEN: The only thing I have heard is that Kazan owns
it now. It does not belong to Warner Brothers.

MIKE: But I think he and Tennessee originally co-produced
it, didn't they?

MALDEN: I think so, and I think it's reverted back to—I
don't know whether Tennessee is part of this, but I know
that Kazan is, because he told me when we discussed it just
four months ago. He said, "I own that movie now." Whether
it means he bought it back, whether he means after a certain
number of years it reverts to him, I don't know what the
deal was.

MIKE: I think Kazan must own it completely now.

MALDEN: I think so, and I told him, "You ought to release
it now, Gadge." Now it would really mean something because—when was that film done? 1955 or '56? That's damned
near thirteen years ago. Definitely. That film was way ahead
of its time because Kazan, during that film, was making a
comment about the Negro situation at that time. So was
Tennessee. They were making a subtle comment about the
Negro situation. And if you see the film you will see where,
I think, one of the comments—if you remember the film, the
Negroes were always in the background, looking at the
Caucasians, at the whites, and kind of laughing, and looking
at them, and the impression I get is that they are saying,
"Look at that, they are listening to that music. That's the
music we had twenty years ago." It is their rock 'n' roll that
is now the whites' music, and they were looking at things

that the whites were doing. We have borrowed so much of their culture and I think that is one of the comments that Kazan was making in that film.

MIKE: It was a good comment to make. Did you improvise many of the scenes in *Baby Doll*? I had always heard that starting as an Actors Studio project, a lot of the script was sort of written from day to day as the actors enlarged and ad-libbed the intentions of the scene—

MALDEN: On *Baby Doll* alone? Are you talking about *Baby Doll*? Or are you just talking generally about Kazan's work?

MIKE: No, on *Baby Doll* in particular.

MALDEN: No, sir, I think that script was very well written. It was a very well written film script, I think, between Tennessee and Gadge. If I'm not mistaken, Tennessee's film script of *Streetcar Named Desire*, he wrote.

MIKE: Well, that was practically the play, just verbatim.

MALDEN: That's right. Someone else putting it into movie terms, technical terms, along with Tennessee. But *Baby Doll*, I think, was completely Tennessee and Kazan, the two of them.

MIKE: I had always heard the actors would—Kazan would give them an intention as to the way the characters relate, and then Tennessee would watch and maybe then write it out on paper, from day to day—

MALDEN: That is not true, not true. Tennessee wrote it. What we said were Tennessee's words. It was a play long before it was a movie and a lot of that play was in that film. Changed a little because he had lived with it longer and was able to develop and improve upon what he had written as a one-act play some ten years earlier, but it was all Tennessee. Where we improvised is—you take the material that

Tennessee had written, and Kazan always likes to work sort of a day ahead; what we are shooting on Monday, we have already rehearsed on Sunday a little, so that we have already rehearsed the scene for Monday, and we are rehearsing also some of the stuff we are going to do the next day, on Tuesday, and we did an awful lot of rehearsing because it was so beautiful outside. We used to set up out in the back yard of that house an interior, let's say the dining-room table, and start to rehearse while the crew was setting up the equipment inside, which takes an awful long time. But we would work with the dialogue and then discard the dialogue as much as we liked and get a kind of improvisational feeling, but always we started from, in this particular film—it can be done the opposite way—but in this particular film we started from the material and worked on that and then if we felt like going beyond that, we were allowed to go and expand. That's the word, I think: We were able to *expand* on what Tennessee had done and then were told, "It stinks, it's not good, let's just stay to the frame," or, "Keep that, that's wonderful." That sort of thing. Let's be very specific about the improvisational aspects: If you remember the film, around the table, the dinner scene—greens, we were eating greens—that's all we had, and suddenly it gets awfully tense and Archie Lee realizes there is something going on between Vicarro and the girl, Baby Doll, who is his wife, and there is something going on there and he doesn't like it and he is beginning to, maybe, say, on the verge of whatever you want to call it—crack, blow his top—and then from there Kazan placed me up against that beautiful chandelier, over that grand piano, which showed that Southern elegance which is not there any more. It was absolutely a framed picture to start with, and then he had a chicken come into the other end of the house. And I stood there boiling. I was supposed to turn around and go with them, and suddenly I said, "Gadge, let me grab that chandelier." Well, he said,

"Sure." Then it got to where the chandelier was so expensive! You know we couldn't do just one take. So they fixed it so that the ball, that crystal part at the end, could come off, and that is the thing that I used to start off the action of that scene. If you could call that improvisation, that is the way that picture was made. I will tell you what was improvised—the moment that we call the "Chaplinesque" thing which hadn't much dialogue at all. It was the scene where Eli Wallach is chasing Baby Doll and scaring her! That was improvised. That "Chaplinesque" kind of thing.

MIKE: That was very outstanding.

MALDEN: That was improvised. One day we said, "What are we going to do?" "He's got to chase her now." "What kind of chase?" And that was all improvised. Everybody contributed, you know, with Kazan—everybody, the prop men, everybody contributes to that.

MIKE: I always thought that you were the type of actor that would fit the role of the Gentleman Caller in *The Glass Menagerie*. I have always seen you in that part.

MALDEN: As a matter of fact, I played the Gentleman Caller. Just on radio, and once we made a tape. It was always an all-star cast. I played the Gentleman Caller with Helen Hayes, with Shirley Booth, with Millie Dunnock. Always on radio. I will tell you what I feel. You will have to help me. Has *The Glass Menagerie* ever been done on TV?

MIKE: Yes, Shirley Booth did it on TV.

MALDEN: She did? I always wanted, and Tennessee said if I could get it done that way, he would give me permission. There was a while when he wouldn't give permission for it. I wanted, a long time ago, I wanted an all-Oscar cast to play it on TV. I wanted either Helen Hayes or Shirley Booth.

Both won Oscars. I wanted Eva Marie Saint to play the girl.
She won an Oscar. I wanted to play the Gentleman Caller.
I won an Oscar. And I wanted either Bill Holden or Marlon
Brando to play the son. In other words, if Marlon didn't
want to do it, I had to go to Bill; this was about fifteen years
ago. In other words, everyone who had won an Oscar would
be in this.

MIKE: That was, I suppose, too soon after the movie for a
TV production.

MALDEN·   Probably, yes.

MIKE: Do you feel that there is an identity between the
Gentleman Caller in *The Glass Menagerie* and Mitch in
A Streetcar Named Desire?

MALDEN: Yes, I think there is a little. Yes. I think that they
are both lost souls, really. I think the Gentleman Caller, in
his braggadocio way and his expanding way, is just a lost
—just so frightened of life! And I think Mitch definitely is
frightened of life.

MIKE: Mitch is like the Gentleman Caller further down the
line. As Blanche resembles characters in earlier plays of
Tennessee's, further along the line. Did you ever spend much
time with Tennessee away from work and at any social
functions?

MALDEN: No, I have seldom had that pleasure. And I would
say that if you can think of it in these terms, seventy per
cent of it was my fault, because at the time when we were
close, the time I had the opportunity to be close to Tennessee, was during the run of *Streetcar*, which was altogether a
period of two and a half, three years: rehearsal, and it ran
for two years, a little before and a little after. That whole
period.

MIKE: Did Tennessee come to Hollywood when they were filming *Streetcar*?

MALDEN: Yes, he did. He was around. Not most of the time, but he was around. And to continue on this "Have I ever . . .?" I regret that I didn't have the opportunity to be more social, and as I said before, seventy per cent of it is my fault, because during that period of time I was shy. I wasn't —I don't want to say aggressive enough—but I was the one that was, and I still am a little bit, you can call it a lone wolf. I was a loner. I didn't make friends easily, and Tennessee was a big writer, and I was just—I thought that I would be imposing at that time.

MIKE: Did you ever feel that he was a shy person?

MALDEN: It took two of us, I think. I think so.

MIKE: But once a person is around Tennessee you feel that he is completely open to almost anyone's company. As if he had known you all your life!

MALDEN: The most honest person I think that I have ever met. Really honest. He is honest to himself, which is wonderful, and expects that honesty from anybody around him.

MIKE: Do you ever think it would be a good idea if Tennessee and Gadge were to collaborate again? Or would you rather not discuss that?

MALDEN: Well, let's see what can come out of discussing it. You know we can always say it doesn't work. I like this— I'm a great one for talking things over!

MIKE: They seem to get along well. Tennessee was one of the hosts of the party when Kazan's book *The Arrangement* came out and he seems to get along with Gadge when they do see each other, and they help each other out. But there seems to be something that keeps them from actually working together again on a project. For instance, I heard that Gadge wanted to direct Tennessee's last play on Broadway, *The Seven Descents of Myrtle.*

MALDEN: I don't know.

MIKE: I asked Tennessee if that was true and Tennessee said, "If it is true, I was never told it."

MALDEN: That's right. Don't believe all that sort of thing. You know we all—it's this business, and careers, and the way it goes—have moments of parting of ways, people going their different ways. The theatre is like: You have a happy marriage for a while, you all come together and it's a great happy family, and suddenly that one is over and it's like a divorce and it is over and each person goes his own separate way, looking for his own career. Tennessee's saying, "I have got to write another one." He gets anxious, he says, "I hope I can write another one." Gadge says, "I have to direct something, or they will forget me," or, "I have got to write my own book now." I think that Gadge definitely has said, "I'm not going to direct anything unless I write it. I'm going to write and direct my own material," which is what he is doing. I don't know whether that is good. I personally don't think it is. I think other people ought to contribute in this form because I think it makes it better. I do feel that because Tennessee and Gadge aren't—I was going to say aren't together—I don't mean aren't together, I mean aren't doing things together, it makes our theatre the worse for it. I think the two of them together were wonderful. I think the proof is that great things, in both their careers, came out during that period. Tennessee's *Streetcar* had a great production; I don't think he can find fault with it. I think that with his *Sweet Bird of Youth* Kazan did a very good production. I don't think he could have gotten a better one anywhere else. I have seen *Camino Real* done other places since, but the original Broadway production was brilliantly put on, I thought, with imagination and the Actors Studio kind of thing. I think Tennessee should be pleased with that, and that was when they were always working together, the two of them.

MIKE: There will be a production of *Camino*, you know, at the Mark Taper Forum in August.

MALDEN: Yes, I know that. I am anxious to see it. I would like to see their idea of it.

MIKE: Yes. I loved *Camino Real* when I saw Kazan's production. That was just after I first met Tennessee.

MALDEN: At the National Theatre in New York?

MIKE: Yes. And before, when it was doing out-of-town tryouts in New Haven, and then down to Philadelphia and then into New York. I had only been in New York for a couple of months, so it was a very exciting introduction to New York and the theatre, to see that play from the beginning. I was so disappointed when it only ran for, I think, three or four months because I think it was a great play but was probably ahead of its time.

MALDEN: That's right; the form, the style, everything about it was way ahead of its time.

MIKE: It's the type of thing that we see more of now.

MALDEN: Absolutely.

MIKE: And Tennessee was doing it in this country sixteen, seventeen years ago.

MALDEN: Right.

MIKE: Very often, when there is a work of art, like the film *The Fox*, they say that if it had come in from Europe as an import there would have been much more of an acceptance of it and excitement about it.

MALDEN: I believe that's true.

MIKE: And I feel the same way with some of Tennessee's works, especially *Camino Real* and the play he had two years ago, in 1966, in New York called *Slapstick Tragedy*, two long one-act plays under the combined title of *Slapstick Tragedy*, which was a really way-out theatre of the absurd. I always had the feeling that if that had come in from France, or Italy, or anywhere in Europe it would have been a big hit. But the very fact that it was an American, done here—

MALDEN: The grass is always greener, is that it? In somebody else's back yard?

Tennessee Williams, William Inge, and Irving Rapper at the home of the author's brother in Brentwood, California. August, 1968. (*Photo by Ernest M. Steen*)

IRVING RAPPER

Irving Rapper should write his own book some day. He keeps his friends entertained with countless stories about Hollywood from the thirties until today. He was nearly always associated with Warner Brothers studio and can spend hours recalling tales both true and legendary about the great stars he has worked with: Bette Davis, John Garfield, Humphrey Bogart, Errol Flynn, Olivia de Havilland, Jane Wyman, Joan Crawford, Claude Rains, Ronald Reagan, Fredric March, and many others.

Irving is a product of the New York theatre. He went to Hollywood in 1935 and worked five years as a dialogue director, having turned down directing offers until he was satisfied with a script. His many outstanding films include Now Voyager, The Corn Is Green, Rhapsody in Blue, Voice of the Turtle, *and* The Glass Menagerie. *The beautiful and sensitive film* The Brave Ones, *about a little Mexican boy and his pet calf, which, when grown, is taken away from him and sent to the bullfighting ring, was directed by Irving during one of his ten suspensions from Warner Brothers!*

Between pictures, Irving spends a great deal of time traveling. His favorite places are London, New York, Rome, and Acapulco. He keeps an attractive apartment in Hollywood, high in one of those new high-rise buildings we are told are safe from earth tremors. It was there that I spent several hours with this long-time friend of mine, chatting about Tennessee.

Hollywood
June 17, 1968

MIKE: You said something about Dana Andrews' being with you and Tennessee on the same ship. Crossing to Europe?

RAPPER: No! Tennessee happened to be in California and wanted to talk to me and wanted to spend a lazy day and I didn't quite understand whether he meant going to somebody's place, some entertainment, or a park to talk things over. So, I finally thought about a yacht. And Dana Andrews, a very good friend of mine, had two boats, and when I told him we would like to meet on the yacht and spend the afternoon going to Catalina, he was very pleased and delighted. He asked us when we arrived, when we came aboard the boat, whether we were good sailors and we both immediately responded No, whereupon he gave us a chicken dinner and set sail and gave us some seasickness pills and we were very happy. The next thing we were being awakened at five o'clock in the afternoon. We were back and we never knew a moment of the trip. So I think it was a very relaxed experience.

MIKE: So you never got to the discussion that he originally wanted in a quiet place?

RAPPER: Never, but then I always found Tennessee to be a very unplanning sort of person, so that I left things more or less spontaneously to him because things that he ever plans to do he never does. Very vague and abstract. When you get to know Tennessee, you let things happen. Let him initiate things because he is the least aggressive person in the world anyway.

MIKE: Was this boat trip during the filming of *The Glass Menagerie*?

RAPPER: No, this was quite afterwards.

MIKE: Oh, after, when Tennessee was on one of his rare visits to Hollywood.

RAPPER: Yes, and I was surprised he still wanted to see me! But we have always had a very pleasant relationship that went on for a long time. I only wished that I had suited him better professionally with *The Glass Menagerie*.

MIKE: Irving, you told me once about Tennessee's having seen *The Corn Is Green* and liking it so much that he told his agent to get in touch with you to direct *The Glass Menagerie*.

RAPPER: Well, I think it was a little bit more the other way around. Audrey Wood, who had known me ever since I was a promising young man in the theatre, had always liked me. And when Charlie Feldman and Warner Brothers approached her about contacting Tennessee, they said they would send me to Italy to meet with him and discuss the production of it. And Audrey, of course, at that time being a great fan of mine, alerted Tennessee in Rome about my coming. And that's the reason Charlie sent me to Europe. Tennessee remembered *The Corn Is Green*. He liked it very much, yes.

MIKE: The first time you met Tennessee, then, was in Rome and that was when he had the apartment there, I believe. He kept an apartment there each summer.

RAPPER: Yes, he loved Italy. He loved Italians very much. He probably still does except he has had so much of it, living there. And I must say he was my first host in Rome and I always look back with a great deal of pleasure to his showing me around the landmarks of Rome. You know, since then I lived there for two and one-half years.

MIKE: Then, shortly after that the film's pre-production got underway?

RAPPER: Yes, we had been using a collaborator, Peter Berneis, who, under Jerry Wald's supervision, was going full steam ahead on the writing of it. And the purpose of my trip to Rome was to get to know Tennessee and also to try to persuade him to come to Hollywood, which he had always resented. You know, he hated business in Hollywood. He hated studios. So, I thought it was almost a coup for me to have gotten him to come back. I thought that he, being a man of great integrity, would certainly want to supervise the writing of the screenplay. But I must add, if I may, that being a very shy, withdrawn person, and *The Glass Menagerie* being his very first experience in pictures, he was certainly most eager, too eager, to transfer all authority and all know-how to everybody entrusted with the picture. Though I must say, everybody surrounding the picture was very experienced, like Jerry Wald and Charlie Feldman. Our greatest problem, of course, was the casting.

MIKE: There is one thing I wonder. If Laurette Taylor had still been alive, would she have been considered for the part?

RAPPER: I'll tell you quite frankly, and I am so sure about what I am about to say because of my very close association over such a long period of time with Warner Brothers, and the same holds true with almost any other studio, had Laurette Taylor lived and wanted to do the picture, believe me, she would have been the last person to be asked because those were not the days of originality or experimentation as they are more probably now. It was always a question of distribution. Of name value. Of box office value. Because even at the last moment, after I had made two or three tests of actresses. Charlie Feldman said, "Irving, how about going to see your favorite actress?" And I said, "Whom do you mean?" He said, "Bette Davis." By the way, I did. Not because I thought she was right for it, but because I thought she was a great enough actress to embrace any characterization. And so I went to see her, but Jack Warner didn't like the idea at all because it was the end of a very, very sad relationship between those two people. So the hunger, the anxiety to get box office, the assurance, the security, to get the right person were prevalent in their minds and, for instance—

MIKE: Bette Davis didn't actually test, though?

RAPPER: No, she was very amenable to doing it provided—

MIKE: Did she personally think that she would fit the mother role?

RAPPER: She thought she was a little too young for the part, but at that time it was just a question of a few years. And I assured her she had such great powers of illusion. And illusion is a word that Tennessee always uses in his plays. I think Bette would have embraced—she may have tipped Amanda, and given a different kind of thing. Different from what I expected. Different certainly from what Tennessee expected. But I think it would have had a tremendous dramatic impact on the play and would have sold more tickets.

MIKE: Who were the people that did test for Amanda, the mother?

RAPPER: I interviewed Ruth Chatterton, and she was very unhappy about the idea of playing a mother. It was Jane Wyman's idea, which I rather respected. Jane had just won the Academy Award for *Johnny Belinda* and she was certainly worth listening to, and—

MIKE: Jane was already cast as the crippled daughter?

RAPPER: Yes, she was cast. And then the second person that I had wanted to cast but had some reservations about was Tallulah Bankhead. This was before all that comic hysteria on television. And she was probably the most brilliant woman, the most brilliant actress, I ever spoke to! And I had covered sufficient mileage!

MIKE: For the part, you mean?

RAPPER: For the part. And she loved the idea because she was born in Alabama and so closely identified with the South, loved all the speech of Tennessee Williams and his drama, of course. She gave herself to the tests! We tested for three long, suffering, humid days in July in New York City. And in all my experience I never saw a crew so staggered by the impact of a performance as they were by the one that Tallulah gave. But Jack Warner rejected the entire idea because of his fear of her drinking. He said Errol Flynn was enough.

MIKE: Then why did he ever allow the tests?

RAPPER: Well, Charlie, Charlie Feldman, insisted on it. Charlie was the co-producer of the picture. And I tell you, it was such a free-for-all game of casting! It was so difficult to cast a middle-aged woman who was a box office attraction. It's easy to talk about it now. But, for instance, if Joan Crawford *now*, or Bette Davis *now*, were mentioned for certain middle-aged parts, you might be inclined toward their direction. But when this picture was made in 1950— '49 and '50—it was impossible to find middle-aged box office women. I am sure they wouldn't have taken Laurette Taylor. With my many experiences with actresses, I can honestly say, with a great deal of conviction, that it was the greatest test I have ever seen or made.

MIKE: Tallulah's?

RAPPER: Tallulah's! Gertrude Lawrence was a sort of compromise casting. Number one: She did have a name, particularly in the theatre. She hadn't done *The King and I* yet, but she had done *Lady in the Dark*, and many brilliant comedy musicals, and a lot of legitimate dramas in which she was quite distinguished, both in England and in New York. But it was purely a theatre reputation that she enjoyed. They wanted four stars: Jane Wyman and Kirk Douglas, a great woman star, and the son, Tom. That was the only thing I prevailed on was to have Arthur Kennedy, who wasn't a star, play Tom. By the way, he was the only one who won a nomination for the Awards. So my thinking was right!

MIKE: He was certainly very good casting.

RAPPER: If I had the whole thing to do all over again, I would never have cast any stars in that picture because Tennessee writes of shy, withdrawn, fragile petals—which I think he describes the girl as, doesn't he? She is like a petal that has to be treated very delicately, sensitively. Therefore, if you cast very important box office names, you immediately inherit the prejudices against them, too. And the crassness of their offstage characters, too. And I think, unlike the robust characters of *A Streetcar Named Desire*, or some of the other people in *Baby Doll*, this was a much more fragile work. He called it a memory play, full of illusions and poetry. So, the less familiar the names would be, the more I think you would hold up the illusion of it. The illusion is destroyed by crass casting.

MIKE: You told me a story about Tennessee's first arriving in Hollywood and the first meeting he had with heads of studios.

RAPPER: Yes, you mean his first arrival at Warner Brothers?

MIKE: Yes, when he and Frank Merlo arrived there.

RAPPER: Yes.

MIKE: Frankie was a very helpful, aggressive person. And he sort of broke the ice for Tennessee, who was usually a shy person.

RAPPER: Exactly. We finally persuaded Tennessee to come to Warner Brothers studio. To Hollywood. And he came, but a little reluctantly. He rather enjoyed his quiet freedom in Italy. And he leaned very much on the friendship of Frank, who was a great pillar of business, particularly for him, because he hated to have any dealings in business. And when he arrived at the studio, we had planned to have a late lunch so the other directors and writers would be out of the way. And Jack Warner, of course, was sitting at the head of the table. And Charlie Feldman and Jerry Wald and I were sitting there. And at last the trumpet blew heralding Tennessee's arrival. Jack fixed his tie, and as the two arrived he got up from his chair. "Well! Well! At last, here you are! Welcome to Warner Brothers!" And he shook the hand of Frank, thinking he was Tennessee, but Tennessee was very, very timidly walking behind Frank, with that familiar cigarette holder tilting from his lips. The mistaken identity amused rather than annoyed Tennessee, which certainly reveals his tremendous humility, which makes for great artistry too, of course.

MIKE: Wasn't there another incident in the studio commissary when Harry Warner was talking and most of the people sitting at the table were a captive audience, so to speak, listening to what he had to say?

RAPPER: Yes, at that time Harry Warner, who is deceased, of course, was the President of the Board at Warner's and he was a sort of patriarchal figure who was entirely dedi-

cated to charities and he would love to indulge in reminis-
cences. He was a magnificent, kindly old man, and being
the head of the studio, and having made Warner Brothers,
he felt everybody had to pay obeisance and listen to him as
a great father. I liked the old man. And Tennessee was
having his second lunch with us on one of those rare visits
he had with us, and Harry was lecturing to a few people
about some moral things. And suddenly our friend Tennessee, I am sure quite bored with the whole thing, was anxious
to get away. And as he passed, so lightly—as he used to
tread so softly, walking away—Harry said, "Just a minute,
young man. What do you do here?" And Tennessee said,
very politely, "I'm a writer," not quite sure whether he was.
And Harry said, "Well, sit down, because this will do you
a lot of good." And poor Tennessee actually had to sit down
with the others, mostly contract players, and listen to all this
lecture, which I thought was so funny.

MIKE: As if Warner had said, "Sit down, kid, you may
learn something."

RAPPER: Exactly, exactly.

MIKE: Which was sincere on Harry Warner's part.

RAPPER: Very, very. I liked Harry Warner very much.

MIKE: And there was a party hosted by Charlie Feldman
at the beginning of shooting. Were there any interesting
things that might have happened there?

RAPPER: Well, they had big cakes of ice made into a
menagerie, like giant glass animals, but it was such a humid
evening all the figures started to melt as the guests arrived
—though it was an ingenious idea.

MIKE: You said if you had *The Glass Menagerie* to do over
again you would prefer casting it with unknown people

because of the fragility of the play. Is there any other feeling that you have about the outcome of the film that you would have changed?

RAPPER: Oh, yes, I think everybody could have been more believable. I think when you are watching great stars, an Academy Award winner like Jane Wyman, a very self-assured fellow like Kirk Douglas, and the mannerisms of Gertrude Lawrence so known to her audiences, I think you are on the wrong approach. Tennessee's people, on the other hand, appeared out of shadows. I can't remember literally the descriptions Tennessee so poetically wrote in *The Glass Menagerie*, but he had such poetic, soft people coming out of obscurity, really, to be beheld by an audience. And that illusion is gone when they aren't fragile, like petals.

MIKE: The system of Hollywood at that time was even more one of casting stars in parts, so you really couldn't buck the system and you had to go along with it.

RAPPER: It was Charlie Feldman's first great property that he was going to produce. And having been the most successful agent in town, practically, he envisioned four great stars, you see. I embraced the idea of Gertrude Lawrence because she made a test which I thought was better than the picture. I had gone all the way to Hyannis to see her in a play and to have her come down to New York to make the test. The first person aware of her resistance to playing a mother's role was Arthur Kennedy, for whom I have a very great respect.

MIKE: Did you see Maureen Stapleton's stage performance as Amanda?

RAPPER: No, although Tennessee told me that in a revival of it he had liked her considerably.

MIKE: You know, most actors and actresses have told me that Tennessee is not too good about casting. He doesn't have an idea about what actors should play what parts, really. That if he liked someone particularly, or had seen him give a fine performance in some other film or play, that he might just say, "Oh, he's a marvelous actor—use him!" without being more specific in terms of the part.

RAPPER: Well, quite frankly, Mike, I always found Tennessee very withdrawn about his own casting of plays. He withdraws completely into a shell and if he likes you, particularly if he likes you, he entrusts everything to your hands.

MIKE: Well, even if he does make a decision, if a person is around who has a strong influence over him, Tennessee could be persuaded to change his decision. I have noticed that through the years. Not only in casting actors and actresses, but also in writers who are assigned to write his screenplays or directors of his stage shows and movies. Sometimes that "influential" person has selfish motives or just plain bad taste.

RAPPER: Coming back to the casting, which is such an important thing in theatre and the screen. The actors really hold the ball in interpreting the writer's work. Despite the director, even on the screen the personality still predominates.

MIKE: Did you see Bette Davis in *The Night of the Iguana* in New York?

RAPPER: No, I didn't.

MIKE: I think that she does have a tendency to be a personality.

RAPPER: Well, it's the force of her personality that's so overpowering and makes her performances so memorable.

MIKE: Did you ever get to know Tennessee very well on a personal level?

RAPPER: Well, I always felt a pleasant relationship between us, almost always. He seemed to be exceedingly amiable and kind and attentive to me. And I thought that was rather generous of him because he was a retiring sort of chap. So his opening up to me, the little opening up he did do, especially when we were together in Italy, made me feel quite rewarded by my trip. He is not a very easy man to know. He's probably the moodiest writer I have ever known. Before I came here to Hollywood, I had worked with Gilbert Miller, who was probably the greatest producer of his day. And we certainly had the great Sidney Howards and Philip Barrys and the Ferenc Molnárs, all the great people that I had met in the theatre before I even came here. I had never known a man who was as gifted as Tennessee Williams to be so shy and to be so withdrawn. That is exactly what he is. He withdraws, practically, from a relationship if he feels its pressure. Don't you agree?

MIKE: Yes, I think he has always been like that.

RAPPER: When we were discussing the preparations of *The Glass Menagerie* in New York we were both at the Plaza Hotel and I used to come down to see him, usually at noon. And there, of course, was that ever-ready long cigarette and always a martini on the table, which frightened me because I don't drink very much at all. When I see a drink at twelve o'clock in the morning—!

MIKE: This was about 1949?

RAPPER: Forty-nine, yes, exactly. Another one like that is Tallulah Bankhead. She's flanked by all kinds of bloody drinks. I want coffee to wake me up, but evidently these are the things that prepare them for the day.

MIKE: Were there any other experiences in Rome when you first met Tennessee that you particularly recall? You say he was your first host in Rome. Does that mean he would have you over to the apartment for dinner, or that you would go out on the town and he would show you the sights of Rome?

RAPPER: I was never in his house. We usually met at my hotel and would have some drinks and we usually toured the city for my benefit. He was very kind. Very gracious. We would either go by a carriage or in his own car.

MIKE: Tennessee would be driving?

RAPPER: No, Frank Merlo. I was told about using the cautious approach—I don't remember if it was Audrey Wood or who—when I was in New York. So I hardly ever pressured him. I tried to let our friendship grow as the days progressed and I did find, as time went on, that we seemed to get on much better and I really felt that he trusted me a great deal. When we went back to the United States, Charlie Feldman was particularly grateful because it was on Tennessee's trip to California that Feldman bought the rights to *Streetcar Named Desire*.

MIKE: When you were getting to know Tennessee as a person, and directing *The Glass Menagerie*, which is supposed to be an autobiographical play, did you feel Tom in the play was close to Tennessee himself? That he was writing about himself and his own family?

RAPPER: As far as his dreams and poetry are concerned, and his aversion to pedestrian work, yes. He was very much Tom. But as far as rebelling, this outward rebelliousness that grew in the play between Tom and the mother, this I couldn't appreciate, as I never saw them together. I did, however, visit Mrs. Williams, Tennessee's mother, and we went out to dinner.

MIKE: In St. Louis? You visited her in St. Louis?

RAPPER: Yes, and his old, old grandfather, a very alert old man whom I enjoyed and who had dinner with me later in New York. But I met Mrs. Williams in St. Louis. She couldn't have been more charming and devoted to me while I was there. She was very lovely. So neither from Tennessee nor from his mother did I ever get any feeling of rebellion. The only way you spell that out is in Tennessee's own imagination and in his own detachment from this association.

MIKE: But you felt when you met Mrs. Williams that the character Amanda was taken directly from her.

RAPPER: Well again, again, there I saw the birdlike quality of the woman and the softer part, but I never saw the garrulous, confused person that was dramatized in *The Glass Menagerie*. I saw a relaxed, mellow woman.

MIKE: Did Gertrude Lawrence ever go to meet Mrs. Williams to get an idea of her characterization?

RAPPER: No. As a matter of fact, Gertrude Lawrence was in the middle of a play in Hyannis, or Hyannis Port, and it was something to get her out of the play to come to Hollywood. Everything else was ready, you see. And it was something, too, to get Arthur Kennedy. He was in *All My Sons* and he had a very difficult producer. I forget his name, another David Merrick. And then I called up Arthur. I always have a dream cast and Arthur's always one of my dream members. I called him in Connecticut one night, where he lives, and said, "Arthur, you've got to come and do the son in *The Glass Menagerie*," and he said, "Kirk Douglas is doing the Gentleman Caller; is there anything left for me to say?" and I said, "Not only that, Tennessee has written three extra scenes." He said, "You're kidding!" I said, "Get on that train or plane tomorrow. We need you immediately." He said, "You mean to say everything in the play—?" I said, "I promise that everything in the play will remain. In addition, you have three extra scenes," which was true. He couldn't believe it. David Selznick had done such a histrionic job in taking a chance on a British girl like Vivien Leigh to do *Gone with the Wind* that I thought perhaps the same thing might happen with Gertrude Lawrence. She was so shy of the part, so frightened of it. Although she was a beautiful figure in the theatre, I felt she feared she was not photogenic by the standards of the screen. She had to be angled very carefully and I must say I remember the tremendous timidity with which she came to Hollywood. She was so worried about everything.

MIKE: Did Tennessee have cast approval?

RAPPER: Oh, I'm sure we would have listened to him. Certainly as a director I would have given tremendous attention to any thoughts that any writer—especially Tennessee Williams—might have. As a matter of fact, if an electrician told me that he didn't like somebody I would listen, because they are the audience.

MIKE: How do you feel now, since Tennessee has written so many other plays, about *The Glass Menagerie*? Would you place it first, second, or third among his works?

RAPPER: Quite frankly, I don't know all of Tennessee's works too well. I do think it is far, far superior to things like *Baby Doll. Baby Doll* to me was brilliant entertainment. It had some wonderful, challenging nuances, but it was entertainment, whereas the other was a penetrating study of four opposite characters, with some beautiful thinking and beautiful writing. I shall always wonder how much of it was my fault as director that it didn't go over better. How much of it was the casting? How much of it was the actual adaptation for the screenplay? And how much, also, was the conventional camera work as compared with the much more creative work that cameras are capable of doing now, which is being accepted by studios, but which wouldn't have been allowed in 1949?

MIKE: I think a lot of it has to do with the fact that *The Glass Menagerie* is a lyrical play which can be more readily interpreted according to the emotional feelings of each individual. I have heard rather lyrical or poetic directors like José Quintero say that *The Glass Menagerie* has never been done properly—even in the original Broadway production.

RAPPER: This will be disputable for a long time. Because you take *Streetcar Named Desire*. That is not only a very well integrated, dramatic, progressive piece of writing; it is a great play. But *The Glass Menagerie* is not a thumping drama.

MIKE: So the final outcome of the film was not completely satisfactory to you.

RAPPER: I received a letter from Stockholm, from the National Theatre there, commending me for the entire presentation! So perhaps the Europeans liked it more than we did. I think one often thinks, unfortunately, of a great play as the particular property of a star who has been triumphant in it, like Ethel Barrymore in *The Corn Is Green,* or Katharine Cornell in *The Barretts of Wimpole Street*, or Alice Brady in her great plays, or Lynn Fontanne in *Idiot's Delight*. And to take something that is played on Broadway by a super artist of Laurette Taylor's stature, and then give it to somebody who is wrongly cast in it is a tremendous gap in casting. If Laurette Taylor had been living then and you had said, "Well, Laurette, let's make a test," I think that that would have been the only way to have made a fair judgment. Successful stage plays often falter on their way to the screen. But, Mike, I did have a successful transference to the screen of not only *The Corn Is Green* but also the comedy *The Voice of the Turtle* and they were done with tremendous fidelity and with great results financially, and artistically.

MIKE: Well, once you did have the cast that the studio heads wanted, did Tennessee spend much time out here watching the filming and helping with the interpretation of it?

RAPPER: Never. Never at all. He came back to go over a few scenes. Also added a few scenes. Some were good, some were bad. And then he went back to New York, and Jerry Wald sent him a rough version of the film. He was very disturbed by the fact that a number of different little phrasings had been inserted. Tennessee was very sensitive even about *a* and *the* and commas, really. He went to a great extent to tell me how Arthur Kennedy should have spoken the last line of the film. "He should have had this much of a pause where he said, 'And so . . . good night.'" I had never made a point of it. I had left it in Arthur Kennedy's hands and I felt I was listening to it for the first time when he said it: "And so, good night." But to Tennessee it was one of the greatest tragedies of the picture.

MIKE: In that case, don't you think if Tennessee is going to feel that way, he should have been there when it was filmed?

RAPPER: Of course he should. That was one of the reasons—

MIKE: So you could know how he felt about it when you still had time to do something about it.

RAPPER: Of course. Who can write Tennessee Williams' *Glass Menagerie* better than Tennessee Williams? And if he wanted help for cinematographic continuity, he should have closely supervised that. If I need help of a cameraman,

I closely supervise his moves. I don't understand the techniques of the camera as much as the cameraman himself does, but when I tell him what I want to achieve, I certainly not only put it in his hands, but I am there every second on top of it and watching it.

MIKE: Is a playwright usually present in Hollywood or on the set when a film is being made from his play? For instance, when *Death of a Salesman* was filmed or *Come Back, Little Sheba* or any of the contemporary plays of *Glass Menagerie,* do you think that Arthur Miller or William Inge was around?

RAPPER: I don't know. I have never worked with them.

MIKE: Or should they have been around, do you think?

RAPPER: It depends upon the degree of acceptance of the script by the director. If the director thinks the script is finished and polished then there is no need for the writer to be around. But nowadays, there are several very bright young men, I forget their names, in studios who have become producing members of the organization. They produce and write. And so, therefore, in their official capacity they watch their work being done on the screen. Now this would be far from Tennessee's make-up. He could hardly supervise or do anything like that. Then there is also the worry, "Shall we change anything that was written so successfully for the stage?" In those days they were afraid to touch anything. Now they do. They change things with cameras and with much more boldness and courage than they had in those days.

MIKE: You think *The Glass Menagerie* was not so much a well-constructed play as it was characters coming out of the dark?

RAPPER: I don't think it was so much a great play so far as all the entities of playwriting are concerned in the classic, academic sense. It was rather a recalling in a man's mind of the memories of relationships around him. These may be poetic, these may have memory, illusion, fantasy, imagination. Whether it strongly asserts itself in a well-motivated and -machinated story composition is a different thing. This is something that will be debatable for a long time.

MIKE: *Streetcar,* for instance, was a play of stronger structure in a classical sense.

RAPPER: Oh, yes, this is exactly what I mean, Mike.

MIKE. People still came out of the dark more or less, but it had—

RAPPER: —great elements of drama—

MIKE: —which shows an advancement as a playwright.

RAPPER: Yes, in Tennessee's writing. Yes, I think you hit it on the head. That's absolutely true. I never thought *Menagerie* had the ingredients of the plays like *A Streetcar Named Desire.* And I remember when I was assigned *Menagerie,* one of the heads of the studio said to me, "Irving, I don't see it as a great movie. It will probably be a prestige piece." Even if it were, I'm sure Tennessee would have settled for it as a great prestige piece.

MIKE: Well, you first met Tennessee in Rome in 1949, then spent time with him after that in New York, preparing for the film, then during the film you had an association with him. What was the last meeting you had with Tennessee?

RAPPER: I saw Tennessee about a year ago in New York at some workshop. I was invited to see a psychedelic sort of play. I found him just recovering from a recent illness. Tennessee never seemed to be a very healthy guy, always seemed to be suffering from some indisposition or another. But he was terribly nice to me. We had a very nice talk.

MIKE: He was more withdrawn?

RAPPER: Yes. You always have the feeling, even when Tennessee is asking you a question, that he isn't listening to your reply. He turns around and you have a feeling that he is lost in another world.

MIKE: Yes, I have often noticed that. A sort of absent-minded professor type.

RAPPER: I suffer from that myself a bit, so it hurts me doubly. And I say, "Well, why, why does he ask me if he doesn't pretend to listen?" But I am sure, of course, he is. He is listening.

MIKE: He is listening to every word you say.

RAPPER: And I must say, he is also like me in a different way. Bette Davis used to say to me, "Irving, you listen only to the things you want to hear." And the same applies to Tennessee. He picks up the shreds of things he wants to hear.

MIKE: Tennessee tells me that Carson McCullers used to tell him that he never was a great conversationalist, but I have always thought him to be a good talker and listener, even though you don't think he is listening. And now I think he is a very interesting conversationalist too. He is always telling anecdotes and amusing stories about people he has known and about his family.

RAPPER: He has always impressed me. I think he has a great faculty of observing. All artists should have a great sense of awareness.

MIKE: Definitely. And he is so funny and amusing himself—

RAPPER: I am always amused by the little Southern nuances in his speech.

MIKE: For instance?

RAPPER: It is always in the nature of conversation, you know. And it would always be the most unhippy, most unmodern phrasing I have ever heard, and yet they have very deep meaning.

MIKE: Things like, "Possess your soul in patience"?

RAPPER: Oh, "Possess your soul in patience" is one of my favorites, but I think it is his mother's.

MIKE: Yes, it comes from her.

RAPPER: The older I get the more I seem to quote my own mother's philosophy, which I used to resent when I was a kid. The older we become the more revered are the things that we have hidden in our lives.

MIKE: More respect for what we should have had respect for all along.

RAPPER: But even ill as Tennessee was that last time I saw him, there was that crazy dance. One of the most peculiar women I have ever seen in my life asked him to dance, and I turned to one of my friends and said, "Oh, God, now what's going to happen?" And strangely enough, with a cigarette in one hand, he danced with her to strange psychedelic rhythms. She danced all around him. She was rather exhibitionistic and silly. And he seemed to glean a great deal of joy and delight from this strange dance which we all enjoyed.

MIKE: I have always felt that Tennessee had that *joie de vivre* that Blanche talks about in *Streetcar*. Such a great lust for living that he never wants anything to end. Even if it's a play he has written, he doesn't want it to come to an end. Any event. As if everything that he's doing is representative of life, and if there is a finality to it he doesn't want to be a part of it.

RAPPER: Well, if you are referring in one way to friend-ship, then I would say that would be a great gift.

MIKE: Yes, it includes loyalty and friendship with Ten-nessee, I think.

RAPPER: Well, he is so abstract I hope he doesn't forget. I wonder how he is ever on time, which he never is, I don't think. Never, never on time, no.

MIKE: And it's gotten worse.

RAPPER: I think he really belongs in a Latin climate. He reminds me of a very close, valuable friend of mine in Aca-pulco, who said, "Next time you come with a watch, I'll throw you out." No, he wants to be entirely oblivious of time.

MIKE: I think he's the same way with places, also. He doesn't want to think that time stops or events stop. And he doesn't want to think that there is just one place that you have to be. He is a great wanderer, with a gypsy spirit of moving from place to place, seeing the world—which I think you have an appreciation for yourself.

RAPPER: Yes, I do. I feel he is very real about these gypsy wanderings.

MIKE: It's a compulsion to have to move and not feel con-fined in one place or one situation. If almost everything has happened that can happen, instead of things just coming to an end, he seems to say, "I've got to leave before it does come to an end."

RAPPER: It gives a lot of meaning, don't you think, to the values he writes about?

MIKE: Of course it does. I have always felt everything he has written is autobiographical. I think there is as much of

Blanche DuBois in his personality as there is Stanley Kowalski. I think he can be refined and sensitive like Blanche
DuBois and I think Tennessee can be just as vulgar and
gauche and insensitive as Stanley Kowalski, on occasion.

RAPPER: I must say, I have only seen the kinder side. And
have hardly ever seen him out of patience. He has always
been terribly kind when I have been with him.

MIKE: I think his kindness stems from the fact that he is
basically a kind person, and if he feels kindness being given
to him he responds with kindness, as most people do. But
even though he is a small man and looks weak and shy, if he
feels that someone is being unkind to him he is quite capable of defense.

RAPPER: He looms large then!

MIKE: Yes.

RAPPER: Reminds me of my favorite story about Claude
Rains. He had a big scene—he was one of my favorite actors
—he had a big scene with Paul Henreid, who was about
six four. Claude bawls him out in the scene and walks away
with smug contempt. I started laughing and had to yell
"Cut!" and Claude said, "What's the matter?" looking at me.
And I said, "Claude, I never realized how short you were
until you left the scene." I think Tennessee embraces that
in character.

George Cukor with Marilyn Monroe. A surprise birthday cake from the crew on the set of the 20th Century Fox film *Let's Make Love*. 1961.

GEORGE CUKOR

George Cukor asked me to come to his home on a Sunday morning. It was a warm July day dominated by the "light-to-moderate" smog that is becoming the daily forecast in Los Angeles. Driving the several miles to George's home, I reflected on the new air of Hollywood. The eye-burning smog, the eye-catching hippies everywhere, the monotonous traffic, the endless tract of houses and jungle-like assortment of small shops, cafes, and dirty-book stores—Hollywood was more a conglomerate of "you name it, we got it" than ever before. Individual style was rarely in evidence.

It was refreshing to arrive at the huge ivy-covered wall that surrounds George Cukor's estate like some medieval castle wall, protecting his privacy from that suffocating new air of Hollywood. Once inside those great walls and sitting in the spacious garden or alongside the athletic-size swimming pool, one feels the atmosphere of Hollywood as it was. The "Golden Age" of Hollywood. The last Garden of Allah. A vanishing life style.

However, after five minutes of conversation with George, one realizes he represents the current state of Hollywood as well as the old. Nothing has passed him by. His impressive energy has persisted throughout more than thirty-five years in the top echelon of the film industry. A man of great wit, charm, and savoir-vivre, *he has probably accumulated more firsthand knowledge of Hollywood than any other person. He has directed most of the great film actresses, including Garbo and Katharine Hepburn and more recently Audrey Hepburn in* My Fair Lady, *which won an Oscar for George. His entertaining manner of reminiscing about the Hollywood film world makes him fascinating to his many friends. It had been about six years since my last visit with George, but he made it seem as if only six days had passed. A few minutes after I arrived we settled down in the shade of the lanai near the swimming pool and began our chat about Tennessee.*

Los Angeles
July 21, 1968

CUKOR: As I told you before, my contact with Tennessee is very tenuous, although I originally met him through Irene Selznick before they did *Streetcar*. She said, "There is this young author. I'm going to do his play. He's coming out here. Could he stay with you a few days?" And he stayed here. And then I met him over the years but never really knew him well. Of course, one feels you know an author very well through his works and I am a great admirer of his, I think he is a most eminent and talented man and a natural-born dramatist and poet. He struck an absolutely new note and was very original. I think he changed the theatre or had a lot to do with it—the taste of the theatre. The boldness, originality was a big influence. He is rather difficult to know. He has enormous charm. As I remember, he has a marvelous sort of giggle. A marvelous laugh. And yet you're kept at arm's length by him. All in all, I met him seven or eight times in my life. What impressed me is that he sees everything from his own point of view. And I think he has a curious kind of self-possession.

I saw him once on a television show. A talk television show. I don't remember just what. But a lot of people were talking on some subject. They were all trying to make an impression and trying to be a little nicer than they were and be a little more interesting than they were. And Tennessee had the candor of a child. He just said everything exactly the way he felt it. He wasn't trying to make good. He wasn't trying to make an impression, which was very interesting. That's what his plays do. And I remember, I think it was Susskind's show, they document these shows, as I remember, and then they take something out of a drawer. Some challenging question. They challenge you. And they said to Tennessee, "You said, Mr. Williams, that you are not going to write any more serious things. In this article, in this interview, you said you are only going to write comedies," or something silly—what they call "thought provocative." And Tennessee giggled and he said, "Oh, that. That article. Well. I remember the fellow who interviewed me. He was a friend of mine. He wanted an interview. And we went out. And we had lunch. And we had a couple of drinks. Maybe a little too many. And I just said that. That's not a deep-seated conviction of mine." Now, most people would have defended that point of view and said, "Yes, I think comedy is the only thing to write." But he just laughed it off. He said, "That day I said that. I had just written a comedy. That's all." He has that candor. Then he told an extraordinary thing about—what was so funny was that everybody else on the program was acting like mad—and he was talking about his grandmother. He said she had been dying, and he said, "My mother insisted I go into the room." And he said this curiously: "Why, I don't know." But the grandmother was past talking and she kept on pointing to something. And, you see, he saw this already in terms of a dramatist. "She kept on pointing and wanting to say something to us. And we couldn't understand what she was saying, but she kept on pointing." And then they said they discovered later that in her corset she had hidden some money and she wanted to tell them about this. But he described this perfectly ordinary scene in the most vivid, interesting way, all filtered through his eyes. And what was funny is the people who were on the program were listening to this thing in a very intense acting way, you see. But he was absolutely candid and funny. Nothing to hide. Nothing to gain. Nothing to lose. And that, of course, is—not of course —but that, I'm sure, accounts for the directness of his plays. He has his own individual vision and he writes that. And that is why it comes out in this pure form that amused me in the television thing. And yet, as he described the scene he wasn't acting or dramatizing but it came out in its most dramatic form, you know. He wasn't acting but you could see this dying woman. So it occurred to me that that's the way he can see life, with that knack of the dramatist.

Then he was in England many years ago and we went down to the country with some friends of mine, an Irish director who makes pictures in England named Brian Desmond Hurst, and Gore Vidal. And we went down to spend a Sunday at Brian's house in the country. It was a perfectly ordinary day and Tennessee talked very casually about his grandfather. The impression that people give is that he was a young man from a small town and had never really been anyplace. Well, he talked about his grandfather. He said, "Yes, I came to England with my grandfather when I was a boy." And you could see that there was background. Although it's very deceptive with Southerners. You can't tell. They all seem full of yams with that curious talk. But not only was he educated, it was the tradition of his family. So it was a wrong idea that he was a young boy of simple and humble origins or whatever kind of origins—aristocratic, as Southerners always pretend to be so aristocratic. But there was a tradition of education in his family. And his grandfather had taken him as a boy to Europe. And he knew a great deal. Much more than most Americans, who put on a lot of dog about it, you see. And there is also an area of mystery about Tennessee. And, as I say, his point of view is very original.

Irene Selznick told me that she went to see a play here. They went to see Jessica Tandy doing a series of one-act plays. This was before *Streetcar*. What was the thing that *Streetcar* was enlarged from? Was it *Twelve Barrels of Hay* or *Twelve . . .* ? What was the origin of *Streetcar*? Wasn't it one of his shorter plays?

MIKE: Yes. *The Long Poker Night* and *Portrait of a Madonna*.

CUKOR: Well, Jessica Tandy played it here. And it was a rather serious thing. And the audience was sitting absolutely seriously and watching this thing, which was rather dramatic. And Irene said there was one person in the audience who was screaming with laughter. And much to her surprise it was Tennessee. Screaming with laughter. And she looked at him and he said, "But don't you think it's funny? It's so funny. It's so terribly funny." Other people would have taken this very seriously. It was rather tragic. But he saw the comic possibilities of it. As I say, the individuality of his point of view.

And, also, to go back to the English episode, he was very annoyed with somebody. Somebody had—and I never saw him angry—somebody had patronized him or something, or somebody had borrowed a book. Things don't annoy him, but he was absolutely furious about whatever this was. And it was curious that he should have been irked by this thing. Everything about him is extremely individual. His writing. His slant on life.

I haven't seen Tennessee in almost fifteen years. Oh, yes, there was one other time. I was making a picture with Marilyn Monroe, and Tennessee and his mother came on the set to see Marilyn. And they were friends apparently. And Tennessee was very funny with his mother. He sort of giggled self-consciously with his mother. And the mother was very fond of Marilyn and made a big show of being fond of Marilyn. And Marilyn liked her. They greeted each other with affection. Marilyn told me, "You know, George, I went to a party and Mrs. Williams insisted on hanging very close to me. She liked me and I liked her but there was something slightly mischievous in the way she clung to me, slightly disconcerting, as though she wanted to disconcert me." I don't quite know what Marilyn meant, but Marilyn was very shrewd. Mrs. Williams herself had a curious slant, and Marilyn got that. She liked her.

MIKE: George, you were always one of Vivien Leigh's closest friends and you were the one who originally cast her in *Gone with the Wind* to play the Southern belle, for which she won the Academy Award.

CUKOR: Yes. I saw the tests, incidentally, that I made. I hadn't seen them since 1939 and they had a memorial to Vivien at the University of Southern California and we were permitted to show these tests, which were very interesting.

MIKE: I thought that perhaps because she had so successfully played the Southern belle Scarlett O'Hara in *Gone with the Wind* that that might have had something to do with the fact that she was sought after to play the Southern belle Blanche in *A Streetcar Named Desire*, for which she won another Oscar.

CUKOR: I have no idea about that. All I know is that she would have been a natural. Also, she was a tremendous star in England and it was a great coup for Irene Selznick, the New York producer, to get her to play the part in London. And Laurence Olivier directed it. So I don't really think, Mike, that that had anything to do with it. She was the leading London actress and it was a leading part and she was box office, and she was a natural for it. She had a very distinguished position on the stage. Maybe it was easier for her to play the Southern part. Curiously enough, it's easier for somebody English to play a Southern part because it's like a whole new language. I believe when Vivien arrived in Hollywood she had never heard anybody talk with a Southern accent at all. It is much more difficult for an American to play a different kind of American. But she learned it as though it were a strange language, you see. And then there was a very nice lady who came up from Atlanta, a friend of Margaret Mitchell's called Susan Myrack, who coached her in that. Mind you, I hear Southern accents played on the screen which are absolutely preposterous. They talk with a mouth full of mush, and it sounds to my ears, not knowing it, absolutely phony. And I think it interferes with the acting. "Yawl gawing heeere." I don't know what the hell they think they're doing. And that passes for a Southern accent. Whereas what was wonderful about Laurette Taylor, aside from being a genius of an actress, she didn't play a Southern accent. She suggested it. She just suggested it. There is nothing worse than going in and just playing any accent all out, because you really can't stand "Yawl gawing—" and all that, which is difficult enough in real life if you get that undiluted. But to play a part—! With Laurette, you knew she was a Southerner. She just touched it lightly. She got the inflections of it and it didn't make the whole part a stunt. She just suggested the Southern accent with a softness in the voice, or however she did it, you know. She didn't do it literally. I think very often actors or actresses who play Southern parts fill their mouth full of molasses and make it awfully tiresome.

MIKE: Yes, that's true, because I coach a lot of actors in films for Southern accents and to get them not to exaggerate is quite difficult.

CUKOR: There was a young lady out here who coached all these people and I never heard anybody talk like that! "You is gawing out heere, you all—" I don't know! Really! Whoever speaks that way, if they do, I should think the people in the South would choke them. Anyway, too much accent of any kind is a bore. The Southern accent is quite agreeable but if it's done all out and not truly done it's wrong.

What they really can't get is the Southern sense of

humor. The wit of the South. That curious kind of slant that's awfully funny that they have, which I think a Southerner has, which is quite different from anything. It's a different kind of wit. It's funny.

MIKE: I think Vivien Leigh did capture that in both of her performances.

CUKOR: She did. She did. She got it and that's what I think is awfully funny. It's a mixture of sophistication and a deceptive kind of simplicity, you know. They kind of talk as though they were farm folk and they're very, very, very sophisticated. The humor has always a touch of homespun in it which is very attractive and funny.

MIKE: Yes. Did you see any of Tennessee when they were filming *Streetcar Named Desire*?

CUKOR: No. No, I didn't. Yes, I may have seen him. I may have seen him at a party. Yes, I'm sure I saw him at a party.

MIKE: But you never saw him together with Vivien Leigh?

CUKOR: No. No, I didn't.

MIKE: I know that he was very, very fond of her and on trips to England he would see her, you know.

CUKOR: I really see Tennessee so little I'm trying to strain to remember the times I have seen him. I'm not sure Tennessee liked me very much! Not that he is unfriendly, but I mean, you know, I just. . . .

MIKE: I think one of the best actresses that we have, Katharine Hepburn, playing in one of Tennessee's films, *Suddenly Last Summer*, was fascinating. And Tennessee thought she was fascinating. He wanted her to have the Academy Award for that performance.

CUKOR: Well, I should think he would have! I should think he would have wanted her to play several parts that she didn't, but I thought she was quite extraordinary in *Suddenly Last Summer*. And as well as I know her, I didn't know that she could be that formidable and that cold. Of course, she had enormous style and distinction in that. The part had a wonderful beginning and then I thought it just fell apart. But she did it with enormous style and authority. I am glad to hear that Tennessee liked it. Well, he should because she did it, you know, marvelously.

MIKE: Yes, I think so, too.

CUKOR: I saw a performance here. I never saw it on the New York stage. I saw it here—the older woman was played by Cathleen Nesbitt, who did it very well. And there was a girl who was quite wonderful.

MIKE: Olive Deering, I think.

CUKOR: Olive Deering! She was absolutely marvelous.

MIKE: She was. Yes.

CUKOR: You saw it here?

MIKE: I did too.

CUKOR: She was marvelous. Quite extraordinary. She came out quite purely and quite terrifying in the play.

MIKE: It was the same part that Elizabeth Taylor did in the film.

CUKOR: Especially, the motive seemed quite mysterious on the stage. There was a wonderful scene, as I remember it, in the play, where for no reason at all she was telling how sane she was and then suddenly she said to the doctor, she attacked the doctor and she said, "Kiss me, kiss me." You knew she was quite mad. And in the film, as I remember it, that was very sentimentalized. The night before she went into some sort of an examination of some kind, she said, "Kiss me," and it was a rather sentimental scene, as though she was going to be executed. Whereas in the play it was so fascinating. Do you remember that?

MIKE: Oh, yes.

CUKOR: That was fascinating in the one-act play. And in the film I suppose they had to use that quite differently. In the play it was chilling, you know, when you suddenly really saw she was dangerous and quite mad. And in the film she was accused unjustly of being mad, which was not nearly as interesting as what Tennessee wrote. It was sort of a distortion of him. I'll tell you who else has played one of his things. I am just talking as a movie audience. In *The Night of the Iguana* I think Ava Gardner was absolutely wonderful!

MIKE: Yes, I did too. I think it was the best acting performance Ava Gardner ever gave us.

CUKOR: Well, I don't. I don't think so. I say I don't think so because I did a picture with her. I think the picture I did was the best! No, but she was wonderful in *Iguana*. She had a kind of real excitement. She was a real movie personality. When she walked across the screen you knew something was happening. It was a remarkable scene when she was in swimming with the two Mexican boys, which she did in the most fascinating way. I thought she was fascinating in that. Absolutely fascinating.

MIKE: Yes, I did.

CUKOR: I was very impressed with her. Tennessee writes wonderful parts for women. Wonderful parts.

MIKE: Well, you know, George, just recently one of my best friends told me, which is a true statement, that Tennessee writes the best parts for women of any writer and that you are the best director of women.

CUKOR: Well, then, we must always leave it that way! Tennessee must write a good part for somebody and let me direct it. No. I think that, you see, in Tennessee's plays the parts are so wonderful there is no end to what you can do with them. I thought the part of Blanche was so wonderful because one is interested in her sensibility, in her education, and certainly she speaks the most poetic way. You feel that she is a high-minded woman doing ignoble things. And that is what is heart-rending and very poetic. You see, he writes these very accurate and perceptive pictures of women.

MIKE: Do you remember Vivien Leigh in *The Roman Spring of Mrs. Stone*?

CUKOR: I didn't see that. Alas, I didn't see that. I would have thought that offhand, knowing the novel, offhand she was—I don't know how the picture came out—but that she was too beautiful. It should have been somebody who was less interesting. More stodgy. You see, you know that Vivien was so beautiful, so attractive. She could attract people. She always had, all her life. She was fascinating.

MIKE: Yes. And Mrs. Stone isn't supposed to have that attraction.

CUKOR: No, Mrs. Stone should have been a rather handsome, slightly uninteresting woman so that one is surprised that she does all this. Vivien—you just know—everybody was in love with her and—so I didn't see the picture, but it was a fascinating story, fascinating.

I think Tennessee's plays can be revived and will be revived in twenty-five years, in fifty years, because I think they're American masterpieces. And they could be revived and played by different people. Played differently, in a wonderful way. I think they will always be done, if we do what they do in England, revive their plays. That Tennessee—so many of his plays can be done. Now they are doing *Camino Real*, which I have never seen. I am anxious to see it here. And also the originality of Tennessee's plays. I mean the original technique, you know, in *Streetcar*, and having the portrait light up in *Glass Menagerie*, and all that kind of thing. In addition to writing beautifully and dramatically, he has such an original and inventive sense and, of course, everything works with Tennessee. He is a real dramatist. If he says a picture should light up, it's just great

MIKE: He has a visual sense, also.

CUKOR: Yes, yes. He is a remarkable fellow.

MIKE: It's so interesting, having that visual sense, that he still doesn't want to write screenplays, which I think is a mistake. I think he should write them.

CUKOR: Didn't he, before he was famous, didn't he have a rather distressing experience out here? Didn't he come out here and just sit around?

MIKE: Yes, I think it goes back to that experience.

CUKOR: I think that threw him higher than a kite. And also I think he is not prepared for the rousting about that the writer gets in pictures. And he doesn't have to be. And he feels, rather practically, "I'll write the thing and it will appear on the stage and God bless them. I hope they make good pictures."

MIKE: Yes. I heard him say once that any good secretary at a studio could put a stage play into screen form.

CUKOR: I'm not quite sure I agree with him but—

MIKE: But that is his attitude.

CUKOR: That is his attitude and it's too bad, but I think it's an attitude that comes out of bitter experiences. And, also, it is a very philosophical attitude. Maugham had things like that. They do the best they can and they cast it upon the waters and hope it will go well. I don't think they are prepared to go through the agony of what goes on for an author of the screen.

MIKE: But Maugham did come out here and try writing the screenplay of *The Razor's Edge*, didn't he?

CUKOR: He did. He did. And I was going to direct it, but I didn't. He wrote a wonderful dramatization of it for no money. He accepted no money. He did it, and I don't think they used a word of it. So you see, I think writers have been badly handled here and that's why they all bear the scars.

It's too bad because I think that Tennessee could write something wonderful for the screen. William Inge told me he read the script of *Boom*, which I haven't seen, and he thought it was absolutely fascinating. He thought that—I haven't seen the picture, but he thought it was Tennessee at his finest.

MIKE: Yes, he told me the same thing.

CUKOR: Inge told you? Well, don't quote me, quote Inge. Well, now, is there anything else, Mike?

MIKE: Another of Tennessee's favorite actresses is Anna Magnani. He wrote two plays on Broadway for her. *The Rose Tattoo* and *Orpheus Descending* were both written for her to play the parts. But she only did the films.

CUKOR: Well, I saw Magnani, with whom I made a picture after that, on the screen doing *The Rose Tattoo*. Incidentally, I think he has the most fascinating titles for his plays. But I thought she was remarkable in that. I thought she was thrilling and funny and she really played the part all out. I thought it was quite, quite remarkable. And how silly of her not to have played it on Broadway, for whatever reason.

MIKE: It was a problem that she didn't know English.

CUKOR: Well, she didn't know English and she did it wonderfully on the screen. In the picture I did, she didn't know English but she has such a wonderful ear that it doesn't make any difference. She is a perverse woman. She is intelligent and a very talented woman, but she is perverse. You don't know what she's up to. On the screen, I thought in *The Rose Tattoo* she was human and funny and quite remarkable.

MIKE: She got the Academy Award for it, of course.

CUKOR: Yes, and well deserved. And then I saw *Orpheus Descending* and I wasn't quite sure about that. I wasn't sure about anything in that picture. I didn't know—I didn't really know—I don't want to seem a cad, but when she was pregnant I thought, "Well, dear, you're a little beyond that," you see.

I would like to correct one thing. When I said, "He writes wonderful parts for women." He writes wonderful parts! I mean, look at the wonderful part he wrote for the boy in *Streetcar*, and he writes, let's say, wonderful parts all over. Like all fine dramatists, all the parts are great and vivid. He writes parts for big talents. They're very big parts and they're wonderful when they're played by people of stature. Because that is what they have to be.

Tennessee Williams, Hal Wallis, and Anna Magnani on location in Key West during the filming of *The Rose Tattoo*. 1954.

Mrs. Edwina Williams, Hal Wallis, Tennessee Williams, Laurence Harvey, and Paul Nathan. Luncheon at the Paramount Studios commissary. 1961.

HAL WALLIS

Hal Wallis has brought several Broadway plays to the screen, notably The Rose Tattoo, Come Back, Little Sheba, The Rainmaker, *and* Summer and Smoke. *The first three became starring vehicles for Burt Lancaster, who was under contract to Mr. Wallis at the time. Lancaster may not have been everyone's ideal choice for each of these films, but he helped assure box office popularity, an important consideration. In two of the pictures the female leads were more important parts and were played by actresses who were brilliant, yet not popularly known at that time by the American public: Anna Magnani in* The Rose Tattoo *and Shirley Booth in* Come Back, Little Sheba. *Both of these actresses won Academy Awards for their performances.* The Rainmaker *co-starred long-time favorite Katharine Hepburn in the role created on Broadway by Geraldine Page. But in general, Burt Lancaster was the public draw for these three films, and the wisdom of Mr. Wallis' casting of a proven star of Lancaster's caliber was confirmed when, in a later film,* Summer and Smoke, *he consented to cast two relative unknowns to star: Geraldine Page and Laurence Harvey. Miss Page had triumphed in the New York revival of the play, and Tennessee was eager that she play the role in the film. Laurence Harvey had become a hot property in Hollywood circles after the English film* Room at the Top. *Even though the film was well made and very good, neither of these newcomers to the American screen was able to attract the public to the box office in huge numbers. However, Geraldine Page was nominated for an Academy Award for best actress. Fortunately, a much larger audience has been able to see this fine film on television recently.*

Hal Wallis, continuously successful, has been one of the top film producers for many, many years. He rarely gives interviews and he preferred not to use a tape recorder. This interview took place in his magnificently appointed offices at Paramount Pictures, with his long-time associate, Paul Nathan, present. While Mr. Wallis talked, I took notes, which I later wrote up in the first person singular to conform to the style of the other interviews in this book. Therefore, the sentence construction is actually mine rather than that of Mr. Wallis.

I have made films from two of Tennessee Williams' plays, *The Rose Tattoo* in 1954 and *Summer and Smoke* in 1961.

My association with Tennessee began in Chicago, where I first saw the stage production of *The Rose Tattoo*. I met Tennessee backstage after the performance. It was there that I told him of my interest in making a film of his play. Subsequently, I bought the property, and Tennessee agreed to write the screenplay.

We had several meetings in New York to discuss the script, and his suggestions and revisions were brilliant. His ideas were invaluable in working out our final shooting script. We had a very pleasant personal relationship, with few of the usual producer-author differences and problems.

Tennessee had written *The Rose Tattoo* originally for Anna Magnani and had hoped she would come to New York to star in the role of Serafina. She was forced to refuse because of her inability to speak English well enough to handle so difficult a role night after night in the theatre.

However, we felt that she would be perfect for the film and that the language barrier could be overcome, since scenes were shot individually and there was no need for a two-and-a-half-hour sustained continuous performance. When the script was completed we flew to Rome and talked to Magnani, for the most part through an interpreter, to persuade her to star in our film. Tennessee, of course, had been a close friend of Anna's for several years. They were very fond of each other and we spent many memorable evenings in her company. She was hesitant about coming to America and doing a film in English, but we had a special script made up for her, the English version on one side of the page and an exact translation in Italian on the facing page. Two months before the film was scheduled to begin in

Hollywood, she finally agreed to come to Paramount and do the film for me. She still spoke English with difficulty and I remember leaving Rome with some misgivings.

Tennessee had decided to come to America with Anna by boat. The trip from Italy to New York took ten days. Every day, all day, Tennessee and his secretary-companion, Frank Merlo, an Italian-American who spoke Italian fluently, worked with Anna, helping her to learn her role in English. She knew what she was saying only because the Italian equivalent was printed on the opposite page of her script. But by the time they arrived in New York Anna knew her lines in English perfectly. The rest is motion-picture history. Anna won the Oscar that year for the Best Performance of the Year in her first American-made English-language picture.

The film was made largely on location in Key West, Florida, and the Chamber of Commerce there was very helpful to us in finding proper locations. I remember we drove all over town looking for a wood frame house that would best fit the requirements as Serafina's home. Finally, I saw one on a corner in an outlying neighborhood. It looked perfect but there was a fence too close to it which enclosed a goat yard belonging to the house next door. I asked my guide from the Chamber of Commerce if he thought the owner of the neighboring house would let us move the fence and provide our own needed goat yard. He said, "Well, I don't think he will mind at all. You see, that's where Tennessee Williams lives."

Tennessee not only let us remove the fence, but he also permitted us to use his house as the dressing rooms for the stars, Anna Magnani and Burt Lancaster.

Tennessee worked every day until about 1 P.M. I would occasionally glance over at his house and see him peering through the curtains of his study on the second floor, watching the shooting. After he finished his day's writing on his new play he would come and join us on the set.

It was an enjoyable location. Everyone seemed to have fun, cast and crew alike. Tennessee and I even agreed to appear as extras in one bar scene which was shot on an actual location in downtown Key West. We stood at a long bar crowded with extras for the scene where Anna rushes in angrily looking for the girl friend of her late husband. She pushed past Tennessee and me to confront the bartender where the dialogue took place. We stood there all day long while the director shot the scene again and again from every conceivable angle. I remember it well, as the temperature was 110° and our "bit scene" was a little more than we had bargained for.

During the filming I decided to fly up to Miami to go deep-sea fishing on a weekend. I invited Tennessee to join me but he declined because he wanted to continue work on his play. It turned out to be a very wise decision on his part, for during my flight to Miami a tropical rainstorm developed. When we finally landed at Miami the runway was flooded, and the plane skidded in on its belly in a crash landing. Everybody got out fast and huddled together at the end of the runway, completely drenched, until officials drove out in trucks to pick us up.

The rain was also particularly heavy when we shot the scenes in the interior of the church. Here again we used an actual interior in Key West. It was one of Anna's most difficult scenes and when we saw and heard the rushes the rain on the roof sounded like a machine gun. We had to re-record the entire scene when we got back to Hollywood, a most difficult procedure because of the high drama of the scene. It was a further tribute to the artistry of Magnani.

When I decided to make a film of *Summer and Smoke* I flew to Rome to see Tennessee, who was spending the summer there. We were thinking of Audrey Hepburn to play the leading role of Miss Alma. She and her husband, Mel Ferrer, had a house in the country outside Rome and they invited us for dinner one evening to discuss the project.

Audrey was a very charming hostess and entertained us as we waited for Mel to get home from the day's filming of *War and Peace*. Finally at nine he arrived and sat down to dinner and a most pleasant evening.

As we left, Audrey literally leaped into Mel's arms as he stood in front of the house. As he held her she comically waved a long goodbye. From the car it looked like a camera shot as we pulled away. Tennessee laughed, leaned over toward me, and said, "Lunt and Fontanne did it better."

Shortly after that, Tennessee and I flew from Rome to Paris to see Montgomery Clift and discuss the possibility of his playing the male lead in *Summer and Smoke*. We had a luncheon together but subsequently for various reasons decided not to go ahead with production of the picture at that time. When we eventually did go ahead we cast the part of Miss Alma with Geraldine Page, who played the part brilliantly in the off-Broadway production at the Circle in the Square. Her film portrayal earned her an Academy Award nomination.

MARGARET LEIGHTON
AND MICHAEL WILDING

Margaret Leighton has been described by Tennessee as being an apparition. ("Oh, she's an apparition!") The dictionary meaning is "a ghostly appearance," but it also says "something remarkable or startling." That she is. Her acting performances are always remarkable and her personality is extraordinary.

When they are in Los Angeles, she and her husband, Michael Wilding, live in one of those large, sturdy, and comfortable Spanish villas in the hills above Sunset Strip. They live graciously, and are obviously a complement to each other.

My appointment to come to their home for taping a conversation was in the afternoon at about cocktail time.

After mixing martinis for us, Michael Wilding excused himself to drive another guest back down the hill. He returned one martini later as Maggie was talking into the tape recorder. The recording session had a feeling of old friends reminiscing about another friend during a cocktail party. I often play Maggie's tape to myself just to listen to the beauty of her voice and speech. The tape began with my usual question, "When did you first meet Tennessee?"

Alan Webb, Bette Davis, and Margaret Leighton. Scene from the Broadway production of *The Night of the Iguana*. 1961. (*Photo courtesy Friedman-Abeles*)

Margaret Leighton
(*Photo by George Kramer*)

Los Angeles
August 8, 1968

LEIGHTON: I think I am right in saying it was in London when I was playing in a play of Terence Rattigan's called *Variation on a Theme*. Tennessee came to see it and said that he had written a play with a part in it that he thought would be suitable for me. Indeed, I was proud later to think that he had thought that, but I didn't do it, to my eternal shame and damnation.

MIKE: Which play was it?

LEIGHTON: It was a play called *Sweet Bird of Youth*, which is no mean play and no mean part.

MIKE: You would have been wonderful in that.

LEIGHTON: I committed sort of mayhem later when I saw it because I hadn't done it. I don't remember precisely when I next met him, but certainly when we started *Night of the Iguana* in New York. I remember clearly the first reading of the *Iguana* and the first reading of *Slapstick Tragedy* in terms of Tennessee. Because I feel, if anything, if it's possible, Tennessee was even more nervous than the cast. They are really tortuous moments for him, I think. We read the *Iguana* in the Algonquin Hotel—in fact, we read both plays there. They were for the same management. We had a kind of suite in the Algonquin and great big tables set up. Everybody sitting around drinking coffee and trying to pretend that it was all very social—and shivering with horror and fright. But Tennessee, I think, probably most of all, because Tennessee is basically, I believe, a very nervous person. This is something I say with some kind of knowledge of the state because I am fairly nervous myself. I don't mean nervous of specific things.

MIKE: But after its opening *Night of the Iguana* received such good notices!

LEIGHTON: Well, there was a lot of water running under the bridges meantime. We rehearsed it for the average time, four weeks. And then we had a rather longer pre-Broadway tour than usual. Usually you reckon, with a straight play, about four weeks. But we had eight and we were out in the Middle West. Thank Heaven! I was very glad of that.

MIKE: Where were you? In Chicago?

LEIGHTON: We were in Chicago for most of the time. I think we were there about five weeks. And we were two weeks in Detroit and a week in Rochester.

MIKE: Did Tennessee remain with the company most of the time?

LEIGHTON: Did he not! He was there every day!

MIKE: Was he working close with Frank Corsaro, the director?

LEIGHTON: With the amount of his writing that was rewritten, altered, replaced, taken out, or put in again, you could have made another play. Tennessee rewrote something every day. He started very early in the morning and the new pages were usually given to us at a kind of preluncheon meeting, perhaps eleven-thirty, twelve o'clock, maybe even earlier. Tennessee, in those days, I think I am right in saying, used to work from something like six to ten or from seven to eleven in the morning. Then we got the material. We used to go to the theatre in the afternoon and work on it, and it went in at that night's performance. And this went on for eight weeks, and he was there every minute of the day. All the time. That, I think, answers your question.

MIKE: Well, I think that was one reason it was such a success then, working toward perfection.

LEIGHTON: Well, it was a kind of tooth-combed play, do you
know? Every line of it was pared and fined down and either
used or not or whatever. I wish I had kept them all. But I
suppose after eight weeks you get kind of punch drunk with
new pages.

MIKE: Did you feel that the play was autobiographical?

LEIGHTON: I think in most cases, in almost all cases with
Tennessee, there is an element of autobiography. He writes
from experience of life.

MIKE: I know that you are one of Tennessee's favorite
actresses and he talks about you quite often, using superla-
tive phrases, and I think at the onset of *Slapstick Tragedy*
that there was no question that he wanted to get you for
those two plays.

LEIGHTON: Well, I'm proud and grateful that he did. They
weren't a success. Every play of Tennessee's is a surprise.
The *Iguana*, to go back to that, I didn't think, when we
opened at the Royale, it would be such a success. I remember on the opening night Alan Webb, who played the grandfather, came into my room after everybody had gone and we
were cleaning up, and said, "Well, Mag, what do you think?"
I said, "I don't think there is a prayer. It's down the spout."
We had had bad notices on tour. There was no question.
Claudia Cassidy, who had been Tennessee's great champion,
gave us such a lambasting in Chicago as you have never
read. I thought that in New York there had been a lot of
word of mouth, which had mostly been dubious. Not only
just the press on tour, but people who had been to see the
play or heard about it or had read it. Tennessee sometimes
prints his plays in something like *Esquire* or whatever it
happens to be before they're played.

MIKE: Before they are rewritten for Broadway production.

LEIGHTON: They're rarely the play that is played. In these cases people have some sort of predisposition about the play. And the word of mouth, I think I'm right in saying, before we came into New York with *Iguana* was not good. And the other play, *Slapstick Tragedy*, Chuck Bowden and Tennessee had asked me to play it certainly a season or really a year before it was finally done. I couldn't do it, for what reason I have quite honestly forgotten. It was a valid reason at the time because they bore me no particular grudge. And as it happened, whoever it was they were hoping would do it didn't. So finally, the following season, I'm happy to say, I did do it. Oddly enough, of those two plays making up *Slapstick Tragedy*—I don't know if you saw them—the play that possibly I wanted to do rather less than the other was the one that was the most recognizable Tennessee. The first of the two. *The Mutilated*.

MIKE: Yes. Set in New Orleans. Yes.

LEIGHTON: I was less keen on this play, and this was the "bigger" part for me. I say "bigger" in quotes to let you know I think it is a stupid adjective. I was fascinated by the second one. *The Gnadiges Fraulein*. I had two lines and three bits of a song or something, I don't know. But that play was, to me, a completely new departure for Tennessee. And a different style of writing. And I think it had a great deal to say.

MIKE: That's why it was so sad when it really didn't catch the fancy of the public or the critics.

LEIGHTON: That's right. When the plays opened, let's face it, neither of them caught the fancy of anybody at all, I think, very much. But the first play did, in terms of the press, who treat Tennessee rightly, with respect. They paid attention to the plays, but really only to the first play. They paid almost no attention to the second one.

MIKE: Do you think the American theatre isn't ready for this type of play?

LEIGHTON: I wonder that. I think the style of the second play was so oblique, was so abstract in—neither of those is the right word, but oblique, I think, is better. It was sort of off kilter.

MIKE: Out of the limits of the physical theatre.

LEIGHTON: It was difficult for the public to grasp. Tennessee's plays always make film sales. I said, "Take it from me," to somebody at large, grandly, "the play that will make a picture certainly won't be *The Mutilated* because that's been seen before. But it will be *The Gnadiges Fraulein,* where you can go into every kind of thing, seeing the whole story and the circus and the girl throwing the fish and the lot."

MIKE: Actually, I have spent quite a bit of time with Tennessee in Key West at his home there and this play, also, I think, is quite autobiographical in a more symbolic way.

LEIGHTON: That's right. Symbolic was the word I was trying to think of.

MIKE: It sort of brings out his suspicions and a bit of his paranoia about the way the people or certain friends think of him in Key West.

LEIGHTON: That's true.

MIKE: Actually, everybody loves him down there. It's all just suspicion on his part.

LEIGHTON: But *The Gnadiges Fraulein* I was really very, very keen on. But I was dogged with bad luck actually on it from beginning until the end. I cracked my shoulder blade the night before we opened, which is no help to anyone, you know! Do you remember the script? Crashing through those fences with a bucket! You have a bucket in one hand and a fence in the other to somehow maneuver, you know, about five times. It was really tough. And I made a mistake, just before we opened, with this damned fence and cracked my shoulder, so I couldn't move one arm at all. I had a sling, I think, for about two performances. And then I lost my voice, increasingly, up until the opening night. And I had a sort of old lady's voice all through the previews. You know, for those silly songs. And on the opening night I had nothing at all, so I thought, well, I don't know what to do. But I had to go on. I was perfectly fit. I had no arm, it's true, but I was upright, you know. Somebody had to do it. Somebody had to go on. And I had my arm in a sling, actually, and no voice. So I had to find another voice, which was a kind of man's voice, somewhere. It was all a disaster. But the part, I was really very, very fond of. If I had a chance ever to do it properly!

MIKE: How did Tennessee feel during the rehearsals of this play?

LEIGHTON: He was curiously—I think that Tennessee was curiously placid and sanguine. For him, not for anybody else, but for him. He wasn't doing pages of rewrites. He wasn't in a great state, seemingly, beyond his usual state, which is fairly great. He had, I think, in that play a director who followed the printed script too literally. By that I mean that in the script it might say a choir of angels enter up left and somebody else comes in down left saying something, you know. Well, this was literally more or less followed on the stage. I don't think directions on paper from an author saying choirs of angels coming on up left necessarily mean what they say. With an author, it's very hard to say, "I don't mean a choir of angels coming on up left." But Tennessee was very sanguine about the whole thing during rehearsals and I think in a sense it didn't pay off.

MIKE: I remember making a trip to London with Tennessee and one of the producers to raise money for the production. And Tennessee's attitude at that time seemed to be, "Oh, it would be such fun to see it on the stage. I don't particularly care if the public likes it or not, I want to see it. It will be fun to do." His attitude seems to be like that more often now.

LEIGHTON: That he doesn't mind what people think? I think he minds very much what people think.

MIKE: I think he does too, but he has a sort of self-protective attitude. But, at the same time, I think it gives him great pleasure to see a play he has written come to life, like it does for any author. And so in that sense he would still rather see it done even if the public isn't going to like it. At least he has had the pleasure of seeing it fulfilled in performance.

LEIGHTON: I think that Tennessee will do *The Gnadiges Fraulein* again in some medium, and I hope that he will have me in it. If it is a movie I doubt he will, because it ought to start with a relatively young girl, I think. I can already think of casting but I am not going to suggest that to anybody! This is a part that I would like to redo. And I think Tennessee, in my limited experience of him, is very tenacious of his work. If a piece of work isn't right the first time, either by his standards or even by somebody else's— that is, if he feels that it has been mishandled in some way or another—he is not going to leave it alone. He is like a dog with a bone. He will dig it up again and redo it. Like *Milk Train* and the *Iguana*. When *Iguana* finally opened on Broadway, it was something like the fourth production. The fourth rewrite. It started as a short story and then it was a one-act play and it was in Key West or in Florida somewhere. It was at the Actors Studio and then it was somewhere else. This was about the fourth time around that he had had a go at it. And Frank Corsaro had been with it since the Actors Studio.

MIKE: Being, in that event, an Actors Studio project, you might say, did it present any problem for you as an English actress working with this sort of New York actor?

LEIGHTON: I loved it. I had played in New York before two or three times. It was the first time I had played in a totally American setup: American author, a new American play, American actors all through. Except for me and Alan Webb. And most of them, and certainly the smaller parts, were actors who had been with it from the beginning at the Studio. And had been out in Florida or wherever it was, and everywhere. It made a tremendous difference.

MIKE: I think it is amusing now since Tennessee has seen you in two of his plays, how often he thinks of you when he's discussing his plays.

LEIGHTON: Really!

MIKE: In casting. I have heard him very often say, "Oh, Maggie Leighton would be marvelous for that."

LEIGHTON: I'm very proud to hear that. The thing that I love about Tennessee as a writer is that he doesn't like spelling things out. He doesn't like laying things on the line. Do you know? What Tennessee will try to scurry out of is his being asked, "What do you mean by this? What does she mean when she says this or that or the other?" which is usually some metaphorical high-flown image that he has dreamed up. He doesn't like having to pinpoint it. And I can't bear being told that sort of thing either. The cat sat on the mat. I think Tennessee gets awfully bored with that. And embarrassed. I think he gets embarrassed.

MIKE: Outside of professional work, do you spend much time with Tennessee? More or less on a social or relaxed level?

LEIGHTON: Yes, a little. But when you are actually in plays it's easier said than done. On tour with this everlasting eight weeks of the *Iguana* we used to meet after the play, socially, talk about it a bit but not really much. By then you have had all day at it. He had been writing it since six o'clock and we had rehearsed it and then played the thing. So that we used to meet and have a couple of drinks in the evening and maybe some food and that was it. And I see Tennessee in New York occasionally, but not a great deal.

MIKE: Tennessee tells a rather funny story on himself: After the opening of *Slapstick Tragedy* you and Michael and he were going in a taxi to a restaurant or somewhere. And after you got out of the taxi, he was still in the taxi, I believe, and overheard you say to Michael, "Poor dear, he doesn't know what hit him!"

LEIGHTON: What does he mean by that?

MIKE: That the play had not been a success and that he was sort of dazed and affected by it.

LEIGHTON: I don't remember that! And I don't remember going into a taxi. He has invented the whole thing! He has invented the whole thing! Now I am trying to think seriously after that play where we went. I am really trying hard to think.

MIKE: Anyway, Tennessee was very amused about it all.

LEIGHTON: I think it is unlikely. Because I would have remembered, and I don't remember going in a taxi with Tennessee. I can't even remember where we went after the opening.

MIKE: What do you feel his reaction was after the reviews weren't too favorable? He seemed to feel depressed or withdrawn?

LEIGHTON: Yes, I think he did. I think it hurt Tennessee that they were badly received. I was hurt for Tennessee, not, frankly, because of *The Mutilated.* I don't really care if he even hears this on the blower. But I did care in terms of the other one, *The Gnadiges Fraulein.*

MIKE: That is his favorite, also.

LEIGHTON: I think that was a fine piece of work. And I think it was highly underestimated then. And I think if Tennessee is the man I think he is, he will do it again, in some form. I think that if he could find somebody with a grain of sense to do it, it should be redone. Perhaps as a film. Or maybe he would rewrite it as a play, or even redirect it as a play or something. It came in for so little attention before, it's discouraging.

MIKE: I remember the film you did of Faulkner's *The Sound and the Fury.* The character that you played reminded me, and I think maybe other people, occasionally of Blanche DuBois in *Streetcar.*

LEIGHTON: Faulkner was writing before Tennessee, I think —please correct me if I'm wrong.

MIKE: Many times you have played these Southern-lady parts. You just finished in *The Little Foxes* on the stage. Do you enjoy playing the Southern-type parts?

LEIGHTON: Yes, I suppose I do. I think so. I don't know that I enjoy playing all of them.

MIKE: The reason I ask is that in my opinion the British actors and actresses do it more successfully than the American actors and actresses.

LEIGHTON: I knew you were going to say that! People have this ridiculous theory that it's easy for English people to speak with a Southern accent. Well, this to me is idiotic because the Southern speech has no consonants at all. I mean relatively speaking. The vowels are extended to the point of madness. The English have distorted vowels and clear consonants. There is no similarity at all. The English have a rather staccato rhythm and sound, melody, if there is one, in the speech. But the Southern speech has a distinctive melody and if you hear the melody in your ear, you can get the lilt of the sentence. I think Tennessee is about the only American writer, American playwright, I know or have ever worked for who has the European—not the English particularly, but the European—sense of tragicomedy. The sort of Chekhovian comedy which is, to me, the best form of theatre. Tennessee is the only playwright, for me, in this country who is genuinely of that school of writing. No. I'll add Edward Albee. It is a truthful reflection of life.

MIKE: Do you think that a play like *Gnadiges Fraulein* would have been a success if it were done in Europe first?

LEIGHTON: Yes. —Darling! Come in!

[*Michael Wilding entered, made a drink, and joined the conversation.*]

MIKE: We're discussing the production of *Slapstick Tragedy*. What were your impressions of it?

WILDING: Well, during the two weeks of previews there wasn't a mass of people flying around backstage, saying, "Darling, this is marvelous." Ominous silence went on. People didn't come round back, which I felt had to mean they were reserving very much their judgment and weren't entirely delighted with the plays. No one seemed to be delighted with the plays. I thought the last one was marvelous —the second one was marvelous. I liked the first one too. Maggie didn't so much, but I liked the first one. But she is more used to Tennessee than I am. So I liked them both, but still there was this kind of reticence going on. So I felt however good the notices were, you know, laughing at things or not, there wasn't any flying backstage to say "Well done" and "How beautiful" and "How gorgeous" at all, so I felt it was sort of dying as it went along. But Tennessee sat there in his box and he laughed at the jokes, which were very funny. Even then I would have thought he would have been rather bored with it by that time, but not at all. And he had a great time there in full view. He wasn't cringing behind or walking up and down behind the stalls or out on the street. I am sure he was dying of fright really, but he sat there and appeared to have a very good time. Which I admire him for very much because he also knew that people weren't flying around to say, "This is divine," "This is great," "This is marvelous."

MIKE: I think that his attitude in enjoying what he had written certainly indicates that he was well pleased with the way it was being performed and directed.

WILDING: Performed, I think.

MIKE: Do you think maybe just hearing his lines spoken out loud was giving him pleasure?

WILDING: I am sure it was.

LEIGHTON: In terms of London, I think the audiences are very perverse about Tennessee because they, by and large, for all my grand words about Chekhov and all that, you know, London audiences as a rule haven't received Tennessee's plays all that well. And I said, as a matter of fact, probably to my eternal shame, No, when they asked me to do the *Iguana* in London, unless they could take over the entire American company and, of course, they couldn't. Because if Tennessee is done by half-English companies, it does something to the texture of the writing. This is a paradoxical thing for me to say, because I was playing an American in New York! You would think playing Tennessee would be like playing Chekhov—a style not foreign really to European actors. But his work never seems to be right when it's done there. Except one play he had which was a flop in New York, I'm told. I didn't see it, but it was a comedy.

MIKE: *Period of Adjustment.*

LEIGHTON: Yes, *Period of Adjustment.*

MIKE: That was a success in New York, but it wasn't a big success.

LEIGHTON: Well, I'm wrong then, but Tennessee always talked about it as a flop there. You know how he goes.

MIKE: They did it at the Royal Court in London.

LEIGHTON: And it was a tremendous smash for the Royal Court. It was a great success.

WILDING: I think Tennessee is like a bullfighter, like Manolete or someone. He has to work close to the horns all the time, to be so successful, and he has been so successful, writing his own poetic kind of Southern thing, or whatever mystic thing he's got. And they, the critics, expect him to be better each time. He can't be better each time. And the critics are the ones who are killing him by making him work closer to the horns. You can't be better all the time. But like a great bullfighter, he wants to be better all the time and braver. And there are the horns! And he can't go on doing it, you know. And I think he gets deeply hurt and distressed by what the press sometimes says about him. Because he has tried so hard, and on he goes, and he doesn't like it too well.

LEIGHTON: It is like I was saying about Tennessee's tenacity, you know. That I think he will redo the play, because he keeps them under the bed! He drags them out and does them again. But the one that I hope he will do again is *Gnadiges Fraulein.*

WILDING: But that's a hard one to do.

LEIGHTON: I don't think any screenwriter should touch *Gnadiges Fraulein.* Only Tennessee. That's for certain.

HERMIONE BADDELEY

Hermione Baddeley travels around almost as much as Tennessee. That is, at least between London, New York, and Los Angeles, Even within one city she is constantly on the move because she has the widest circle of friends of anyone I know. She is a party-going and -giving girl, but she is also a dedicated, hard-working actress.

My first contact with Hermione was in 1964 in Spain, where she was visiting her former husband, the Right Honourable David Tennant, at his villa in a mountain village near Málaga. A mutual friend, Gerald Hamilton, was her guest there after having been my house guest, and he had her telephone me in Madrid, where I was working on a film, to inquire of Tennessee's whereabouts. Tennessee had been reported as traveling in Spain and she wanted to invite him to stay at the villa. Unfortunately, I had had no correspondence from Tennessee since he had written several weeks earlier from Key West that he was coming to Madrid to see me. He wanted me to spend the summer traveling about Europe with him. He never showed. But a Barcelona newspaper reported that he was in that city. Tennessee told me later that year in New York that he had gone from Barcelona to Tangier to visit Jane and Paul Bowles, and that he was traveling with his long-time dear friend Marian Vacarro. Hermione and I were both sorry to have missed him.

Hermione has become one of Tennessee's favorite friends. There are many reasons for this: She has a sustained and vociferous wit (Tennessee says she is the only person who can outtalk his mother), she makes a hardy fun-loving drinking companion, and she has a great amount of genuine affection for Tennessee. Tennessee loves her.

At the time of the following conversation Tennessee was

on an extended visit to Los Angeles and we were all together a great deal of the time. Hermione was in town for some work at the Walt Disney Studio, where she is under contract, before going to New York to star in the musical The Canterbury Tales.

Hermione Baddeley with Tennessee Williams in Italy for the Spoleto Festival of Two Worlds and the world premiere of *The Milk Train Doesn't Stop Here Anymore*. 1962. (*Photo by Roloff Beny*)

BADDELEY: So far I have found when one meets a real genius they are always marvelous. And they never disappoint you. I was lucky enough at the age of fifteen to meet H. G. Wells and George Bernard Shaw and then, far later on, Winston Churchill. After that the most exciting of all for me was Tennessee Williams. Tennessee has a wicked sense of fun when you meet him which is never boring, which just makes other people forgotten when you are with him. He has a touch of the wild-boy sense of humor, which at times reminds me of Dylan Thomas. But Tennessee of all these people has the greatest quality of humanity, which is just very wonderful, this quality. And I consider myself extremely lucky to have played in one of Tennessee's plays after being in America only one year and a half. This was put on during the New York newspaper strike, otherwise it would have run as long as *Streetcar Named Desire,* I am quite sure. The audience reaction was more than I have ever felt with a play. Watching the great production of *Camino Real* at the Mark Taper Forum the other night, again and again I found myself saying, "This is the present-day Shakespeare." These wonderful, glorious sentences, pouring out from the poet-playwright, that one longs to memorize. The fantastic melting of words and sentences. The feeling is just as one has with the great Shakespearean plays. And you have to go back to the book again and again to remind yourself. Tennessee's plays have many deep layers and meanings of thought. Indeed, again as with Will Shakespeare. That is why I think all his plays should be tried out for many months before they go to such harsh critics as London and New York. The actors have to prepare and also the director must be prepared for many months before. It is only fair. There's so much to take in and master. When Tennessee said to me once that I was so very like a favorite actress of his called Laurette Taylor, I was overjoyed and oddly enough I knew he was right. I love him as a friend and I adore him as a playwright and poet.

MIKE: Hermione, when you say the production of *Milk Train* seemed to you, as a person playing in it, to receive very good audience reaction each evening, and that it could have run, do you think, therefore, that the producer should have let it stay on?

BADDELEY: Oh, quite definitely, because that play was climbing and climbing, although this terrible blackout of papers was going on. I mean there were several other great plays on. Bill Inge had one that came off in three weeks. So, you see, we really were going along well.

MIKE: Also, when you say that Tennessee Williams' plays have so much in them that they should have longer periods of rehearsals or out-of-town tryouts, do you think that with the economic situation in our theatre that something like that could still be justified?

BADDELEY: Yes, well, you see, *Milk Train* did have just that very thing. We had the most wonderful reception in Spoleto. So that is why I knew it was good. But of course there were always people who love to attack him because he is just too good. People like that have to have attackers. They've just got to.

MIKE: It seems to me that a Broadway producer who is presenting a play that has made a pre-production sale to the movies should use some of that movie money to rehearse the play longer before it reaches Broadway and to really make the play a beautiful production.

BADDELEY: Well, I think you've got a great idea there. You really have.

MIKE: I am sorry that hasn't been the situation more often, but it seems to me the state of the American theatre is just to make that extra dollar, and there is a lack of appreciation for works of art on the part of producers, usually, nowadays.

BADDELEY: Yes.

MIKE: But I would like to ask you more about Spoleto, where *Milk Train Doesn't Stop Here Anymore* had its initial production.

BADDELEY: Tennessee was there for the festival. He was so delighted because *Milk Train* was the most successful of that year. And, in fact, we received sort of applause rather like the opera, you know. Ten, twelve, fifteen curtains. It was ecstatic. Claudia Cassidy came over from Chicago and she just went all out about this play. You know, she really loved it. And Tennessee said, "What? She thinks it's wonderful!" And everybody was very excited about it.

MIKE: Was Tennessee working closely with the director, Herbert Machiz?

BADDELEY: Yes. Very. Herbert was, I think, excellent, really. He was a little bit muddling over the other parts. I think he worried a couple of the actors, but by and large I think he did a wonderful thing. And he was especially right with me. He knew just how to handle me.

MIKE: But Tennessee was giving rewrites at this time?

BADDELEY: Right the way through! And most of them were a great improvement. And as I say, I know that play would have been just the greatest hit in New York if only they had—I know Martita Hunt said to me, "When I played *The Madwoman of Chaillot* they came to me after six weeks and said, 'We're taking it off.' But I stamped my foot down and I said, 'You've got to give this play a chance.' And as you

know, it turned into a big hit." And she said, "You should
have done this with *Milk Train*. Your play with the strike on
is doing better than we were doing with *The Madwoman of
Chaillot*." I was just not firm enough about *Milk Train*.

MIKE: You told me a story once about Liz Taylor and
Richard Burton coming to Spoleto to see the production of
Milk Train.

BADDELEY: Yes, they came on the only night we were off!
And they were so sort of hot and tired. They had come
all the way from Rome and they looked so disappointed.
Mr. Menotti gave a special party for them. They kept look-
ing disappointed that we couldn't put on a special show.
Anyway I think they did see the play later in New York.

MIKE: Well, I am sure that neither of them had any idea
that they would do the film *Boom*, which is loosely based
on *Milk Train*.

BADDELEY: No, I don't really in all fairness ever think that
they thought of this as a prospective vehicle for them. They
really came over because they heard it was very exciting.
And they wanted, particularly Richard did, to see me in
the part.

MIKE: Were any rewrites done for the New York production?

BADDELEY: Well, it was such a great hit in Boston and
Philadelphia that there were very few rewrites. When we
got to New York that was it really. But then, of course, it
was removed during the newspaper strike. And then David
Merrick called me and said, "This should never have been
taken off, with your wonderful performance. I won't have it.
It's a great play and I shall put it on again. Let me know
when you are available." I said, "Unfortunately, I am going
to Hollywood to do *Mary Poppins* and *The Unsinkable*

Molly Brown but I will be free in four to five months' time."
"Splendid," he said. "We must do this play again." And then
to my horror I found, in the middle of one of these movies,
that it was indeed being re-presented by David Merrick,
with Tallulah Bankhead in the part! I was a little bit hurt.
But I imagine what happened was my agent said, "Miss Baddeley is unavailable." Agents are very hard. They thought
it had been taken off in New York and that's that. Then it
wasn't fair what happened after that. It was very unfair to
The Milk Train, which is like a problem child, you know,
that must be looked after. That's why I want to do it in
London. I would like to bet you it would be a big hit in
London.

MIKE: What would you describe Tennessee's reaction as
being when *Milk Train* failed? Although you yourself got
good personal notices.

BADDELEY: The first New York production of *Milk Train*
didn't get bad notices. It got good notices. I got fabulous
notices. They merely said, "This isn't Tennessee Williams'
best play," and perhaps I slightly overshadowed it because
I was a new actress and all that. But they love to pick on
him and bicker. They love that. That is part of his greatness,
I think. They've just got to attack him a little. What was
unfair was the second production, of course, which was just
badly handled.

MIKE: What was Tennessee's reaction at this time? Was
he very hurt or withdrawn by it all?

BADDELEY: Well, he was disappointed when the producer
removed it from the Morosco. And indeed Mildred Dunnock
wouldn't believe it. She said, "This play is such a success!"
It was going beautifully, you know, really well. And at that
time you would expect half-empty houses, you know. But
however it was, by word of mouth, it was going well. This

is the trouble. I mean that's what's so sad. And Tennessee was hurt because he went away out of town, you know, thinking, "This thing is running." But it was never never a flop or a failure as people like to say. I was in *A Taste of Honey*, which ran for a year on Broadway. I would say it went far better than *A Taste of Honey* did when I was playing that. The audiences simply loved *Milk Train.*

MIKE: Wasn't Frank Merlo still alive when *Milk Train* was done in New York?

BADDELEY: Frank was, but he wasn't able to be around enough.

MIKE: He was very ill at the time.

BADDELEY: He was very, very ill. And we all feel that he was tremendously influential in pulling together previous plays, you know. Making excellent suggestions when pulling them together.

MIKE: Tennessee always had a feeling of security with Frankie.

BADDELEY: Frank was ill at the time and that was very bad luck. There was a great amount of sadness surrounding that. And yet, all the way through it Tennessee was wonderful about it really. But Tennessee was happy about the play. I remember his having lunch with Herbert Machiz and me after the opening night. And, you know, he was joking and saying, "Oh, she's pulled off all the notices," and all that sort of thing, and you knew he was pleased.

MIKE: So you think the play will be done in London?

BADDELEY: Yes.

MIKE: So often Tennessee has done rewrites of plays that had not been successful. The classic example is *Orpheus*

Descending, which had previously been *Battle of Angels,* and neither version was too successful. Then a film was made of it called *The Fugitive Kind,* which also was unsuccessful. Some people say that at a certain point things should not be dug up again or rewritten.

BADDELEY: If I were the average public, every play of his would be an enormous success. I think that it is a great tribute to him, as he is so much above, you would think, the average public, that his movies are usually such great, great box office draws. I mean he is really a very unusual person.

MIKE: So, you would say a play that hasn't been well received may be because it didn't have the correct production or didn't have enough exposure to the public to catch on, rather than the fault of the writing?

BADDELEY: You see, with him, as I keep saying, comparing him to Shakespeare, the parts are tremendous. You have got to be as big as the play to be able to do them and say them and put them over. You have got to have great directors. They're not just little anythings. His plays are so tremendous. But I found myself saying to him the other day, "You're terribly lucky, Tennessee, to be recognized in the way you are." Being such an enormous genius, rather like Strindberg, whom every critic turned down and yelled and screamed, "This dreadful man," you know, in his day. And poor Shakespeare had a battle of a time. It has only been Laurence Olivier, and a few others, who have brought Shakespeare to the screen even.

MIKE: You see Tennessee fairly often, then, as a friend of his, I know. Do you find him amusing to be with and someone who is very diverting and entertaining?

BADDELEY: Well, I feel just like you obviously do. I just absolutely love his company. I sort of giggle inside every moment I'm with him. He seems to make every moment funny and every ordinary event amusing. And I mean he is the type of person one doesn't often meet, although there are a few that I have found. And you can't resist them. I mean they are just too wonderful.

MIKE: He does have a unique sense of humor that you seem to be very much in tune with.

BADDELEY: Yes, that's it!

MIKE: Did you first meet Tennessee in America or England?

BADDELEY: Well, a friend of mine saw *Baby Doll* in London and she said, "I loathe most movies but my goodness, there's a good one on around the corner." We didn't know Tennessee then, but we went to see this. Then about a year later I was just preparing to go into the country. A car was outside, and I was just leaving. And there was a knock on the door and this friend of mine, Maria Britneva, arrived with Tennessee Williams. I mean it was absolutely astounding to me. This wonderful creature standing there with his cocktail shaker. A beautiful, shiny, silver cocktail shaker. And he said, "Nobody makes cocktails properly in this country. This is really cold and I brought it with me. And I brought a play called *The Rose Tattoo* because Maria says you're the one actress in England who'll really be able to take on this part." I was flabbergasted, but very delighted. So he put the play on the table and said, "Read it during the weekend and tell me what you think of it." So I said, "Well, I don't have to tell you. I know about *The Rose Tattoo*. And we must ring up Mr. Binky Beaumont on Monday and say that you want it done and I will do it." And he agreed. He said, "This must be done." So at that moment Laurence Harvey, who had moved into my house—he'd lost the key to his flat and he was staying with me—and he wandered in there sort of looking startled when he saw Tennessee. I never knew whether he knew it was Tennessee, but I think he felt something, and he saw the script on the table and I am sure he was very anxious to know whether there was a nice part for him in this play. Because at that time Laurence Harvey was completely unknown. He was doing little B films around London. And, indeed, I was in one of them. So that was how we all met, and we went on this rather crazy but rather wonderful party with a maharaja who was the person waiting in the car in fact. Of course we had dragged him in and he was at Tennessee's cocktails and we were all very happy by now and it was a most beautiful weekend. The disappointment was ringing up Binky Beaumont the next day and hearing that Binky Beaumont, being a great admirer of Tennessee, and he likes me very much as an actress, he said, "Well, I can't think of anything more interesting than you two together but I wouldn't dare put on *The Rose Tattoo* here because of the religious angle." It was a very tricky play to do. And so I remember Tennessee making a wonderful remark. He said, "Oh, I feel very sorry for very good actresses in this country."

MIKE: Maybe Mr. Beaumont didn't want to take a chance since *The Glass Menagerie* had not been a success in London with Helen Hayes starring and John Gielgud directing. I don't think it was a very big success, was it?

BADDELEY: Well, I just can't think why. That is one of the mysteries. I think it must have been a very difficult time in the London theatre world or something like that. Or they were at the wrong theatre. Mind you, they were at the St. James Theatre, which people were talking about having pulled down. But I remember being amazed at that not going well because I wanted to scc it and it was off before I could see it.

MIKE: How do you feel about mixed casts? That is, British and American actors playing together with their different accents?

BADDELEY: I think it is marvelous. I think the more mixed you get it the better. If you can act, you can act! I don't think it matters and I think it is so irritating, this Equity business. I can only think that in England they are so frightened in such a small country that they will be overrun. But I think there should be a fair exchange the entire time. Because obviously the public likes the exchange. For thirteen years the American musicals absolutely ruled the waves completely in England. Nobody ever thought of going to an English musical because the American ones happened to be the best. Now in New York they are taking a lot of English actors and English plays because they are the best at the moment. Don't you agree?

MIKE: I do. Very much.

BADDELEY: I get so irritated by this. You must exchange. With these two countries with the same tongue! I mean it is ridiculous!

MIKE: The same tongue, but the accents differ. Especially in Tennessee's writings. So many of his plays are set in the American South.

BADDELEY: I don't think that matters. You know, Vivien Leigh and Margaret Leighton told me it's so easy to fall into the "South." Actually, oddly enough, no one can ever utterly get an accent because something strange about nature keeps this thing to themselves. But they can give a beautiful feeling and impression. Just like some Americans I know give a pretty good Cockney accent and British-officer accent. And I think it should be encouraged.

MIKE: Hermione, are you very familiar with Tennessee's poetry? Not many people know that Tennessee has written as much poetry as he has.

BADDELEY: The point is that he is such a great poet and yet the plays have overshadowed it. We all think of him, you know, in terms of the theatre and movies. But if he only stayed a poet he would still be glorious. To me it is better even than Dylan Thomas. To me it is most wonderful poetry. But poetry is usually kept for a little group of special people—although it is accepted more now. But I hate that sort of prissy poetry attitude, don't you? What I loved the other day at that little party was the way his brother, Dakin, read it! Four or five poems, without making an entire evening of it. But casually done. And then Tennessee said, "Now let's shut up." Don't you agree? I don't personally enjoy planned poetry readings. But that is what is so gorgeous about the Williams family. They have grown up with poetry. The mother knows Tennessee is a poet. He can't help it. That comic song—"Gold Tooth Woman"—that the brother did at the piano! He's just born like that. And he is a natural, unaffected, gorgeous poet, isn't he? But you know, I can see him when people come up to him and say, "Oh, will you come and read your poem?" Well, I can see him absolutely giggling and saying, "Oh, we don't want to do that." I mean he is absolutely something. For me he is a perfect mixture. If he will only watch out for his health, because Tennessee is, we feel, in for further recognition. The young people of today dig him. They seem to understand him. And this says a lot for our new young group. I've overheard young people in cafés and at parties talking so excitedly about the production here of *Camino Real*.

WILLIAM INGE

William Inge at the beginning of his career was somewhat of a disciple of Tennessee's. He has always been Tennessee's closest playwright-friend. In August, 1968, I drove Tennessee to Bill Inge's house in the hills above Sunset Strip for their first visit in a long time. It was a warm and sentimental occasion. They embraced and Tennessee said, "I have always had a special love for you, Bill." A few days later Inge asked me, half jokingly, "How is Tennessee? Does he still love me?" understanding quite well Tennessee's ambivalence toward everyone he knows, his duality of feeling. In the past few years I know of no one, from his mother to his maid, toward whom Tennessee has not at some time or another felt antagonistic. However, that is far from being his typical behavior. He's usually a very nice, gracious, and kind person.

The present-day Inge appears to be more at peace with himself than ever before in my sixteen-year memory of him. He writes every morning, reads a lot, swims, and continues his favorite hobby of collecting paintings, which he buys, sells, and trades with a connoisseur's enthusiasm.

In the fall of 1968 William Inge became Professor Inge at the University of California, at Irvine. His classes, naturally, are in playwriting, and his presence on that campus is one reason UCI enjoys an increasing reputation of having the best liberal-arts department in the West.

I sat on the floor of Inge's thickly carpeted living room, manipulating the tape recorder. His West Highland terrier, Toby, playfully interrupted occasionally as Bill and I talked about the person who has tremendously influenced both our lives.

William Inge in front of the Liberal Arts Building of the University of California at Irvine. December, 1968. (*Photo by the author*)

Los Angeles
September 12, 1968

INGE: It was in October of 1944 when I first met Tennessee. I didn't know then whether to call him Tennessee or Tom. First I would call him one name and then the other. I usually call him Tenn now. I was living in St. Louis at the time and working on a newspaper there. I was a drama and music critic and I did feature stories on public personalities, artists who came to town, and I had had a note from a nice old lady in town who was a friend of Tennessee's that he would be in town, that he was going to have a play in production soon called *The Glass Menagerie.* And the lady thought I should do a feature article on him. So I called his home and made an appointment and we met. I did the article and we became good friends. I don't think he had many friends left in St. Louis. It had been quite a few years since he had been there and he told me he had never enjoyed life in the town. And most of his memories in St. Louis, I think, were un-happy ones. So I think I showed him a good time for a couple of weeks. We were very close for those two weeks. We enjoyed quite an intimate friendship in talking with each other about our lives, what we hoped to make of them, and he told me something about his play *The Glass Menagerie.* But he was cryptic, understandably. No artist likes to talk much about his work. He said it had something to do with the lives of his own family, that it was a play drawn from his own life. And I continued to see him. I had to cover the concerts in town, the symphonies, the plays, the movies, so I would take him with me every night I had to go to some place. And we enjoyed each other's company enormously. Then he left for New York for rehearsals of *The Glass Menagerie,* which was to open in Chicago Christmas week of '44. I had told him I thought I could be in Chicago that week to see the play and I did make it. I arrived there for its first weekend showing. It had opened on a Monday and I saw its first Friday-night performance. It's an irony now to recall that the play at that time was far from a success. Tennessee was very discouraged. So were the others in the company. They had received good reviews from, I think, all the Chicago critics, but the public had not yet taken to the play. They weren't doing good business. I went to see it and I sat in a half-filled theatre, but I watched the most thrilling performance of the most beautiful American play I felt I had ever seen. And I still feel so, I think, in all honesty. I had the feeling at the time that I was seeing what would become an American classic. And I sat in the theatre with Tennessee and another friend of his from New York. I think it was Donald Windham. Yes, it was. And they, of course, had lived very close to the play. Tennessee and Donald were good friends then and saw quite a bit of each other and they were close enough to the play that they could sit there in the theatre and laugh about little things in it, and make fun of little things in the production that they didn't quite like. And I couldn't stand this because I was being overwhelmed by this experience. I had no way of knowing just from being with Tennessee for a couple of weeks—I was expecting a good play, yes, but I didn't know that I was going to encounter a work of genius. And I didn't know either that I was going to see this marvelous performance by Laurette Taylor. It was the finest piece of acting—I don't think to this day I have seen a piece of acting as fine as hers. She was thrilling and terribly exciting to watch. And the play itself was written so beautifully, like carved crystal, and so it was a stunning experience for me and it shocked me a little, too, to suddenly see this great work emerge from a person that I had come to know so casually. And so I—suddenly—I held him with a reverence I think—that made the casual geniality of our friendship almost impossible from then on. I think from that time on we were always a little self-conscious with each other. The play was a great experience for me, too, in that it enabled me for the first time to see the true dynamics between life and art. Tennessee had told me just enough of his life that I could see through the symbolism of the play and see how he had arrived at this work. How he had achieved it. How he had ground it out of his own living and experience. And as sophisticated as I thought I was at that time about art—I had been a student of the theatre and literature for all my years—I was just thirty-one at that time, I think— for all of my supposed sophistication in cultural matters I never had seen—I never felt—that simple dynamism between life and art. I had not really known, I think, where art came from before that experience. That's why the experience will always be one of the greatest experiences of my life and that's why I'll always revere, I know, the man who gave me that experience.

MIKE: Do you feel that in Tennessee's other works there's also that strong corresponding relationship between his art and his life?

INGE: Yes. Yes. All art comes out of life. We know that. Even fantasy comes out of life. The surrealistic comes out of life too. But yes, I think I have seen in just about all of Tennessee's plays some connection, remote or otherwise, between the work and his life. But I don't think any of his plays is quite as personal as the *Menagerie*, although *Menagerie*, when you see it, does not strike you as a too personal play in any way at all. It's a real work of art. It's not what you could call an indulgent piece of self—it's not self-indulgent, is what I am trying to say. It is out of self, but it's conceived in terms of universality.

MIKE: The pains of being unhappy in St. Louis and having had an unhappy family life there influenced Tennessee's genius to write a play like *Menagerie*. Do you think it is worth having those painful experiences if they make one an artist capable of producing something like that?

INGE: Well, an artist hasn't any choice, really. He can't ask himself, "Is it worth it?" An artist can only deal with his life and I don't know what the statistics are on the matter but it does seem that most artists, most creative people, have had miserable personal lives, at least such a high percentage of them do that we do have to stop and admit the fact that there is some relation between suffering and creation. But an artist can't say, "Is it worth it?" Oh, yes, yes, he can. He can say, "No, it's not worth it! I am going to end it all and not put up with this damned existence." But usually he feels, "No, I've got something to deliver." An artist usually feels that he has to justify his existence in some way. I think almost every real artist I have ever known has felt that in some way. That he has to justify his existence.

MIKE: After you met Tennessee in St. Louis and then saw him in Chicago, didn't you, within the next couple of years, make the move to New York also?

INGE: Let's see, I met Tennessee in '44 and I wrote my own first play that following spring. It was a play called *Farther Off from Heaven*. It was a simple family story. You know, having seen this relationship between life and art in Tennessee's work, I felt that I knew where to look for something in my own life to work with. So I wrote a family play. Today it seems a very immature thing. But it holds together and it's, I guess, a piece of some little value. I sent it to Tennessee. At that time he was visiting Margo Jones down in Dallas. Margo was just about to start her Dallas Theatre. She thought she was going to start it in '45. It turned out she wasn't able to start it until '47 and she did open her theatre with my play and it came off successfully down there. But I went on writing and it was not until 1949 that I went to New York. I went to New York with *Come Back, Little Sheba* in July of 1949 and considered myself a working playwright from then on. I wrote three plays before I was able to write *Come Back, Little Sheba*, before I had the writing equipment to do it with.

MIKE: When you moved to New York, Tennessee was also living there, and you saw each other fairly frequently, I believe, didn't you? You had a lot of mutual friends there in the literary world.

INGE: Yes, I saw quite a bit of Tennessee in the early fifties. But he was always a great traveler and he would never stay in one place very long. And I'm just the opposite. I get in a place and I stay, and I stay, and stay. I travel very little.

MIKE: I have always thought it interesting that you have never been outside the continental United States, having been born and reared in Kansas, the heartland of America. You have stuck to this country constantly.

INGE: Yes, I don't know if it's a—I have read of one other writer who is that way. A very good writer, a woman, who died a few years ago. I can't remember her name right now. But she tells somewhere of how she feared leaving this country, as though she might destroy the very—she didn't want to pull up the roots that she felt her writing grew in. And consequently she had never taken a trip abroad.

MIKE: Is that also your attitude?

INGE: It's something I subconsciously fear. Consciously I know that it's nonsense, that a trip abroad isn't going to pull up my roots. I guess I can only say that I really haven't been concerned about going abroad. It stays in my imagination as a terrible ordeal: packing trunks, and making reservations on either an airliner or a steamship, and then getting from one country to another, one city to another, not knowing about accommodations, and so forth. It just seems like it stays in my imagination. When I fantasize going abroad, it's an ordeal. My main concern is to get as much out of myself as I can while I live, to produce as much as I can, and I have never felt that I needed a trip abroad to enrich what I have to write about. I think perhaps I feel that a trip abroad would be frivolous of me.

MIKE: Why do you think Tennessee has always felt such a compulsion to move about and travel?

INGE: He is a restless person, physically restless. And I think much of his moving about is pure physical restlessness. I think he does need the diversion that travel gives him, and then, of course, he has always been able to move about with a great deal of comfort. He is very well known abroad, and his plays are very loved abroad, and he's a man with a great international reputation. He can go anywhere with comfort. And that helps one too, I think, in traveling.

MIKE: How do you feel about the way Tennessee's plays, as well as your own, have been transposed to the screen? Do you feel that in general Hollywood has done well by your plays?

INGE: I guess with my first three plays I had better luck than most writers. *Come Back, Little Sheba, Picnic,* and *Bus Stop* all came out very well in films. I never saw *The Dark at the Top of the Stairs* and I never saw *The Stripper,* which was based on *A Loss of Roses.* But those first three films of mine were handled, I think, very well.

MIKE: When they were being filmed, did you watch over them and were you in contact with what was happening?

INGE: No, I didn't go near the filming of any of those pictures. I just stayed in New York and went on working. The only thing I did was to send out to the producer of *Come*

Back, Little Sheba, Hal Wallis, a list of scenes outside the house. You see, the action of *Come Back, Little Sheba* was all contained in the one setting, the inside of the house of Doc and Lola. And I had a letter from Hal Wallis asking me if I would suggest scenes for getting the action out of the house so that they could make the movie move. So I did that. I sent him a list of about twelve scenes that I had in mind to take place outside the house, and when I saw the movie I saw that all my suggestions had been used.

MIKE: Do you prefer usually to have a Broadway cast perform the movie roles?

INGE: No.

MIKE: It doesn't particularly make any difference?

INGE: No.

MIKE: For instance, with *Picnic*, which was done so beautifully in New York and which was also a beautiful film, did you agree that the principal parts should be played by stars as they were? To use box office values, in other words?

INGE: Well, that was out of my hands. I wanted them to use younger people, but they made a very big success out of it, and I think made a very good picture out of it, using stars. Certainly I liked Roz Russell very much as a schoolteacher, and I liked William Holden. He gave a totally different nature to the part of Hal, but I thought he gave it a value of his own that worked very well in the picture. Tennessee certainly had wonderful luck with *Streetcar.* He got a beautiful movie out of that. A magnificent movie.

MIKE: There he had actors who had performed the same parts on the stage and the director who had done it in New York.

INGE: Yes, he had the same director, Kazan, and all the people he used were people who played it on the stage.

Vivien Leigh had played it in London, and the rest of the cast had played in the New York production. I don't know right off now what other movies of Tennessee's I've seen, if they had been as successful. That certainly is the most successful picture.

MIKE: I think *Suddenly Last Summer* was very successful also.

INGE: Oh, yes, and *Cat on a Hot Tin Roof* came off very well.

MIKE: Do you think that sometimes Hollywood accentuates any violence that might be in Tennessee's work to make a film more interesting and have more action?

INGE: Oh, yes.

MIKE: So that the movie public sees a slight distortion of what Tennessee might have originally intended.

INGE: Yes, I think the violence in his plays has sometimes been exaggerated in films. I don't think it was in *Streetcar*. I suppose that's why *Streetcar* still stands out in my memory as the best film made of his work. I don't know that it is my favorite of his plays at all. I think as a play I might prefer *Cat on a Hot Tin Roof*. Certainly I have the greatest love and respect for *Night of the Iguana* too. I think it is a marvelous play.

MIKE: Your favorite, really, was *The Glass Menagerie*, and his others come after that.

INGE: Well, let me put it this way: I'm not sure that *The Glass Menagerie* is my favorite in that I think it is his finest play. Perhaps in a sense it is his finest. It certainly holds a unique place in Tennessee's work and we do have to look at his other plays somewhat differently. And so I suppose it is useless to compare them. I don't want to compare *Glass Menagerie* with *Night of the Iguana*. They were totally different and it's unfair to the plays to try to compare them. But I know that I was very deeply moved by *The Night of the Iguana.*

MIKE: Which among your own plays do you prefer?

INGE: I really have no preference at all. I really don't. I think I prefer, though, the plays that failed. There's something about the later plays of mine that failed that make them rather dear to me. But maybe I'm like a mother favoring faulty children. I don't know.

MIKE: Tennessee has this tenacity of rewriting plays that have failed, and even if they've failed the second time, still rewriting them. Do you do the same thing? Or do you think it's right to do this?

INGE: I haven't—oh—yes, I rewrote *Loss of Roses* after it failed on Broadway, but the Broadway production was a mishmash. I had not been able to control that production at all, so I rewrote it for the Dramatists Play Service when they bought it. And I am very proud of the play now. It does stand as one of my favorites in my own work. No, I don't rewrite as persistently as Tennessee does, and I admire him so much for the way he does persist. For instance, *The Milk Train Doesn't Stop Here Anymore.* There were two productions of that on Broadway and I didn't see either one of them. I was busy. I had a play of my own during one of the productions of that. I think it was the first production. I was working on *Natural Affection.* We were doing that and played right across the street from each other. And I had not heard very good reports about *Milk Train.* Some people said it was a wonderful play but just hadn't been handled right. That was the first play of Tennessee's that I didn't go to. When I am working on something of my own, it's sometimes hard to go see another play. So I kind of purposely stayed away. And then I was out of town during the second production of *Milk Train.* And I have never read it. And then a couple of years ago at Christmas time I was in New York and a friend of mine, a mutual friend of Tennessee's and mine, asked me to read a film script called *Boom.* I looked at it and the title page said, "Based on the play *The Milk Train Doesn't Stop Here Anymore,*" and I took it with some hesitation. I somehow had the feeling, I'll admit, that the theme of the old woman and young boy was one that Tennessee had worked on before and I was expecting really not to like *Milk Train.* I think that's why I stayed away from it. I thought he was just rechewing old material and so I kind of snubbed it. And then when this friend presented me with this film script, he said, "Please read it. I'm going to have something to do with some part of the production of it, and I would like to know what you think of it." I was living at the Algonquin Hotel for a few weeks, so I took it back to my hotel room that night and read it, and I read some of the most beautiful writing that Tennessee had ever done! I read a beautiful, flawless, deeply moving film script! And it was not a story about an older woman and a young boy, although these characters were in the screenplay. It was a story of a woman's facing death and of the young man who, like a good angel of death, comes to help her, out of his own humanity. He comes like, really, like an angel. He's a little superhuman. Or, I don't know, a little—well, he is an angelic young man. He is almost unreal. But there is great beauty about him, great beauty of person, and a really beautiful understanding. And I was so deeply moved by that screenplay when I finished it, I'll admit, tears came to my eyes and I felt so miserable for having discredited Tennessee. For having thought that in that play he was just doing over old material that he should be leaving alone now and forgetting. And here I found he had written a beautiful new script and I'll go on record as saying that he has never done finer writing than existed in that script! And then I went to see the movie of it. I think I spent about twenty-five minutes at that movie. It took me about that long to find out that the people who had produced that movie had understood nothing of it. They had not seen or felt its poetry. They had seen none of the beauty in the script, of the script that I had read. The flawless, flawless film script had been changed and had been destroyed. All the beauty in the script had been destroyed. And then it was so disheartening to hear on television and read in the newspapers and magazines the critical reactions to it. Of course it is always so easy to blame the writer, and I think I heard Miss Judith Crist on television tell what a lousy script Mr. Williams had given this great director, Mr. Joe Losey, to work with. That was the attitude that all the critics took. That Williams had turned out a very poor piece of writing and that this great director, Mr. Losey, had done the best he could with it.

MIKE: Actually, it was more the other way around.

INGE: Oh, yes, yes, of course.

MIKE: The script was brilliant and the director and producers didn't quite understand the poetry of it.

INGE: The people who worked with the play all struck me as gross, mundane, and totally unable to understand what they were dealing with.

MIKE: Do you also include the Burtons in that?

INGE: Well, they are actors. I don't think they were right for the part. The play had to be reconceived to fit them.

MIKE: Don't you think that Richard Burton would have a lot of control or influence over a director and would be quite influential in the interpretation of the screenplay?

INGE: Oh, I suppose he would. Yes, yes. I suppose. But I don't know because I knew nothing about the production.

MIKE: I was very disappointed about the way they advertised the film, as if it was another *Who's Afraid of Virginia Woolf?* type of vehicle, which had been such a big hit as a film with the Burtons. Pictures outside the theatre of Liz Taylor and Richard Burton screaming their lungs out at each other. Sort of imitating the publicity of *Virginia Woolf.* As if they thought, "We had one success with this type of thing, so maybe we can have another." And really, *Boom* had nothing to do with that sort of anger between people.

INGE: The whole story of *Boom* was about an aging woman, or an aged woman. I think Tennessee listed her age at sixty-five. She was a dying woman and it was hard to see Elizabeth Taylor as a dying woman even though she was spitting up little splotches of red now and then. But she was dressed like something out of an early Cecil B. DeMille picture. Grotesquely. And then, of course, the part of the young man should have been played by a young man, I felt, to be true to what the author had conceived. But that's neither here nor there.

MIKE: Do you think that perhaps since the play had not been successful in New York and no movie company was bidding for it, that perhaps they had to compromise by getting box office people like the Burtons and then try to tailor the play to fit them?

INGE: I suppose. I suppose Tennessee settled for the only kind of production that he could get, which is a shame, because there is no one in the picture industry who's going to buy a good property. The movie producers buy headlines, not properties. They want to buy something that has a big name, that has made a big splash, whether it's right for the films or not. Now, if you noticed, the play *Luv* was bought and produced for films. When I walked out of *Luv*, which I enjoyed enormously, I thought, "Here is one of the finest

American comedies I have ever seen in my life. And it's a piece of pure theatre and how smart this young man is to write so purely for theatre." I thought to myself when leaving the theatre, "This play could not possibly be turned into a movie." And then, sure enough, less than a year later, I think, I heard that someone had bought it to make a movie of it and I thought, "How in Heaven's name are they going to make a movie of *Luv*?" But you see, they weren't thinking of the property. They don't care about the property. They want a title. Well, of course, that's why Hollywood makes so many mistakes. They buy titles whether they make good movies or not.

MIKE: How much would you say a writer's Broadway agent has to do with putting these materials into the hands of Hollywood, or the improper people? Shouldn't an agent control these things or are they sometimes burning the candle at both ends, serving two masters?

INGE: Well, I really think—naturally, an agent wants to make the most money that he can for a client. Usually, an agent wants secondarily to get a good performance, or a good production. Sometimes it works the other way. You will find agents who won't settle for a high fee, but who won't settle for a movie sale until they are assured of a good production. I don't know if Tennessee had any choice in this matter. But I would still love to see the movie that he wrote.

MIKE: In your own experiences in films, have you felt that Hollywood has messed up plays you have written?

INGE: Well, I felt this: If Hollywood buys a play that has not been a big success, then they want to change everything around. They will not stop and study the play and try to figure out why it was not a success on Broadway. And they should know by this time that Broadway success has very little to do with movie success because the movies have quite often turned unsuccessful plays into marvelous films and they have turned sometimes second-rate novels into fine films. Now for instance, in my own work, certainly *Loss of Roses* suffered from not having been a Broadway success. They played around with it, and changed the era that the play was written in. I never saw the movie because friends told me that it was not good and so I just didn't bother. It hurts too much to see something of your own destroyed. So I just stayed away.

MIKE: I think very often Hollywood will buy your name, or Tennessee's name. And if it's a short story or, as you say, a play that hadn't done too well like *A Loss of Roses*, they are buying your name value and reputation as a playwright to use as a box office draw, in addition to using box office stars. And I think that very often when that happens they're really not genuinely interested in the property, or the material, and they distort what you have written.

INGE: Yeah, that's true. My name meant something on the screen during the fifties. Tennessee's still means something. But you see, Hollywood doesn't like to advertise the writer. They don't—the Hollywood structure now seems to be deliberately built to ignore the writer's importance. They don't want to become a writer's medium because if it ever did become that it would destroy the whole structure of the film industry as it stands now. Now it's a director's medium and no writer is ever any better than his director in Hollywood's eyes. That's too bad.

I still love to write for the theatre. And I probably always will feel, upon certain times, that there's something I want to write a play of. I still want to work in the theatre but I no longer regard it as an enjoyment. I love television as a medium. I don't always love what I see on television. But last night for instance was one of the most beautiful productions I have ever seen on television. That was Jonathan

Miller's stunning production of *From Chekhov with Love*. It was beautifully handled. There was some element of genius in that whole concept and the actors, of course, were very good. But it was really a director's show. Mr. Gielgud was splendid, but the vision, the way Mr. Miller visualized —that was so beautiful. And it was so wonderful to see such a fresh, glowing work on television, so I feel that when you do see something good on television, it far surpasses what we see in the theatre. And television is a different medium even from movies. It's a medium that is related to both films and theatre but it does seem to be a little closer to the theatre than to films. The best *Hamlet* I have ever seen—and, of course, many scholars and critics will holler when I say it—but the only *Hamlet* I have ever truly enjoyed without sitting there and feeling self-conscious watching a classic was the television *Hamlet* called *Hamlet at Elsinore*. I thought it was so gripping.

MIKE: You're more or less saying that a well-done television show, well written, well cast, well produced, well directed, is as important as something that would be done in a film or on Broadway?

INGE: Oh, yes, because it's our only true mass medium now. There is, of course, an awful lot of slop on it. But there is an immediacy about it that makes even the slop and the junk that you see somehow more interesting than most of what you see on Broadway.

MIKE: Do you think television will become an origin of plays as Broadway has been? Plays which community theatres, colleges, or universities could perform on the stage?

INGE: Oh, yes! You have to remember there already exists some television literature: the dramatic literature that was written for television back in the forties and early fifties. You know, that's when television gave birth to some fine writers.

Paddy Chayefsky, Horton Foote, and Tad Mosel all came out of that period. And their works, the works that they wrote for the *Kraft Theatre* and *Playhouse 90* and maybe one or two other programs, still exist in print.

MIKE: Do you think that the commercial situation in the theatre, television, and the motion-picture industry is too accentuated by making money and less in tune with the writer or the artist?

INGE: Well, yeah, of course, but that's what's wrong with our whole society, you know. When we have only the profit, the financial profit, motive, life isn't going to be very idealistic. And ideals are going to suffer and we are all going to lead pretty mundane existences. It seems like what we are doomed to. No one wants to give up the competitive society that we live in, but yeah, it hurts, it hurts our theatre and our films, our television. Just as it hurts, I think, every department of our lives.

MIKE: I have always thought that the entertainment industry attracts people who want to make fast money by putting deals together. People who weren't really educated to the theatre or really in love with the theatre, but more in love with a fast way to make money.

INGE: Well, yes. I have seen people who get their creative kicks out of making a deal, you know, out of setting up a big movie deal. I think there are some agents who, you know, they feel if they make sort of a big deal, they get some creative satisfaction out of that, and then quite often some of these big deals that are brought off, the results are miserable. Some miserable movie comes out of all this glorified office warfare that goes on.

MIKE: Unfortunately the people that are doing this are the people who are in control of what the public sees and maybe are responsible for the state of the theatre not being any better than it is now.

INGE: Yeah, well, I know, I know what you mean. I used to be awfully bitter at the world because everyone wasn't idealistic. We just have to face the fact that very few people are truly idealistic. We do live in a society that gives survival not necessarily to the fittest, but to the most aggressive and to the most ruthless.

MIKE: So there's a point when an artist, like yourself or Tennessee or any other writer, would have to compromise in order just to survive.

INGE: Well, I can't think of any instances right now where I have had to compromise. But maybe it's a compromise as soon as you sit down at a typewriter and start writing for an audience with an audience in mind. I don't remember any compromises in *Streetcar* or *Cat on a Hot Tin Roof.* And so it's still possible to create, really, to create without compromise, but it's the exception, I suppose, rather than the rule.

MIKE: Do you think that a writer like Tennessee should turn to films now with the state of Broadway being what it is? That he would find a creative outlet in films?

INGE: Well, I—I just don't think films is a writer's medium now. No, I think he would be unhappy working in films. And we know that he had a hard time selling that beautiful script *Boom.* We know that he got it done the only way that he could. So, as I said before, Hollywood is interested in buying headlines instead of property. It's too miserable a life to work creatively for an industry that doesn't appreciate you.

MIKE: I feel that way about Broadway, more or less, now. I don't see where a really artful playwright belongs right now.

INGE: Well, I don't know. I have been away from the Broadway scene for so long now I really don't know what it is. It may be just as bad on Broadway as it is out here.

MIKE: Of course there is off-Broadway, and smaller theatres, and European theatres.

INGE: Oh, I think there are many avenues open to Tennessee. I think he should produce off-Broadway now because the most creative things are happening off-Broadway. I think also there's the broad field of prose for him to enter and I think, I think he might even write memoirs or recollections

MIKE: Since his last play was on Broadway, *The Seven Descents of Myrtle*—he was so hurt and disappointed that that production was not better and the play wasn't successfully received—he turned completely to poetry for several months.

INGE: Well, it does seem kind of futile now to write plays. It used to be that anything he wrote he could depend upon getting as good a production as possible. Now the chances of anybody getting a good production are getting slimmer all the time. I think Broadway is losing its good actors and its good directors. Broadway right now belongs to the young, to the very young kids who are starting out with some kind of wild new idea, some way-out concept of a show. For them it is very alive. They are just starting their careers. The American theatre has always been a theatre of the young. Playwriting—we have never made playwriting a real profession in this country because it's never been a profession that a man can grow old in. We have never appreciated any of our playwrights' more mature work. We finally appreciated O'Neill's late work after one of his late plays, *A Long Day's Journey into Night*, was done in Sweden with great success. Then we were kind of ashamed. But I can remember back in the 1940s O'Neill was all but spat upon in the theatre.

And the reviews of the first production of *The Iceman Cometh* were so belittling, so snide, so contemptuous of this fine writer that I think these men did break his heart. They did it callously, without knowing what they were doing. They did not see the greatness of that play inside the, from what I hear, unsatisfactory production that it first received. And no critic has ever been able to see the merits of a play apart from its production, and that great play of O'Neill's— and I think it is his greatest play, *The Iceman Cometh*—was really just, it was looked upon—it was written about as if it were the work of some—of a total has-been. It was really looked upon with contempt.

MIKE: In a way, I think, Tennessee has experienced that same attitude by the critics.

INGE: Well, everyone gets it eventually. Now O'Neill is dead, so we can revere him. We can revere our dead playwrights and our young ones but when our playwrights get over that first—when they grow out of that first burst of youthful energetic talent and want to mature and grow old along with their work, this country won't let them. So Tennessee has been really very fortunate. He has lasted a much longer time in the theatre than O'Neill because O'Neill was discarded and forgotten as a playwright. And he was in total eclipse for about twenty years, really, until Sweden did *Long Day's Journey into Night* and then out of guilt it was done again in America and then another production was done of *The Iceman Cometh*. Finally we saw what a great play that was, so the man did have a rebirth. But it was too bad it happened after his death, and he died a miserable man. Most people, most creative people in the theatre, die unhappy people.

MIKE: When you say that perhaps Tennessee should turn to prose now, you mean you think the prose he has already written is good work and he should continue with it?

INGE: Oh, yes, he has his stories, you know. He could do like Chekhov and write more stories and he could write memoirs and recollections and maybe even novels, I don't know. But I think it would be a more peaceful work now and I think he would get personal enjoyment out of it.

MIKE: And he could also continue working with his poetry.

INGE: Oh, yes, of course.

MIKE: How have you felt about writers purposely injecting pedantic statements or attitudes into their work, or comments on the social situation, or trying to give the public what they think is best for them, or teach them something that they think they should know?

INGE: I have never liked pedantic theatre. I think we are always going to have writers who are writing out of the social situation they are in. I think it's a limitation on some writers to conceive man only in his relationship to the social order. Because we all know that human life itself is bigger than the social order that we find it in. So I think in terms of—it's a limitation to write of man only as a member of the social order that exists. Because when that social order changes, as it is bound to do, the play is suddenly going to be found lifeless. The most enduring plays are those that—those that deal with man in his relationship to time and eternity.

MIKE: Which is usually writing that comes from the heart rather than from the head.

INGE: Well, I don't know. Yes, I suppose so. Of course, art also comes out of humility. I remember Barbara Baxley once telling me about seeing Tennessee and Kazan walking together down the street in downtown New York. They had just come out of a rehearsal together. And she said when she first looked at them she could have taken them for tramps. Kazan needed a shave and was dressed in sloppy clothes, and Tennessee was dressed very casually and looked tired and then she kind of laughed to herself, and she thought, "These great men, they're so talented that they don't have to walk down the street beautifully tailored, exquisitely groomed, smelling of cologne. They are so great that they can afford to appear as humble as they do." And certainly Tennessee is a man—is an artist—who has never exploited his own success in a way to affect his work. His creation has come out of that humble person. He was always a humble man. He may have very ostentatious mannerisms, he may be playing a part like Oscar Wilde did, and other writers. He may have a flair for exploiting personal foibles and eccentricities, but when he sits down at the typewriter or with pen in hand, there's that humble self that does the work. I don't know why that is necessarily. But it's—I think the creative self is the self that is always aware that it moves in a world much bigger than itself, and I think the greatest talents among writers are men who have always perhaps not professed or admitted a belief in God, but have always had some feeling of a supreme being. We know there have been some great writers who have been atheists. But with, I think, the greatest writers, Tolstoy, Shakespeare, there's always a metaphysical something about it. There's something that transcends the purely material lives, or life that we live in. And Tennessee does have that spirit. I don't know if he is religious or not.

MIKE: Yes, he is.

INGE: I think that he is. I have never talked to him about religion.

MIKE: He believes in God very strongly.

INGE: I am sure he does. And whether he knows it or not, I think, I could tell by his plays that he does. And there is always, in most of his plays, the suffering spirit that gives his plays their beauty and appeal.

MIKE: When you are with Tennessee do you feel, as I do, this tremendous sense of humor come out, and that he is enjoying making people laugh, or laughing himself?

INGE: Yes, he does have a lust for life. And he does have his own very special brand of humor that I don't always get, that I don't always get immediately. I usually get it on the second beat. But I know it's always there. He is never without humor. I don't know of any of his plays that are without humor. And I know that nothing repels him like a production of one of his plays in which the humor has not been seen. I know how really repelled he is when peope don't get the humor of his writing.

MIKE: I have heard Tennessee say that with the most ugly things in life you have to find something about them to laugh at, otherwise it would be so heartbreaking you couldn't endure it.

INGE: I have felt that, yes. I have felt there are circumstances in his life that he must laugh at because if he didn't he would fear that they would destroy him.

MIKE: Even circumstances that he observes, that don't actually touch him personally—ugliness in the world, or other people's misfortunes or deformities—he observes so keenly that he looks at it with a sense of humor to keep from being too saddened by it. I know recently at the hotel where he was staying in Hollywood, there were about thirty paraplegics on holiday and they were around the lobby and about the swimming-pool area all day and, you know, quite awkwardly maneuvering themselves. It was a very, very sad thing to watch. But Tennessee turned the whole situation into something that was comical in order to make it hu-

morous rather than to be heartbroken by it. He is so hyper-
sensitive to things like that, that as a self-defense from
becoming saddened, he jokes about it.

INGE: I know exactly what you mean, yes. Well, there is
a certain emotion called hysteria, and there is in much great
art a quality of hysteria—when we don't know whether to
laugh or cry. Because there is such a fine line between the
tragic and the blatantly comic that—it's such a fine line that
quite often we will have a split reaction, or a kind of hysterical reaction. When you mentioned the paraplegics it made
me recall a time when I was in college and a friend and I
took a trip into Kansas City to see some play. I think probably Katharine Cornell was there playing something. This
was back in the thirties. We were both college students. And
so we looked forward to these trips to Kansas City because
it was the city closest to us and it was the nearest thing we
could find to New York, I suppose. So going into Kansas
City for a weekend to see a play, or to shop for some new
shirts or neckties, or maybe a suit, a pair of shoes, was very
exciting. So we had spent the morning shopping for shirts
and getting our tickets arranged for the matinee we were
going to see in the afternoon. And then with all this excitement we went into a cafeteria, into a big crowded cafeteria,
and we took our trays and found ourselves a table, and we
were just getting ready to eat when a man with a spastic ail-
ment brought his tray to the table next to us and suddenly
went into a spasm and the tray flipped and everything on
the tray just splashed and spilled all over the floor. Well, a
spastic, of course, is a very unfortunate person. Yet the whole
incident somehow had the nature of Mack Sennett slapstick
and the two of us started laughing. And we couldn't understand—we kept analyzing it, trying to figure out why we
were almost convulsed by this ludicrous incident. Well, such
a person is doubly unfortunate because he does appear very
grotesque to us. And it's hard, it's hard to feel the tragedy of

a person unless we can find beauty in that tragedy, unless we can find meaning. It's hard to find any meaning in his misfortune or to find any beauty in it because his behavior is that of a—really a comic—and so I am sure that Tennessee's humor is a humor that comes out of suffering. And there are some things—there are many things in life too sad to face without humor. We have to laugh at them to keep from destroying ourselves in tears.

MIKE: I think it is also a beautiful thing when you can find humor in your own grotesqueness, or what you think is your own grotesqueness, which Tennessee has done a bit now with *Slapstick Tragedy*. And the fact that he is blind in his left eye and he can write parts where characters are blind in an eye, which is almost a spoof on himself—a humorous attack on his own grotesqueness. As if by laughing at himself or making himself comical, he can escape the misfortunes that he may have come by, physically or otherwise.

INGE: I am glad you mentioned that because I think that quality of—or that ability to laugh at oneself is the greatest human quality that man can possess. And very, very few people have it. And it is such a beautiful quality in human nature when you do find it. And yes, Tennessee has it. He can do it. He can laugh at himself. And he can let you laugh along with him at himself, which is very graceful too.

MIKE: However, I think he usually has to initiate it. I think if somebody else were to laugh at him without his first having the idea himself, it would be quite a different situation. But his humor, which also shows a certain amount of courage, is one of the best qualities, I have always felt, that Tennessee possessed.

INGE: Yes, I loved that one play in *Slapstick Tragedy*. *The Gnadiges Fraulein* I thought was a beauty. I never got to see the first one because I went to its opening night, and I had a play then that was playing previews, so I had to be at my play for an early curtain. But I loved *Gnadiges Fraulein*. I thought it was just marvelous. Tennessee's writing is getting more and more personal, I think, nowadays, and in some ways, although his later plays haven't had the solid kind of blockbusting power of *Cat on a Hot Tin Roof* or *Streetcar* or even of *Night of the Iguana*, there is a personal thing about them that is so beautiful, that I do wish more people could get with and respond to. Certainly I felt *The Gnadiges Fraulein* was just a beautiful conception and the humor in it, the personal humor that no one saw, no one— no critic really dealt with what that play was about. Harold Clurman was the only critic who realized there was anything personal in the play. But it was a marvelous comedy.

MIKE: It is unfortunate that critics can make or break a play on Broadway.

INGE: Getting back to my first seeing *The Glass Menagerie* in Chicago the Christmas week of '44, the producers of that play were very, very chagrined because they felt certain that they had a flop on their hands. I think it is theatre history now that the Chicago critics did get busy. This was one time when critics did save a play. They did get busy. They did extra features about the play. They did make a very serious effort to sell that play to the public and they did succeed after about two or three weeks and the crowds started coming and they sold out for the rest of their engagement in Chicago and moved on into New York with glory. But the Friday-night performance that I was at, Tennessee was so embarrassed to have what was considered then a failure, that he couldn't even face his producers. And I was a newspaperman then and I had a press pass, so he didn't have to ask them to let me into the theatre and he was too embarrassed to anyway, as though it was a good thing I had my press pass with me. I did go back to St. Louis and write a story about it and a fine review of it. But I'll never forget when we entered the theatre, the three of us, Don and Tennessee and I, and the two producers with cigars stuck in their mouths were standing on the other side of the lobby and honestly, they looked at Tennessee with such hatred, with such contempt, because they thought he had delivered them a flop. And it was just another incident of the cruelty of theatre, the hardness of commercial theatre that we have to endure, and of course, I suppose two weeks later when the crowds were coming in and they were selling out, I suppose they were—

MIKE: Buying more expensive cigars!

INGE: Yes, and probably treating Mr. Williams a little nicer. Another reason I think Tennessee might not like working in films, if he lived out here, I don't think he would like the company. A writer in Hollywood has to—or I'll say most writers, certainly a writer like Tennessee could not move very comfortably in the existing social structure of the movie profession. I don't think that good writers get along very well in the company of movie directors and actors. In a social setting, they are still giving a show. And they usually select their company from—or try to select their company from—among the existing luminaries of the particular time. And consequently a serious artist in Hollywood has to look long and hard for serious friends. The big social functions out here are rather preposterous affairs of show and ostentation and everyone is trying to create an impression. And I know, to Tennessee—he likes comfortable company and contemplative conversation. And out here finding friends is difficult because of space, for one thing. You may find a fine friend but he or she may live twenty miles away from you and getting together can be very difficult. Yes, social life out here is difficult because of the structure of the society and of space too.

MIKE: Does that affect a writer's work also?

INGE: Well, it certainly affects a writer's work if he sells out to the existing social structure—oh, of course, it destroys a writer to be at society's beck and call. A writer has to live for his own values and if he starts trying to keep up with the Joneses, the Getzes, or whoever out here, he destroys himself. For one thing, even the most successful writers are paid small fees in comparison with those of big-name actors and directors. So writers are seldom able to travel in the same society as actors and directors for financial reasons. There are writers, however, who eventually become producers, and some of them even become directors. Some of them become very good directors. But that's something else. Tennessee is a pure writer. A real writer. He will never be a director and he'll never even want to be. He could never be bothered with the problems of production. They couldn't concern him and shouldn't. So he will remain a real writer, a true writer, for as long as he lives.

MIKE: No matter where he is, do you think?

INGE: Sure.

MIKE: You're not saying that Southern California will kill a creative writer?

INGE: Oh, no, no. A writer, if he lives here, has to be strong enough, though, to live by his own values. A writer has to do that wherever he is. But the battle is not as arduous in New York, or in Florida, or in other places as it is out here, where a writer, or any serious person, has to face every day the kind of ridiculous fanfare of the movie industry. One is always affronted out here by the existing values and the social values and they are, of course, deplorable.

MIKE: Don't you think there now exists in Los Angeles, however, a theatre set as well as the movie set?

INGE: Oh, yes. There is a theatre set in Los Angeles and there is an intelligentsia that moves quite independently of movie society. But as I said before, distances out here being so far one may find that, you know, he has an invitation to dinner at a friend's house and he wants to go, he knows he ought to, he'll enjoy himself there with good talk and good people and so forth and good food, but it may be twenty miles away. So he arrives there at seven-thirty and he usually leaves at ten-thirty or eleven in order to get to bed before midnight.

Felice Orlandi and Alice Ghostley on the patio of their apartment in Hollywood. 1968. (*Photo by the author*)

ALICE GHOSTLEY
AND FELICE ORLANDI

Alice Ghostley and Felice Orlandi recently made Los Angeles their home, although they keep strong ties with New York and the Broadway theatre. Alice makes frequent television appearances as an actress and as a singer. After her long operatic training, her career began as an entertainer in various Greenwich Village cabarets. She was one of the stars in New Faces of 1953, *a very successful Broadway revue which was later put on film. In another Broadway show called* All in One, *Alice sang Leonard Bernstein's short opera,* Trouble in Tahiti. *Felice appeared in the first part of the same show in Tennessee's one-act play* 27 Wagons Full of Cotton, *playing the part which Eli Wallach later played in the film* Baby Doll. *Felice is a very accomplished actor and is also finding new success as a script writer.*

While Tennessee was living in Los Angeles during the latter part of 1968, Alice and Felice were two friends he saw quite often.

Los Angeles
October 4, 1968

ORLANDI: I guess the best way to talk about a person that you know is just to try to remember where you first met him. I met Tennessee by accident, actually, in Rome in 1949. And it is exciting for me to think, and I'm grateful to know, that we are still friends after all these years. It's been almost nineteen years, I guess, hasn't it?

GHOSTLEY: Almost twenty.

ORLANDI: I used to see Tennessee in the Café Doney before I met him. I had a room where I paid twenty-five cents a day and somebody pointed out this building where Tennessee Williams lived. Of course, I knew who he was; I had seen *Streetcar Named Desire* seven times in New York. I had ushered for it in Pittsburgh, where I went to school. So I saw the play altogether about sixteen times before this summer that I'm referring to. But I eventually met Tennessee there, at the Café Doney. He used to go there frequently with friends and he was as gracious then and as kind a person then as we all know him to be now. He had a lovely apartment that many people were always welcome to. The amazing thing about Tennessee that I've learned over the years is that initially when you meet him you get the feeling that he's shy and kind of reserved and so forth. But it's just the contrary, I think. Through that shyness, which is certainly there, he has an amazing ability to deal with people and be very open with people, you know, in his way. Perhaps it's a bit more quiet than a lot of other people, but certainly more pleasant, don't you think? I've seen him handle crowds of people at parties, and the thing that makes him amazing is that he never tries to be impressive. Don't you think so, Alice?

GHOSTLEY: That's it! That's it! He absolutely is himself. There's no attempt to impress anyone. He enjoys himself, I think.

MIKE: Alice, did you meet Tennessee about the same time Felice met him?

GHOSTLEY: No. I met Tennessee in 1950. I was working in a club, a little tiny club in New York called the Fireside Inn. One day he came with Frank, and I think it was the most exciting night I ever had! The idea that he was sitting in that room! And I could see him because it only seated fifty people.

ORLANDI: Didn't he request a song?

GHOSTLEY: Yes. I think it was "Oh, Dear, What Can the Matter Be?" because at that time I was doing folk songs and everything that people do now, but they weren't as popular then as they are now. But he loved them. Dear, did you say you exchanged money in Rome for Tennessee?

ORLANDI: Well, we used to do a lot of illegal things there. Not a lot, but one thing. I met a number of people—of course, I was born in Italy and I speak Italian, and I used to wear Italian shirts, so I fit right into the picture, right? But I sat at the Café Doney and I was always desperate for money, and the thing that kept me alive was that I would exchange money for Americans on the black market. You know, that sounds very illegal, but I think everybody was doing it in those days, in 1949. But I exchanged some money for Tennessee and officially that was our first meeting, you know, committing an illegal act like that. Which is kind of humorous to me.

MIKE: Could Tennessee speak Italian then?

ORLANDI: Yes, he was speaking Italian then. Certainly well enough to be understood and to order food in a restaurant.

But then we would meet occasionally. I think one of the reasons Tennessee liked Italy, and that many people like Italy, is that it is a very casual place and you would simply bump into people in this café, Café Doney. And Tennessee was there frequently and with friends. And he was a very gracious kind of person, you know. He was very free to invite people to his place for lunch and frequently he had ten or twelve people there for lunch, you know.

MIKE: Did Frank do the cooking?

ORLANDI: Frank was there, yes, although I don't remember his cooking there but I do remember it in New York. I don't remember whether he cooked in Rome or not, but Tennessee seemed awfully content and I can well understand why he likes places like that, and Key West. But then he has a way of making his own life, I think, which is a lot more than most of us are able to do. He seems to make his own life and his own world and he expresses and shares that world as well as anybody I know, if not better. There are so many humorous things about Tennessee that are difficult to repeat because they're not gags as we know them and they are not jokes, but I find his humor in his observation of other people, you know.

GHOSTLEY: In three sentences he can describe a person and you know exactly what the person looks like, what he likes to eat, what he wears, where he's lived. His command of the language, and the lean way he says things! There's no waste. I thought of that again when I read *The Seven Descents*, the last play, which I loved.

ORLANDI: You wanted to be in it too, didn't you?

GHOSTLEY: I did, desperately. But right from the beginning of that play, all of a sudden there are off-stage voices and you hear two people talking and just within one speech you know exactly what those people look like. He can set a character in a whole town almost in just one speech. You almost don't have to know how to act to act Tennessee Williams, I think, because he has it there for you in the words, everything.

MIKE: Can a director feel the same way? That a script directs itself?

ORLANDI: I would say No to that. First of all, before we go to anything else, I did want to insert this: I was talking about Tennessee's sense of humor and his ability to kind of crystallize a million thoughts in your head. Suddenly, he can say five or six words and crystallize all these rampaging thoughts in your head. For example, I wasn't there when this happened but somebody told me about it who was very fond of Tennessee and appreciates him. Tennessee was introduced to somebody at the opening of *Camino Real* down here at the Mark Taper, and this person, this man, was wearing a Nehru jacket with a medallion on a chain, and they were introduced and they shook hands, and Tennessee looked up at him and said, "What is that you're wearing, young man?" And the man said, "This is a Nehru jacket." And Tennessee said, "Mmmmm, you look just like a wine steward." And all of a sudden every Nehru jacket I have ever seen—

GHOSTLEY: Every time you see people in Nehru jackets they look like a roomful of wine stewards at these parties!

MIKE: I was there that evening and Tennessee liked the Nehru jacket and a few days later bought one for himself!

GHOSTLEY: Oh, he did! Isn't that marvelous.

MIKE: Then on another occasion he wore it to the Mark Taper Forum when he was going to see the play again. The final performance, actually. And his old friend Paul Bowles was there and he hadn't seen Paul in several years and Paul took one look at the Nehru jacket and bent over toward Tennessee and said, "Well, you're in pajamas. I knew it would come to this."

ORLANDI: So he gets it back too, doesn't he? But, Mike, I interrupted you. You were going to ask something.

GHOSTLEY: About the directors.

MIKE: Yes. Alice said Tennessee's scripts are very playable for actors. Do you think the director finds it just as easy to stage his scripts or his plays?

ORLANDI: Well, I don't think great plays, such as many that Tennessee has written, are easy to act or easy to direct. Because I think the better the play, the more work I have to contribute, say, as an actor, or you have to contribute as an actor, or a director has to contribute, you know, to realize that play. Tennessee is in kind of a sphere of his own as a playwright, you know. I think he is the greatest American playwright who ever lived. There are very few directors who can stand up to him on the same level, you know. Kazan was certainly a successful director for him, and José Quintero. I must say, when José did *Summer and Smoke* it was a beautiful production and I think there was a very happy marriage between playwright and director then. But I think very few—you see, I think like *Camino Real* is such a magnificent play that I can't even pass judgment on it until I see it ten or twelve times. It really is quite honestly beyond my comprehension. It is certainly beyond my comprehension to the extent of what it is.

MIKE: Yes, each time you see it you get something new from it which you didn't realize before.

ORLANDI: So I think it's tremendous work that has to go into any Williams production.

MIKE: I agree with that. The greater a part, the greater an actor or actress you have to be to perform that part, and the director would have to be a greater director to—

ORLANDI: To realize it. To even understand it. Because *Camino Real* is beyond a lot of us, and I don't understand that it's a masterpiece, but I certainly feel that it is.

MIKE: When you did *27 Wagons Full of Cotton* in New Orleans in 1954, didn't Tennessee take over as director of that for a brief period?

ORLANDI: Yes, he did, right. We opened there, and there was a period of about a week when we didn't have a director and Tennessee very reluctantly took over the direction. We certainly were not reluctant to have him, because it was a rare experience where a playwright of his caliber would be there to talk about the play. And I must say it was prob ably the most rewarding, exciting week of rehearsals I have ever experienced. And in a way, it was intimidating because he would talk about the characters in such a manner and then I would have to get up and rehearse and I could never quite reach him, certainly. But he was wonderful. And I think he, perhaps more than any other director I've worked with, had a kind of patience for actors. Without ever having been a director, he understood the patience that an actor needs from a director to work.

GHOSTLEY: Well, that's rare, really.

ORLANDI: I don't mean they just have to wait until open ing night before I start making my major contribution. But we were in the process of rehearsals and he had a fantastic understanding of what my problem was as an actor.

MIKE: Alice, you have never so far acted in any of Ten nessee's plays, have you?

GHOSTLEY: I never have, no. But I would love to do a lot of them.

MIKE: Do you think that Tennessee has been happier in New York, or Italy, or Key West? That is, do you think places matter much to Tennessee?

GHOSTLEY: Well, I do think places do matter to Tennessee.

ORLANDI: I would guess so. I would guess places matter. You know, like Ernest Hemingway. I remember reading once that he said he could write better in certain places than he could in others. You know, like he liked Key West, and he picked Key West, Toronto, and Montana. And I have a feeling that Italy was a good place for Tennessee. I think that Key West was. I certainly think, now having spent as much time as I have in Los Angeles, that Los Angeles can be a good place for Tennessee. I also think it depends on people that are around him.

GHOSTLEY: Yes, I think that has a great deal to do with it. Absolutely.

ORLANDI: We get nostalgic for places because of people that we were there with, I think, frequently.

MIKE: I was always a little puzzled why he never bought a house in New York, since he was there most of the year, every year. But he never really felt that it was home or tried to make a home in New York as he did in Key West.

GHOSTLEY: Well, I think also a place like Key West lends itself better to buying a home. Somehow buying a home in New York—

MIKE: Well, not right in Manhattan, but perhaps upstate or in Connecticut.

ORLANDI: Now that you mention it, that's kind of odd that he wouldn't do it because it seems to me he would have liked that.

MIKE: He always moved from apartment to apartment in New York. His gypsy spirit was in evidence in the one city of New York. He was a wanderer.

GHOSTLEY: Yes, he is a bit of a gypsy. But I always felt he was very happy in New York when we were all part of a gang, back in the fifties especially.

MIKE: When the Circle in the Square was flourishing?

ORLANDI: When the Circle in the Square did *Summer and Smoke*. We had a company there and when I first started working there we got three dollars a week, which was transportation money. And then we did a play called *Burning Bright*, which ran sixteen weeks and we thought that was phenomenal! So we got ten dollars a week. And shortly sometime after that, José decided to do *Summer and Smoke*. I should interject this: José was going to do *Summer and Smoke* right after *Burning Bright* and he asked me to play Dr. John. Well, I was busted broke and I couldn't afford it, so I had to go out and get a job. And so help me, this is the absolute and sincere truth! I am so glad today that I never did that part because another girl and I were going to do that show and it wasn't Gerry Page. And I feel that if I had done it with this other girl we would never have seen Gerry give that magnificent performance in that magnificent play. And I think the combination of José and Gerry Page and the set designer, Keith Cueridon, and everybody in that cast, was a magic team. I think Tennessee somewhere in his soul had met all these actors before in his life, you know. Somewhere in his past life, because it was as if he had designed and cut a suit for each of them individually. At that time if you weren't acting in a play, you were doing something else. And I wasn't in it when Gerry did it, of course, so I was selling soft drinks. I got to see that play over two hundred and fifty performances. It was just as fresh and exciting for me on the two hundred and fiftieth performance as the first. Tennessee used to come down there occasionally and look at it.

MIKE: That production gave the play more recognition than it had received originally on Broadway.

ORLANDI: That's true.

MIKE: It really brought the play into its own.

ORLANDI: But I saw that play also in Cleveland when it first was done, you know. And I was thrilled by it. Another thing, when I first read *Glass Menagerie* I had just gotten out of the service. I got a copy of it out of the library and got on a streetcar to go home. And I had just finished reading the last page and looked up and I was on the other end of the streetcar line, you know. I had gone long past my stop. That was before I met Tennessee. But to see his plays and know him is a remarkable thing because he told me once—I told him I was interested in writing, you know, and he said to me, "If you write, then tell the truth." And he repeated that two or three times and I have never known anyone personally, on a personal level, who expresses his own truth as well as Tennessee does. You can sit in a room with him all night and just exchange maybe ten or fifteen words, and it's a far more rewarding experience than talking. A lot of us, you know, just talk, and we say nothing, really, by comparison. I remember one time when José called me and asked me to go up and have dinner and he said, "We'll have dinner and then we will play poker." So, well, I couldn't imagine José playing poker, you know. The idea of him holding cards and even adding five and two is beyond me. And then he said, "Tennessee will be here." And that was an equally large shocker because I couldn't imagine Tennessee playing poker, which was kind of naïve of me, I guess. But I went up there and sure enough, they were going hell bent for leather, you know, playing poker and arguing with each other as poker players do. And a green light was over the table. I felt like I had wandered into a small Las Vegas. And the thing about Tennessee and José—and they both play poker the same way—they never drop out. They'll stay if you have four kings and all they have is two deuces! And it is a kind of a bluff with them too.

GHOSTLEY: What was the thing one night that made Tennessee decide to stop playing? What was that story?

ORLANDI: Well, this one night Tennessee threw his cards down on the table and he had nothing cardwise to speak of, and he said, "I'm going to quit. I'm going to stop. You're all a bunch of thieves and bandits."

GHOSTLEY: And degenerates!

ORLANDI: Yes, "And degenerates." "Thieves, bandits, and degenerates." Right. And he had the lowest hand at the table, you know. He had no reason to get upset.

MIKE: Was he really upset or just being funny?

ORLANDI: Well, he—you know—he wasn't—

GHOSTLEY: He always says things even though—he never says anything mean. Tennessee never does. But anyone else saying them they probably would be, you know. It is hard to describe in a way, but there's always a twinkle. There is always a great deal of gentleness and innocence in how he says things, like "The Good Gray Goose has gone."

MIKE: He calls his mother the Good Gray Goose.

GHOSTLEY: Yes.

ORLANDI: That was an exciting thing, to meet her with Tennessee Williams at the party you and your brother gave, Mike. Couldn't you see some Amanda in her?

GHOSTLEY: With her little red shoes, her gloves to here— elbow length.

ORLANDI: But quite the lady, wasn't she?

GHOSTLEY: Oh, yes.

ORLANDI: What did she say to you?

GHOSTLEY: She said, "Oh, I just enjoy this party with all these Southerners. Well, at least we all seem like South-erners." Which I loved. She is a darling woman.

ORLANDI: And another thing. Another night. José and Ten-nessee lived in the same building, you know, on Seventy-second Street on the West Side in New York. I had had kind of an unpleasant experience at one time in my life, and I had seen Tennessee shortly after that and apparently he had heard about it and we just exchanged a few words about it, but I felt somehow he really understood what had hap-pened to me. And then we would see each other occasion-ally. And he came to see a play I was in, that José Quintero had directed again, and shortly after that he gave me a play to read. A two-character play to read. And I guess it affected me as much as any other play he had ever written, if not more, you know, for reasons that I won't go into now because they would just take up too much time. But it obvi-ously was a very personal expression on his part and it touched upon the experience I had had, that very unpleas-ant experience. And when I took the play home to read and opened the cover and saw the cast list—it was a two-character play, of course, a man and his sister, and the man's name was Felice. I thought to myself, "Well, gee, I've never heard of anybody else called Felice." Of course there must be thousands of Felices somewhere in the world but I took it as a form of flattery and then I thought, "Well, don't be ridiculous. The name is very appropriate for what happens to the character in this play, in a way symbolic if a word can be symbolic." But then about six months later—recently, as a matter of fact, out here, he said to me—we were sitting, having some coffee, Alice and I and a couple of friends with Tennessee, and he looked at me for a long time and he said, "You know, I took the liberty of using your name." And I thought to myself, "Well, how foolish of you, Tennessee. You know, if you drop my name at one of the studios, it won't do you any good." He was referring to the play, you know. He hardly needed my name to help him. But so there might have been some connection. But that is the thing about Tennessee, you see, you never know, but he is absorbing you like wild.

GHOSTLEY: He said something the other evening to the effect that he didn't observe people, if I understood it correctly, because I couldn't believe it. I said, "Oh, I think you, of all people—"

ORLANDI: I thought he said, "People think I don't observe." Isn't that it?

GHOSTLEY: Oh, was that it?

ORLANDI: There was that twinkle in his eyes, because he laughed and I'm sure the thought on his face said, "Well, I do!"

GHOSTLEY: He has a kind of sixth sight into people somehow. And Felice, you were saying the other day he really is a semanticist?

ORLANDI: It's about semantics, you know. After all these years of knowing him and so forth, I'm still stunned by the way he's able to describe certain things, and his insight into situations and people is so astounding and the way he can draw them. He paints with words like a great painter paints with oils. He is just absolutely incredible. And it's a thrilling experience to hear him talk. It's absolutely thrilling, you know. I am sure that never occurs to him, obviously, but I would rather sit and listen to hear him talk than do a lot of things.

MIKE: You're saying that his language in his private life is like his language in his plays.

ORLANDI: Socially, right. He just can't help but use the right word or the right combination of words.

MIKE: Which is his distinct way of putting words together.

GHOSTLEY: That's the genius in him.

ORLANDI: He does it with the ease that a great painter does it with oils. I don't think he could construct a bad— I don't think he could put a group of unattractive words together if he wanted to. I think that's where he would stumble, whereas most of us stumble trying to put the right words together! He is an incredible guy to listen to. And to repeat, his sense of humor, which is absolutely extraordinary, is very difficult to do because it comes like bullets at you, you know. In a quiet, pleasant kind of sense. Maybe that is not a good description, but his sense of humor is constantly there and illusive if you try to capture it or try to copy it. It's very distinct.

MIKE: Yes, I have heard him tell stories that you really laugh a lot at. And then you try to tell somebody else that same story and you don't get a laugh at all.

GHOSTLEY: That's right. Yes.

ORLANDI: He has built-in protection, right?

GHOSTLEY: You can't steal from him.

MIKE: What was the name of the show you did together in New York? Was it called *Three in One*?

GHOSTLEY: *All in One.*

MIKE: *All in One,* yes! Felice, you acted Vicarro in Tenn's one-act play *27 Wagons Full of Cotton.* Then, Alice, after intermission you sang Leonard Bernstein's *Trouble in Tahiti.* Then the third part of the evening was Paul Draper in a dance recital.

GHOSTLEY: It was drama, dance, and opera.

ORLANDI: And I must say, and you say it with me, Alice, or it will sound egotistical, but we got really wonderful reviews and we ran eight weeks.

MIKE: I know. I saw it.

GHOSTLEY: Oh, you did, Mike?

ORLANDI: I'll tell you, that was so discouraging, in a way. It was interesting too that people would come back, that we had a lot of repeats.

GHOSTLEY: That's right.

MIKE: Wasn't it a limited engagement, though?

GHOSTLEY: No, it wasn't.

ORLANDI: It might have started out that way, but after the reviews came out, and they were really extraordinary reviews, you know, we were all grateful for that. And as a matter of fact, Alice and I went out and bought an apartmentful of furniture on the basis of it. The producer came back and said, "We've got a smash hit on our hands." And we were really going to swing. And we went over to Bloomingdale's and just bought hundreds of dollars of everything, you know.

MIKE: And charged it.

ORLANDI: And charged it like crazy! But I didn't care. I would rather have been in that play for those eight weeks than I guess any other play that I have ever been in, for whatever length of time they ran. It was the only Tennessee Williams play I have ever been in.

MIKE: Wasn't that also the beginning of the Actors Studio project to take that play and expound on it until, finally, it became the film of *Baby Doll*?

ORLANDI: Well, perhaps that's so. I wasn't a member of the Actors Studio in those days, although I was studying with Lee Strasberg in his private classes. But I think you're right there.

MIKE: The success of that play when you were doing it stimulated the interest in it so that it did become a major work rather than a one-act play. And evolved into *Baby Doll*.

GHOSTLEY: Because I remember that Kazan got back into town and he was beginning to work on this, or starting it, or casting it or something. And the day he arrived was the day we closed. So he never got to see that. It was a bit disappointing. He was off to the Continent or something at the time. But, you see, I think had they done a publicity push on it, it would have run. If they had done what the Chicago critics or somebody did for *The Glass Menagerie*.

PAUL BOWLES

Paul Bowles lives an exciting life. I don't mean exciting in terms of action or adventure. He is too tranquil for that; in fact, he is Buddhistic in nature. I mean he lives a stimulating and unusual life in terms of his familiarity with people and places of the world. He was perhaps the original dropout when in the 1930s he left the University of Virginia to begin his world travels by way of Europe. Since then he has had homes in Mexico, Morocco, and Ceylon, and shorter residences in several other countries.

It is understandable that this intelligent man who dropped out of college but dropped in on the entire world was invited by San Fernando Valley State College to be a visiting lecturer and hold seminars on existentialism in 1968–69!

While in California, Paul had a penthouse apartment on top of Shangri-La, a 1930s building overlooking the palm trees of the Santa Monica Palisades Park and the ocean beyond. As we talked about Tennessee, we sat in the sun on his terrace, enjoying the sea view, which reminded him of Spain and North Africa. That, in turn, reminded him of his wife, Jane Bowles, who was convalescing in a Catholic hospital in Málaga. She was waiting for Paul to come collect her for their return to their home in Tangier after his one-semester teaching obligation.

Paul and Jane Bowles were married in 1938. At that time Paul was already composing incidental music for Broadway plays, but neither his writings nor Jane's had yet been published. A couple of years later in Mexico, Jane was at work on her novel, Two Serious Ladies, *when the twenty-nine-year-old Tennessee appeared on the scene. Thus began two of the very closest friendships of Tennessee's life.*

Paul Bowles on the balcony of his apartment in Santa Monica, California. January, 1969. (*Photo by the author*)

MIKE: Paul, you first met Tennessee in Acapulco in 1940?

BOWLES: That's right. He came to the house. We lived on the Avenida Hidalgo there. And one morning we were just about to go out to the beach, and the servant came and said there was a gentleman at the door and I went, and he said, "I'm Tennessee Williams. I'm sent here by Lawrence Langner. He told me you were here. The Theatre Guild is going to do my play *Battle of Angels*." I said, "Come in, but you must excuse us because we are about to go to the beach for the day and since we have been invited, we can't take you. But here is the house. Here is the patio. Here are hammocks. Here's a new bottle of rum and there's plenty of Coke. You just call the servants and they'll bring you whatever you need, books." And when we came back at five o'clock in the afternoon, he was lying in the hammock, and he'd drunk a good deal of the rum and lots of Coke, and was very happy and was reading books. And that's how we got to know him. Actually we hadn't spoken with him at all before we went out. It seemed like a rather seedy way to treat someone, but there was nothing else we could do. So we just turned the house over to him. Left him in it.

MIKE: Did he stay as your house guest during the time he was in Acapulco?

BOWLES: No. No. He was staying in a hotel there, not far. I think he was staying at the Miramar, up at the Quebrada, which was at the top of the same street we lived on. We lived down near the square. It has changed enormously since then but this was long ago and it was a small town. And he stayed on awhile. And then I had to go back to New York to do the music for *Twelfth Night* for the Theatre Guild with Maurice Evans and Helen Hayes. So I went back and

I didn't see him again at all. I stopped in and heard a rehearsal of the music to *Battle of Angels*. It was very fine. And then I heard it had closed at the Plymouth in Boston. Never got into New York at all. Just too bad. And I didn't see him again until December '43, when he suddenly appeared one night at my New York flat with Donald Windham and Margo Jones and the script which he called *The Glass Menagerie*. He left it with me and said, "We have a production lined up and you'll only have the weekend. If you can write the music for it over the weekend, it will be fine." And I had no contract. I had nothing. But I did, I wrote the music over the weekend. And Monday it was all done. That was quick! And then the show did come off and I flew out to Chicago, arrived in a terrible blizzard, I remember. It was horrible. A traumatic experience. And the auditorium was cold. Laurette Taylor was on the bottle, unfortunately. Back on it, really. She had got off it with the first part of the rehearsals but suddenly the dress rehearsal coming up was too much. The night of the dress rehearsal she was nowhere to be found. And finally she was found, unconscious, down behind the furnace in the basement, by the janitor. And there was gloom, I can tell you, all over the theatre because no one thought she would be able to go on the next night. She pulled herself together and gave, as you know, an historic performance the next night, and from then on. It was marvelous. And on opening night in New York, George Jean Nathan sent her a bottle of Scotch, a pinch bottle, and she sent him a little wire saying, "Thanks for the vote of confidence."

MIKE: The Chicago reviews of *Glass Menagerie* were all good ones, weren't they?

BOWLES: They were very good, yeah. But no one in New York knew it was going to be a hit from that, because it had critical success but not popular success in Chicago.

MIKE: Then you also did the music to *Summer and Smoke?*

BOWLES: Yeah, that was in '48, five years later. The autumn of '48. And, let's see, I came over to this country and went on the road with them. Yes. We went to Buffalo. Gypsy Rose Lee was along on that. I don't know why. She accompanied the show with her husband, Julio de Diego, the painter. That was a very enjoyable junket, the whole trip. We went to Cleveland and we went to Detroit and then came in to New York.

MIKE: Margo Jones directed it, didn't she?

BOWLES: That was Margo, yes.

MIKE: Well, why would you need to travel with them? Were you writing additional music during the out-of-town trials?

BOWLES: Sometimes, certain cues. But the composer always goes on the road with the show. I've been with all my shows. I don't know why. Because oftentimes it's unnecessary. But they seem to feel happier if you're there. In almost all shows there are changes required, up to and sometimes after opening night.

MIKE: When you say you came to this country to do *Summer and Smoke,* you mean you came here from Tangier?

BOWLES: Yes, that's right.

MIKE: What year did you move to Tangier, Paul?

BOWLES: I moved there definitively in '47. Then Tennessee came over to Tangier the winter of '48–'49, yeah, after the show went on. I remember he had a Buick Roadmaster with a convertible top which went back automatically. But it didn't! And we had some horrible experiences. We tried to get through the frontier, I remember, from Tangier into the Spanish zone. We got there late and it began to rain and the thing balked and wouldn't shut. We had to get all the luggage out into the customs shed, and there two small Spanish soldiers were looking at it and they took out Tennessee's suits, his underwear, his shirts, his typewriter, manuscript paper, razor, and they confiscated it all. And they were holding his suits up and saying, "This one will fit me." "I like these pants." "I'm going to take this." They were just taking everything. Stealing it. So we packed everything back into the car and went back to Tangier. And then Tennessee made an indignant call the next day to the American consulate and told them about it and they got busy and three days later we started out again. The consulate had called the frontier just before we left and when we arrived they threw the gates up and were screaming, "Diplomatico! Diplomatico!" We went straight through. Never stopped us at all. Didn't even have to show our passports. We got all through the Spanish zone to the border of the French zone, and then they asked us for our gasoline coupons, which we should have got at the Spanish frontier. So we didn't have any. So we had no gas, and we stayed there four hours trying to finagle some. And finally we got enough to go on to a horrible little town called Petitjean and we had a real mess as a result of not having enough gas to get on to Fez. And Tennessee got very frightened because it began to pour rain, and the sides of the mountains were coming down with mud blocking the roads, the mountain passes. And he just went through hell until we got to Fez. He was worn out by the time we got there. He just stayed in the hotel for two weeks without budging.

MIKE: Was it just you and Tennessee?

BOWLES: No, Frank was along. The three of us. And Frank did most of the driving, fortunately, because Tennessee had vibrations in those days and complained about them a lot and when he would take the wheel he would say, "I feel

them coming on." And then he would have to move over
and let Frank take the wheel.

MIKE: What about your return trip from Fez back to
Tangier?

BOWLES: We never made it. I stayed in Fez and he and
Frank drove on to Casablanca and took a ship from there to
Italy. And I remained the whole winter down in Fez.

MIKE: Where was Jane at this time? In Tangier?

BOWLES: I'm trying to remember. No, no, she wasn't in
Tangier. She was, I think, in Paris.

MIKE: Did you ever do much other traveling with Tennessee? Didn't you travel with him in Italy some?

BOWLES: Yes, yes—oh, Lord! In the—let's see—it was the
summer of '53; I motored up to Barcelona and met him there.
And I had with me Ahmed Yacoubi and Mohammed Temsamani, two Moroccans. Temsamani was the chauffeur. And
Ahmed had trouble with his passport. He couldn't get a visa
in order to go through France, so the only solution was for
him to fly with Tennessee from Barcelona straight to Rome
and I had to go by car. And so that was done. When I got
to Rome, Ahmed and Tennessee had already been there several days. And Tennessee had arranged with Luchino Vis-
conti for me to do the music for a film there, which I did. It
was called *Senso*. Alida Valli and Farley Granger. I remember we were very lucky to get another flat on the same floor
as Tennessee in the Via Firenze. And every night I would be
working hard because I worked hard all summer. Day and
night. And everyone else would be going out to the movies.
The American movies. And I felt very put upon to have to
stay at home alone every night. But I did, all summer.

MIKE: Didn't Tennessee keep an apartment in Rome each
year?

BOWLES: He did. I don't think he was always on the Via Firenze, but he did have that one for several years. He loved Rome. He was there all the time in those days. You couldn't drag him away. I went on to Istanbul. That was the year I went to Istanbul to do a piece on it for *Holiday* magazine. And when I came back to Rome Tennessee was still there. And then we motored back up through Italy, France, and Spain, all the way down to Tangier.

MIKE: Did you get to know Anna Magnani in Rome with Tennessee?

BOWLES: No, no. I've never seen Anna Magnani at all. And there were a lot of people there, but not she. We also went down to Positano, I remember, and stayed there awhile. And Maria Britneva was along. I can tell you!

MIKE: What about another female companion of Tennessee's, Marian Vacarro? Didn't she often travel with him?

BOWLES: Yes, she came to Tangier on two separate occasions with him. Once in '61, I think, and again in '64. That's right, yeah. She was very amusing.

MIKE: I think she's always been one of his closest female friends, along with Jane and, of course, Carson McCullers and Maria Britneva and Lilla van Saher.

BOWLES: We spent a weekend out at Carson's once, I remember, at Nyack. Tennessee, Jane, and I with Carson, her sister, and her mother. But Reeves was not around. Reeves McCullers. I saw Carson again in Paris a few years later and I think that was the winter Reeves committed suicide, very shortly afterwards. But Tennessee was not in Paris then. I've seen Tennessee in so many places and under so many different conditions that it's like a patchwork quilt. It's very hard to get any chronology straight. He's suddenly here, and then he's suddenly there, and I happen to be there and see him.

But to remember exactly all the various years and where I saw him is impossible.

MIKE: With Tennessee liking to travel so much, did you ever feel he was very good at languages when he'd be in the various countries?

BOWLES: Not at all, naturally. No, no.

MIKE: He speaks some Italian, doesn't he?

BOWLES: Some. He is not a linguist. Oh, no. Not at all. He always used the present-infinitive verbs instead of the proper forms. And I think that people abetted him in that when he was speaking with Italians. They would use it too, because I suppose that they thought it was easier.

MIKE: He was always very popular in Italy, wasn't he?

BOWLES: Oh, yes.

MIKE: And didn't you feel that he was rather down-to-earth with people he'd meet and would accept people as friends rather readily? There was nothing snobbish about him.

BOWLES: Oh, no, never. He is never snobbish.

MIKE: He was always giving an immediate feeling of friendship.

BOWLES: Too immediate. Yes. I think he was too friendly, really, with people too soon. He often regretted it later but he has a natural outgoing manner.

I have noticed that Tennessee always seemed to have friends in every city where we happened to be and I suppose the fact that he had these friends helped make the place bearable to him because I know he doesn't really like to travel. For someone who moves around so much, he's surprisingly unaware of his surroundings. And I've always suspected that he was more eager to get away from where he was than he was to get to another place, really.

MIKE: Do you think that to get to another place would also be a desire to get to other people? That his eagerness to leave one place is also an eagerness to leave the people that he may be with at that particular time?

BOWLES: Oh, I think very much it is an eagerness to leave the people. I am not sure that he's eager to get to the other place to see the other people. No. But I think he suddenly is fed up with a place and the people in it and feels that somehow any other place, or nearly any other place, will be more acceptable at that moment than the place he's in. So he leaves where he is and goes—it doesn't matter so much where, because he always changes his mind at the last minute anyway.

MIKE: And never finds the place which he thinks will be the ultimate place. The place to really remain, or the situation to really remain in.

BOWLES: I don't think he has ever found it, no. Not at all, because he is inherently extremely restless.

MIKE: Of course, that could be beneficial to a writer: never to be content with any place or situation. Keeps them on the go and will influence their writing in a positive way.

BOWLES: Surely. I don't see anything wrong with it at all. It is simply that he is never very interested in the place itself that he is in. I suppose that is a concomitant of being more interested in the people of the place he is in than in the place itself. That's natural.

MIKE: But to feel a compulsion to move about that often could be within himself an unpleasant feeling. Don't you think?

BOWLES: It probably is.

MIKE: A lack of being able to be content.

BOWLES: I don't think he is ever content for very long. And as far as compulsive behavior goes, it's always unpleasant because you're doing it before you have time to anticipate it. Half the pleasure of anything is anticipation.

MIKE: But Tennessee also could be called a compulsive writer. And I think, even though I have heard him say that writing is a torture to him, it is his life. I really think it's a pleasure to him, that particular compulsion. He may deny it, but I think he really enjoys it.

BOWLES: Of course he does. It gives him satisfaction. Whether or not he actually enjoys the moment of writing or not, I don't know. I suspect that he does enjoy that too. It certainly is satisfying to him.

MIKE: The next play of Tennessee's you wrote the music for was *Sweet Bird of Youth*.

BOWLES: Yes, it was ten years later, actually, I set *Sweet Bird of Youth*. I had the script in Tangier and I worked on it for about a month and then went to America. I continued working on it on the ship, I remember, the old *Vulcania*, going across. I went straight to Philadelphia, where Gadge was already rehearsing. The thing was in rehearsal, and it needed some more cues and bridges and tying up, so I finished the actual composition there in the theatre between rehearsals. The score was completed only two or three nights before opening night in Philadelphia. It worked very well, I thought. More successfully than the score for *Summer and Smoke*.

MIKE: Did you think the play *Sweet Bird of Youth* was drawn very freely from Tennessee's own life and experiences?

BOWLES: Yes, I do. Well, he said it was, so I'm not betraying a confidence by saying I think so too. How close the parallel was I wouldn't know. I should think very close, but certainly the ideas came from what he had been living during those years.

MIKE: And the last play that you did the music for was *The Milk Train Doesn't Stop Here Anymore.*

BOWLES: That's right, yeah. That was in the autumn of '62.

MIKE: Did you do that work in Tangier?

BOWLES: Let's see. No, I didn't at all. I had Virgil Thomson's apartment in New York in the Hotel Chelsea and I wrote it there. Almost all of it. And then I moved over to Oliver Smith's house in Brooklyn Heights and finished it over there. And we recorded it. That was done on tape. Also, *Sweet Bird of Youth* was recorded. I think that was the first time that I allowed them to actually use tape instead of live performances because in the old days the reproduction wasn't good enough. It costs exactly as much, as you know. You have got to pay your musicians every night for every performance anyway, whether you tape it or use them. Once tape got good enough, then you had a better performance really when you recorded it because you knew exactly what you had every night and everybody played perfectly because it was done in the studio. That play was well recorded. *Milk Train* was a much more difficult thing to fit music to, I thought. And I didn't like the script as much personally as the other three plays that I worked on. I still don't like it as much. I never believed in the character of Chris Flanders for a minute.

I remember in '46 Tennessee gave me some lyrics and asked me if I would like to use them to write songs. One was called "Gold Tooth Woman," I remember that. I didn't use that. But I did use four called *Blue Mountain Ballads* which I set to music: "Heavenly Grass," "Lonesome Man," "The Cabin," and "Sugar in the Cane." They made a suite which Schirmer published separately. They sell very well. They have gone on selling now for twenty years. They have gone into the repertory now. And then I did another one called "Three," which was published. And then he gave me one which I like very much called "Her Head on a Pillow," which I did set in '49 in Tangier and promptly mislaid. It was gone for about fifteen years and then I found it on the bottom of an old bag, a valise, and brought it out but I never did anything with it. Now I have lost it again. There is only that one copy. It is somewhere in Tangier. It is probably the best of all the songs of his that I have set. He writes excellent lyrics. The poetry I find harder to read, if you want to distinguish between his lyrics and his poems, his free-verse poems. I also did a series of six songs on commission from a singer, Alice Esty, who wanted to give a concert in Carnegie Hall five or six years ago. I chose a series of poems of Tennessee's which makes its own cycle. They are free verse. And they also set very well. But I chose them myself. I like to use as many Anglo-Saxon words as possible and as few foreign words, naturally, for the prosody. So I picked out the ones that suited my purposes best and made a song cycle of them. And I have never heard those, unfortunately. I would like to. I enjoyed setting them very much.

MIKE: Do you think that any of Tennessee's long works, his three-act plays, could or should be set to music, or made into musicals?

BOWLES: Certainly not musical comedies. No. Well, it's problematical whether one could make opera out of them or not. They would lend themselves much better to straight opera than they would to musical comedy. I don't see that they're musical-comedy material at all. I can't think of one that would make a good musical comedy. Not one. I can conceive of an opera though, a lyrical opera of *The Glass Menagerie*. It's not unthinkable. It would have to be very delicate. It could be done. But I don't see the point, really, of adapting Tennessee Williams to grand opera. They are wonderful plays. You don't need anything more.

MIKE: Since you're a writer as well as a composer yourself, Paul, I think any opinion you would have on Tennessee's writing would have more value than most people's.

BOWLES: When I first knew Tennessee, of course, I wasn't a writer. I was only a composer. And I didn't start writing until the mid-forties. But as soon as I did, Tennessee immediately took up cudgels for my work and went out of his way to write reviews of my first two or three books in *The New York Times* and *Saturday Review* and various other publications. He couldn't have been a better friend. No one I know has so consistently stood behind my writing as Tennessee all during these years.

MIKE: I believe he has the same attitude toward Jane's writing also, doesn't he?

BOWLES: Very much, very much. Perhaps even more, I don't know. He loves Jane's writing.

MIKE: Has he ever written reviews for any of her work?

BOWLES: I don't think he has ever reviewed them. But he has written blurbs for them, certainly. Several times.

MIKE: I think he was quite a strong promoter of Jane's play, *In the Summer House*.

BOWLES: Oh, yes. He had great admiration for it from the beginning, always. We were on the ship, Tennessee and I, going to Europe one time, and I stayed in my cabin and wrote a story called *The Delicate Prey*. And so then I gave it to him to read on the ship. And I remember the next day he brought it back and said, "It is a wonderful story but if you publish it, you're mad." And I said, "Why?" He said, "Because everyone is going to think you are some sort of horrible monster when they read it." And I said, "I don't care. I have written it and I'm going to publish it." And he said "You're wrong, you're wrong to publish it. You will give people the wrong idea." But I disagreed with him on that. Perhaps now everyone does think I'm a monster. I still disagree with him. I think if you write something, you should publish it.

MIKE: Well, I think that is certainly his belief now. I am surprised that he wouldn't have always had that same belief.

BOWLES: Well, it shocked him, the story.

MIKE: Well, certainly he has written stories that are shocking.

BOWLES: Absolutely. Think of *Desire and the Black Masseur*. That's pretty shocking. Or even *The Mysteries of the Joy Rio*. No, my particular brand of shockingness shocked him more because it was mine and not his, I think. That's all. And it was just a friendly admonition on his part to try to dissuade me from publishing it.

HUME CRONYN

Hume Cronyn is a man of many talents. During his long and colorful career he has been an actor, director, producer, writer, and teacher. He was born in Canada of a prominent pioneering family, and in the 1930s his love of the theatre brought him to New York. He immediately began getting parts in plays. Although he is a highly sought-after charac-ter actor in Hollywood since films like Brute Force *and* The Postman Always Rings Twice, *he always returns to the legiti-mate stage when he can discover a suitable script.*

Now that Alfred Lunt and Lynn Fontanne are in retire-ment, Hume Cronyn and Jessica Tandy are, probably, our leading husband-and-wife acting team.

Hume was in Hollywood to play a role in the film The Arrangement *when I obtained this interview.*

Hume Cronyn

CRONYN: Tennessee Williams is not someone about whom I can talk with any sort of authority. I suppose I met him over twenty-five years ago. And in the intervening period I sat down and had a drink or a meal with him perhaps five times. An average of once every five years is not very good! I'm more comfortable talking about his work. To begin at the beginning, Tennessee's plays first came to my attention through Audrey Wood, his agent all these years. I used to see quite a lot of Audrey in the late thirties, and I was searching for plays, finding writers. I was just beginning to become interested in production and direction. And she gave me these one-act plays, which I immediately fell in love with. It's a matter of eternal shame and regret that those nine one-act plays which were written by Tennessee and all of which, I think, finally comprised the *27 Wagons Full of Cotton* collection were plays that I never managed to get on the stage at that time. It's not very different now. At least on Broadway it's not very different. It's difficult to persuade people to invest in a bill of one-act plays. At that time all I needed was about eleven thousand dollars. That was for a full-scale Broadway production. Today eleven thousand dollars wouldn't get you a production off-off-Broadway. I raised about seven of it but I couldn't get it all. And there was no such thing then as off-Broadway. There was really nowhere else except the commercial theatre to do those plays. It was a whole different institution then.

MIKE: Was this before Tennessee had ever been produced on Broadway?

CRONYN: Yes. This was before that first exciting thing that happened for him in Chicago when Claudia Cassidy gave a tremendous boost to *The Glass Menagerie*. This was all prior to that. I peddled these plays around, as I say, without any

success. I was going to give them up, but Audrey asked me
if I could manage to hold them under option for an added
six months because that was during Tennessee's very hard-
up period. He was traveling around somewhere in the South
and I remember Audrey telling me stories about him, which
did make it sound as though he needed whatever help he
could get. He was having trouble with his eyes, as I remember it, and he was traveling pretty much by bicycle. At any
rate, I held the plays for a full year and then let them lapse.
I'm not quite sure where I first met Tennessee, but I think it
was in Audrey's office. I remember he came to New York. I
have a feeling it was his first visit to New York and I met
him briefly and then, of course, once *Menagerie* was underway, he was off to the races. But when I first presented these
plays to people, the reaction was very mixed. Even the name
Tennessee Williams was one that sounded dubious. And the
whole business of a bill of three one-acts was difficult. I think
the only time in that period when it worked was when Noel
Coward did *Tonight at 8:30* with Gertie Lawrence.

MIKE: I think it is fascinating that you were one of the very
first people to recognize Tennessee's art, and I think it indicates how much a man of the theatre you are. You still are
quick to perceive new material, new writers. It is something
you have been rather consistent in.

CRONYN: Well, I was certainly a very early admirer of
Edward Albee, and also Bill Inge and Bill Hanley and some
others. I'm not essentially a producer. I've been involved in
production as a producer or co-producer only four or five
times in New York. I have only directed half a dozen plays.
I don't think I was particularly wise or perceptive in that
time. It was simply that, for me, the plays had a particular
kind of magic and very obvious poetry. Tennessee's been
spoken of time and time again as a poet, and yet I don't think
he has been given his due in those terms. These plays all had
certain things in common, a marvelously lyrical quality and

a wonderful evocative use of music, even when only frag-
mentary. As I was saying, I saw something of Tennessee
when he first came to New York, when I had the plays under
option. The next time I really saw anything of him was when
I came out here in 1942 and was under contract to M-G-M.
Tennessee was put under contract and given an assignment
to write a film for Lana Turner. I saw him a few times then,
and at that point he was doing the script for M-G-M but he
was also working on a play. I am not sure which one it was,
but I think it was *Glass Menagerie*. But he came to the house
a couple of times then, had meals with us. And he didn't
enjoy what he was doing at the studio very much, but he
was grateful for the contract and the money he was earning.
I don't think the film he was writing for Lana Turner was
ever made.

MIKE: But M-G-M's early investment in Tennessee paid off
after he became successful and they filmed *Cat on a Hot Tin
Roof, Sweet Bird of Youth, Night of the Iguana,* and *Period
of Adjustment!*

CRONYN: Sometime after he left, probably a couple of years
later, I directed Jessica in *Portrait of a Madonna* in which
she had an enormous success out here. Tennessee, Kazan,
and Irene Selznick saw her in it and that certainly had something to do with her getting *Streetcar*. A lot of people feel
that *Portrait of a Madonna* is a sort of blueprint for *Streetcar*,
which is not so. At least I don't believe it is so. You'd better
ask Tennessee. But the character of Miss Collins is really a
lot closer to the character of Alma Winemiller in *Summer
and Smoke*. When *Summer and Smoke* was produced—Tennessee doesn't know anything about this—but when the play
was produced, it didn't get very good notices but it did get
a good notice from Brooks Atkinson. And I remember I sat
down and wrote to Mr. Atkinson. I have written to him only
twice in my life and one of the occasions was to thank him
for the notice he had written for this play, which I thought

was a beautiful play. It was not nearly as sensational or effective or as good a play as Tennessee had written before.
But if Tennessee had been new—if this had been the work
of an unknown writer—everyone would have exclaimed
over it. And this is, of course, a problem that every good
playwright faces. As soon as he has written one good play
or, God help him, two good plays, then everything he writes
subsequently must measure up to or surpass what he's done.
He is constantly in competition with himself. And that's
desperate. You can't do creative work that way. I mean,
you've got to be able to fall on your face and then, if you
can, come up with a master work once in every decade and
if you live any good length of life, you've really done very
well. I mean, if you can leave three outstanding plays! Tennessee's whole influence in the theatre, too, of course, is
remarkable. He represents something in the theatre of the
twentieth century which is monumental. I still think he's
our outstanding playwright. I know that in the last few
years he's gone through periods which have been very difficult for him personally. Obviously he's not told me so. I've
had one or two conversations with him only, but I have been
aware from people who were close to him. I never have
been close to Tennessee. It's something I regret. He's a man
who alarms me, rather, because he is so acutely shy. Perhaps
"shy" is not the right word, but on the occasions when I have
sat and talked with him I've found it rather hard going and
always felt that he did too, and that doesn't make for any
sort of close relationship. But that has nothing to do with my
admiration for him. I think that personally he suffers certain
furies and a kind of anguish that's very hard for anybody to
understand who isn't inside his skin.

MIKE: I've always felt that even though Tennessee is just
a human being like the rest of us, everything is more intensified to him. Any feelings that any of us have are extremely
exaggerated within him, so that it does make him a bundle

of nerves sometimes and could also make him tormented in certain areas. But it's also what makes him the genius, the sensitive writer that he is.

CRONYN: God, what a hell of a price to pay though, isn't it? I wouldn't for the world trade places with Tennessee! Not for the world! I am simply a workaday character actor but I wouldn't swap for all the gift and talent and skill. Perhaps that sounds smug of me. I certainly don't mean it to.

The last time I talked to Tennessee was just about a year ago. It was a conversation on the telephone. I had read a new short play of his—a full-length play. I don't know why I said short. *The Two Character Play*. I had read *The Two Character Play*, which I found impressive. I thought it was terribly difficult to do but I thought it was impressive and that there was some marvelous writing in it. And that, in a fashion, there was more revelation of Tennessee in that play than in anything of his that I have ever read. We even went to England to see a production of it. That was the principal thing we went for. I thought the production was disappointing. I also felt that it was going to be extremely difficult to do that play justice. It should be done again and done differently. I thought it was something that Jess and I might attempt but I was frightened by what I saw. However, I talked to Audrey about it and then talked to Tennessee about it on the telephone. And in the course of the conversation said, "How are you?" And I remember him saying, very frankly, "I'm not at all well, Hume, I'm not at all well. I'm feeling miserable." And I think that part of the problem recently is that current success has escaped him. It's as though he were writing on a different plane, on a different level, and somehow the form and pressure of this time is escaping him and he is seeking desperately to find some way of expressing himself to the world of today, and particularly to the young people of today. In *The Two Character Play* that quality came over very, very strongly. I mean that terrible effort to reach out to say what had to be said. The whole setting, the dark theatre, the sense of being locked in, the quality of alienship, if there is such a word. There was only one person in the world with whom he had any kind of relationship at all, or either character had. And even that was half fantasy. It was a dream world in which somehow two people were baying the moon.

MIKE: That's the best explanation of that play I've ever heard given. You really hit home with that interpretation.

CRONYN: However, very unlike Tennessee's other work—and I am talking in theatrical clichés—it lacked a basic conflict. It was narrative. The drama was constantly being narrated after the fact. It did not develop and happen before you.

MIKE: Yes, it really has no plot. It's more like a duet, or concert between two people.

CRONYN: But the two people were very often traveling parallel roads. So that the emotion had to be generated in terms of what was remembered by them. It did not happen there at the moment, and the violence of their experience wasn't a violence which took place in front of you so that you participated. It made it a terribly difficult problem for the actors and the director too. But my God, what a marvelous writer! What a gifted man! You know, all his gifts, all of them, were reflected in the short plays.

MIKE: That's true. He's frequently gone back and expanded on his short plays and short stories to create major works.

CRONYN: Right. Right. In '42 or '43—the chronology of the things I'm telling you gets all mixed up—I know after he'd left Metro, I took one of his plays and submitted it to Judy Garland and she would have been superb casting. That was, ah, ah, all I can think of is *A House by the Railroad*.

MIKE: *This Property Is Condemned.*

CRONYN: *This Property Is Condemned!* His stage direction was that it should be set against Hopper's portrait of "A House by the Railroad." It isn't a portrait. It's a drawing of a house by the railroad track and one of the best works of Hopper. Great one. Wonderful mood. Nostalgia and sadness about it. And Judy Garland as that child, which she could have played, would have been just marvelous. I'm not sure she even read it because I had to send it to her at the studio. It was probably intercepted somewhere along the line. Of course it was later made into a film. And I never saw the film but I believe the emphasis of the film was largely on the sister, who never appeared in the play but was important as an off-stage character.

MIKE: But she becomes the star of the film. I was the dialogue director on that picture.

  If it is true that Tennessee is groping to express himself in a theatre today which isn't too receptive and has an economic situation in which other talented playwrights find it difficult to have a successful Broadway run, do you think perhaps Tennessee could say what he feels he needs to say through short stories and novels?

CRONYN: I think it would be impertinent for me to even express an opinion of it. I have one, though! And that is, "My God, the man is a *playwright!* He is also a novelist, a short-story writer, essayist, and poet. He has done all these successfully, but the most difficult of all the forms, and the greatest form, is the one for the theatre. And he is a master of it. And the fact that not everything works now is no reason to abandon that form. I am no longer close enough to Audrey Wood, and I see Tennessee rarely, so I don't know what his experience has been except that it has been disappointing. And there has been a rejection of some of his work and some of it has been received with—not hostility, but with the complaint that there is a quality of repetition. It's simply that the time is out of joint for his work.

MIKE: The atmosphere of theatre, the Broadway theatre now, seems to make it difficult for serious, poetic playwrights. The audiences seem to want big productions of musicals and comedies. That, along with the competition of films and especially television, has lessened the popularity of serious theatre.

CRONYN: I have been hearing that a long time. The situation is particularly acute now, but it will change. I don't know what will bring about that change but I have seen these cycles before. At the moment, motion pictures are providing a damned sight better level of entertainment, using provocative, fresh material of greater topical impact than you are getting in the theatre. What do we get now? One or two plays a season that seem to have real substance and worth. Of course there must be some unknown plays that aren't being seen but I don't believe very many.

MIKE: Bill Inge thinks the mass medium of television is the most important medium now.

CRONYN: But the standard of television is so bloody awful!

MIKE: He says there is a literature of television that will become more and more important.

CRONYN: From the mid-forties to mid-fifties? I don't see anything revolutionary now on television—not in straight dramatic form. Of course I must admit that you don't even see a television set in this room!

MIKE: At the moment I certainly can't imagine Tennessee writing directly for television.

CRONYN: Nor can I. I wish I could think of more to say about him right now. I can only repeat myself, singing his praises.

JESSICA TANDY

Jessica Tandy was the first in a long line of British actresses to star as Tennessee's heroines when she immortalized Blanche DuBois in the original production of A Streetcar Named Desire. *The latest in that line is Lynn Redgrave, who is starring in the title role in the film version of* The Seven Descents of Myrtle.

However, Jessica Tandy is rarely thought of as a British import because she has lived in America since 1942. She and Hume Cronyn have been a husband-and-wife theatrical team for more than twenty-five years. Part of that time was spent under contract to various film studios, where they were called upon to play supporting character roles. But in the legitimate theatre the Cronyns have starred in many plays on Broadway and on national tours. Memorable are The Fourposter, A Delicate Balance, *and their work at the Tyrone Guthrie Theatre in Minneapolis.*

Jessica Tandy
(*Photo by Editta Sherman*)

Jessica Tandy in
Portrait of a Madonna. 1947.
(*Photo courtesy
Friedman-Abeles*)

Hollywood
November 19, 1968

TANDY: Well, we had corresponded before he came to see the play. We actually did that revival of *Portrait of a Madonna* for him, really. Because of the interest there was in *Portrait of a Madonna*, I had become a possibility for Blanche. Irene Selznick had hired me for Blanche and then Hume and I thought, "Well, it's an awful pity, but they're really buying a pig in a poke. Maybe we should do that play again for him to see." So we did revive it for a few extra performances so that Tennessee could see what he was getting. I must say the first night of the revival was absolutely disastrous because everything went wrong. We hadn't been playing it for several weeks and I had been making a picture in the meantime and was shooting all day. We hadn't really had as much rehearsal as we had before and everything seemed to go wrong. I was absolutely suicidal afterwards. I thought that was not at all the best performance we'd given. Irene Selznick was there, Kazan, and Tennessee. I didn't see Tennessee afterwards, though. Apparently there was a big party afterwards so they could all go off and discuss it, but they didn't ask me. It kind of seemed like a knell of doom. In fact, the next day I just went out and drove my car because I thought, you know, they obviously are all going to say, "We made a dreadful mistake," and I actually called Kazan and said, "Look, if you want to change your mind—I quite understand how you all feel. You don't have to feel bound to me." And he said, "Don't be ridiculous, we still want you." Which was a great surprise to me. But this isn't really telling you about Tennessee. We really didn't have any contact, actually. He came to see the *Portrait of a Madonna* and, of course, I was delighted he was there and very frightened. But I don't really know what he thought about it. After that, at rehearsals for *Streetcar,* I was delighted to see that he came to every rehearsal. He was there all the time, although it must have been agonizing for him to see the awful growing pains that actors go through. If the author is involved with you it's a closer relationship, and that should be. But Tennessee didn't really communicate with us at all. He communicated with Kazan, who directed the play, but he didn't really talk to any of us, at least not to me, about it all. I think he is a very, very, very shy man. I think he is not able to be outgoing.

MIKE: Was he doing rewrites on the script during rehearsals in New York?

TANDY: Not really rewrites. No. It was really a very well finished script by the time we started the first rehearsal. He really had done his work thoroughly before we started. It was a little over-long, I think, and I think a tiny bit was cut out of it. But I think when we opened out of town, there was a great deal of talk about shortening it a little bit because it was quite a long evening. But it wasn't possible to shorten it because he writes so poetically, so musically, that you can't chop it. It's impossible. You could perhaps take out a word or three, three words here, four words there. You can't really. We all tried to think, you know, if that were possible, but it really wasn't.

MIKE: Was the out-of-town opening in Philadelphia?

TANDY: New Haven. Then Philadelphia, Boston, and New York.

MIKE: When Tennessee came to Hollywood to see you in *Portrait of a Madonna,* were other members of *Streetcar* already cast?

TANDY: I don't think so, but I don't really know. No, that was quite a little while before we started rehearsals.

MIKE: Since Blanche was the main character in the play, it would be more important to cast that part first, I should think.

TANDY: I don't think there was anyone else cast at that point. It was several weeks, really, ahead of time. There was something else I was going to tell you about *Streetcar*. Oh, yes, I remember. You asked if there were any rewrites. I remember one day that Kazan turned back to Tennessee, who was sitting at the back of the theatre, and said, "Tennessee, I need a few lines here for the people upstairs because they've finished their dialogue down at the ground level, but as they go on upstairs, they should continue the conversation. So would you see about that?" And around fifteen minutes later—we thought maybe tomorrow he would come back with it—he came down with a piece of paper and told them actually what they had to say. And I was absolutely overcome. I thought, "How marvelous!" Just like that he got it! And then a little later I was reading some of his earlier plays, some of the one-act ones, and there I found that dialogue. Tennessee had obviously said, "Oh, well, I can fit that in here." And, of course, it was marvelous. It did fit, thank Heaven. But it was kind of awesome when he did it. Those were very happy rehearsals, as a matter of fact. It was marvelous to be working on a play of such quality. Before you actually open in a play in New York there is absolutely no knowing at all whether the play will be successful or not. Right down to the wire. Even though I've opened out of town and maybe there's been a great deal of excitement. You don't really know if you are a success or not until you get to New York. That's really where it's at. But nevertheless, the quality of that play was so absolutely remarkable that it never bothered us whether it was going to be a hit or a failure because it was so fascinating to work on. And Kazan is a remarkable director with a great sensitivity to everyone's needs. I think he understood very well how to get the best out of all of us. And also out of Tennessee. And make us all contribute everything that we had. He's a very strong director with a very great deal to give of himself. To every production, he gives. But I have never found that he squashed anybody's creativity.

MIKE: I think he brings it out.

TANDY: Yes, he brings it out and uses what he can. And he is quite—ruthless isn't the word, but he's quite—all right, let's say ruthless, but I don't really mean ruthless. I'll try to think of a better word than that. He can say immediately, "No, that's all wrong," and that's finished! There's no argument about it. It would be silly to argue about it because he really has a marvelous eye for what fits and what doesn't into the whole production. It was fascinating to do it.

MIKE: Did you have any problem learning the Southern accent?

TANDY: Well, I worked on that before I ever started with a Southern girl and then also, you see, Lucinda Ballard was doing the costumes. And I used to spend a couple of hours each morning before rehearsals, or most mornings before rehearsals, at the dressmaker's because Lucinda is a girl who likes to make the clothes on you, so to speak. And so I would be pinned up one day and it would be done and all the pins would come out the next day. And all the time she talks. She has a marvelous Southern accent. But the most difficult thing for me was that in order to be audible you have to sound all the consonants because otherwise the people at the back are not going to know what you are talking about. On the other hand, one of the characteristics of some kinds of Southern speech is that the consonants are softened and even sometimes left out. And also it seemed absolutely imperative to play fast, not to indulge oneself. It's such marvelous language that one could go very slowly and it would be absolutely delicious, but it would not really have the underlying pulse that the play demanded. So one had to speak fast, distinctly, and Southern. And to do it all together was quite difficult!

MIKE: At the end of the opening night's performance, didn't they bring Tennessee on stage?

TANDY: Yes, they did. And I was the most surprised girl in the world. I never thought he would come. I thought he would be much too shy to come. But he did, as a matter of fact, and I was delighted. It was a wonderful, wonderful night and it was his night! My goodness! Of course he already had a great hit with *The Glass Menagerie*, which is a beautiful play. I don't think that play was as well realized —except for Laurette Taylor's performance—as *Streetcar* was, but I think it's a beautiful piece of work.

MIKE: Did you spend much time with Tennessee after rehearsals, going out to discuss the part—

TANDY: No, no.

MIKE: —the interpretation of the role?

TANDY: No. I would have adored it, but no, not at all.

MIKE: He felt he should leave all that to Kazan as director?

TANDY: I don't know. Maybe he did, but I think also he's really very shy, you see. I wouldn't feel that I could go and ask him if he didn't take any part in the talks, as it were. And after all, I suppose at the end of an eight-hour day, everyone is exhausted and you have got tomorrow. You've got studying to do to try to learn the thing.

MIKE: You played Blanche for about eighteen months, I believe.

TANDY: Yes.

MIKE: Did you ever play it with any other actor playing Stanley besides Marlon Brando?

TANDY: Yes, I did. Marlon was ill or off for a week or something at one time, I'm pretty sure, and they brought in Jack Palance. Luckily for me I had a clause in my contract that said I could have a six-week vacation after the first season, otherwise I would have been dead. So I left for six weeks and Uta Hagen came in and played my part with my company. And she went on and did the Chicago company with Anthony Quinn. We were a very happy company. When I say that, I don't mean we had a lot of joking to and fro between dressing rooms, but I mean we worked well together. I found it absolutely exhausting, that part, although I love to be in a play when I'm never off the stage because of the progression. I hate to have to play a scene and then have to go sit in my dressing room for twenty minutes. I like to have the continuity of it. But that was physically very, very exhausting! And mostly I think it was because, you see, I had a fight with the audience every night because as time went on the audience got less and less sensitive. There was always an element of the audience who thought it was absolutely hilarious. Any bad language, you see, would be terribly funny, or anything kind of sexy would be hilarious. It was only some of the audience, but it was very disrupting and awful when playing the part not to be able to hold them all. My only real contact with Tennessee was about that very thing. When we had been running, oh, quite a long while, Thomas Hart Benton wanted to do a painting which I think David O. Selznick had commissioned for Irene Selznick as a Christmas present. I posed for him. And he did the painting, but I never saw it. But the manager came to me at the theatre one night and showed me a photograph of the painting, which filled me with a certain amount of horror

because if you knew nothing at all about the play, and you
looked at the painting, it looked exactly like a couple of
two-dollar whores waiting in the room for the boys to finish
playing poker! It had nothing of the deep feeling of the
play. What's marvelous about the play is that there are so
many opposites all going at the same time. It isn't just vi-
olent, or just lyrical. It's violence and lyricism all at the same
time. And they intermingle. And they're absolutely depen-
dent on each other. And no scene has one color; it's a million
colors. *Look* magazine apparently wanted to put a photograph of the painting on one page and then we were all
going to pose, as we never did in the play, exactly like that
on the opposite page. And I said No because that would
make it look like I thought that was really like it was. Irene
Selznick was very upset about that. She thought it was
marvelous publicity, which, God knows, we didn't need. We
had standees at every performance all the time. She was so
put out about that. She said she would ask Tennessee what
he thought and he wrote me a charming letter in which he
said he quite understood why I didn't want to pose in my
underwear, which, of course, was nonsense because I was
on stage in my underclothes every night. It couldn't have
mattered less. But this is rather darling. He said that he
thought perhaps Blanche herself would say No at first, and
then she would say Yes. So I wrote him a very long letter
back saying, "This is what I think Blanche is about: . . . and
every night that's what I try to play, sometimes in difficult
circumstances. And I don't want to destroy that. I want to
keep on with that." And he wrote back immediately and
said, "You are right. I had forgotten that that's really what
we had set out to do." Words to that effect. And there was
no more talk about it. We never did that publicity for *Look*,
which really didn't matter at all, because as far as publicity
was concerned, we certainly didn't need it to help the play
and it would, I think, have been a detriment to the people

who did come with a more sensitive understanding of the play.*

MIKE: Tennessee told me that he was once asked by an actress who had played Blanche, "Of all the actresses who have played Blanche, who do you think played her the best?"

TANDY: Oh, God, what a daring thing to say!

MIKE: And Tennessee answered, "Why, Jessica Tandy, of course!"

TANDY: That's sweet of him.

MIKE: And he still says that. Because I asked him recently if he thought that, and he said Yes.

TANDY: Well, I would like to think that's true, but I think also the first impact is sometimes the greatest, and also he'd watched it take place, as it were.

MIKE: You were the creator of the part, so he identified you more closely with it.

TANDY: And, you see, we are not really creators, or only to a small degree are we creative. Our creativity is really to —providing we have scripts as well written as Tennessee's— it is to dig every bit of good out of them and make sure the form and content is fully realized as the author intended.

MIKE: Well, obviously Tennessee thought that about your performance.

TANDY: Well, that's marvelous. I couldn't be happier that he thinks so. It's something I'll never really forget. But, you know, many years ago I was in another play in England. It doesn't really matter what it was, but the authoress had written a scene between two people which I wasn't in, but

* The correspondence appears at the end of this interview.

I watched the rehearsal. She had written stage directions of one sort or another and at some point she wrote: "[His eyes flashed]." And the two people who were playing the scene didn't realize she was at the rehearsal and they thought this was hilariously funny and they said, "Go ahead, flash your eyes." "Am I flashing my eyes?" Awfully funny! And she came down to the footlights and she said, "I'm not asking you to flash your eyes or do anything with your eyes. I'm only telling you what happened when it happened in my head first. And that's why I put it there." And I thought, "My God, isn't that marvelous!" Because I think stage directions of an author, in varying degrees, should be followed. Don't fool with George Bernard Shaw because he really knows exactly where everything he writes should go. You'd better try to do everything he says because you're not likely to come up with anything better. And the things that an author says about his play, I think, are of great value to the actor as pointers, as things to open up all kinds of avenues.

MIKE: But not necessarily to be taken literally.

TANDY: Not necessarily to be taken literally at all.

MIKE: Do you think that in Tennessee's stage directions he's indicating an emotional feeling only?

TANDY: He does much more than that. He indicates musically too. And the rhythms of everyone's speeches! You can't mess around with that script. No speech of Stella's could possibly be said by Blanche, and vice versa. He really writes absolutely individualistically. There is no possibility of saying, "You say that instead of her, because it will be more convenient." It couldn't be done. He really has thought most carefully about it and I am sure that there is music in his head because there is a great deal of music in all of his plays. Music plays a great part in *Portrait of a Madonna*, with those old, old records.

MIKE: I think it is interesting in reading Tennessee's plays that his stage directions also have poetry.

TANDY: Absolutely.

MIKE: Even his technical instructions are written with lyricism.

TANDY: His poetry seems inevitable. And, as I said in the beginning, he presented us with a finished script. I think very often now an author will say, "I'm sure there are changes to be made but I don't want to do that yet until we actually get into rehearsal." And that worries me, because if he is sure there are changes to be made, I think he should make them first. And anything that comes later would come out of a complete script. They would be minor things. Probably not important. Tennessee finishes his homework. He certainly did on *Streetcar*, anyway, I can say.

MIKE: You did *Portrait of a Madonna* on television, didn't you, with Mr. Cronyn directing it again?

TANDY: Yes, that was for the Actors Studio. And we also did it as a part of a program we toured, just Hume and I, of all kinds of things from Ogden Nash to Shakespeare to Browning.

MIKE: That was the tour called *Face to Face*.

TANDY: Yes. *Madonna* is really a superb play. It's got everything in it. It's a perfect little jewel of a play. A lot of Tennessee's one-act ones are. He really mastered the one-act play.

✿   ✿   ✿

DEAR JESSICA:

I have been appointed intermediator in the delicate matter of persuading you to pose for a photographic duplication of the Thomas Hart Benton painting which our Lady Producer is to be surprised with at Christmas. I have seen a picture of the painting. It looks marvelous and of course Benton is a very outstanding painter. I can see how Blanche's dress, or lack of it, might offend you, but I am assured that you will not have to be so anatomical and I suppose the idea is an excellent piece of promotion. Myself I don't see it is vulgar, but I cannot swear that my sense of vulgarity is the most impeccable in the world.

Ever,

TENNESSEE

P.S. I believe Blanche *would*—after some initial protest.

DEAR TENNESSEE:

You have the wrong impression of my objection to posing for a photographic duplicate of the Benton picture.

Eight times a week, and to progressively less sensitive audiences, I have to make clear Blanche's intricate and complex character—her background—her pathetic elegance—her indomitable spirit—her innate tenderness and honesty—her untruthfulness or manipulation of the truth—her inevitable tragedy.

My protagonist Stanley—my executioner as you put it—is comparatively simple and easy for an audience to understand.

The setting is a wonderful mixture of the qualities of both these characters—decayed elegance and sheer unadulterated guts.

I share your admiration for Benton as a painter, but in this painting he has chosen to paint, it seems to me, the Stanley side of the picture. Even in the set, you are more conscious of telegraph poles than scrolled ironwork.

There has always been a part of the audience who obviously expects a sexy, salacious play. I don't want to do anything which will lead future audiences to think that they are going to see sex in the raw, as it were.

I respect Mr. Benton's right to paint any facet of the play that he sees and to exaggerate it in order to make clear his impressions.

Please believe me when I say that Blanche's lack of dress has nothing at all to do with my objection.

I suppose the idea of printing the two photographs is an excellent piece of promotion. It is bound to bring a lot of people into the theatre, but we have no empty seats and, in my opinion, such promotion is not very far removed from the marquee of *Open City, a* truly great picture in my opinion, which was advertised as the "most fearless sex picture ever made," or words to that effect—and I would hate to help in any such scheme.

Print the Benton picture—and don't bother with the *cache-sexe* that is being offered as an inducement —but no duplicate photograph. If *Look's* interest is really in Mr. Benton's painting, they should be content.

There, Mr. Intermediator, is my initial protest. What do you say to that!

Truly affectionately,

JESSICA

DEAR JESSICA:

Many, many thanks for your letter on the Benton picture. You are so right that it really makes me ashamed of having lent my casual support to the idea. What you say about Blanche suddenly recalls to me all of my original conception of the character and what it was to me, from which you, in your delineation, have never once drifted away in spite of what I now realize must have been a continual pressure: that unwillingness of audiences to share a more intricate and special and sensitive response to things: their desire to participate more safely, familiarly, in the responses of an animal nature. I have almost forgotten (perhaps under this same pressure) that it was Blanche whom I loved and respected and whom I wished to portray, though I have never, please believe me, forgotten the exact and tender and marvelously understanding way that you brought her to life.—I have such a divided nature! Irreconcilably divided. I look at Benton's picture and I see the strong things in it, its immediate appeal to the senses, raw, sensual, dynamic, and I forgot the play was really about those things which are opposed to that, the delicate half-approaches to something much finer. Yes, the painting is only one side of the play, and the Stanley side of it. Perhaps from the painter's point of view that was inevitable. A canvas cannot depict two worlds very easily: or the tragic division of the human spirit: at least not a painter of Benton's realistic type. Well, I am still an admirer of the painting, but, believe me, still more an admirer of yours for seeing and feeling about it more clearly than I did at first, and I should have felt the same way.

With love,

TENNESSEE

Deborah Kerr and Peter Viertel (*Photo by William Eccles*)

DEBORAH KERR
AND PETER VIERTEL

Deborah Kerr is a perfect example of the song "A Pretty Girl Is Like a Melody," and the favorite melody of her husband, Peter Viertel, should be "I Married an Angel." I had never met Deborah Kerr prior to this interview but everyone said, "You'll love her, she's an angel." I couldn't agree more, and she is more than an angel. She is vivacious, intelligent, chic, and talented. She is the answer to any man's dream!

Deborah and Peter make their home in Switzerland. When in Los Angeles they usually take a house on the beach. Peter is an ardent surfer, and after spending all morning at his typewriter, he often heads for the Malibu beaches. He is the author of White Hunter, Black Heart, *a thinly disguised account of the making of John Huston's film* The African Queen.

When I went to see them at the Bel-Air Hotel, Deborah had a rare day off from her heavy film schedule on The Arrangement.

KERR: As I remember it, I first met Tennessee outside of the Ethel Barrymore Theatre with Elia Kazan when we were rehearsing *Tea and Sympathy*. As you know, Kazan and Tennessee were great chums, and whether he had been to a rehearsal or not I don't really remember because I don't think he wanted me to know that anybody was there. But I remember they were together in the street outside and I said, "Hello" and "How do you do?" and that's all. That was the first time. Then I didn't meet him again until *The Night of the Iguana* in Puerto Vallarta. I arrived later than the rest of the company. Richard Burton and Ava Gardner were already there working, and Tennessee had arrived earlier, too. Even then I didn't really see him very much. Dorothy Jenkins, who designed the costumes for the film, was someone who knew him quite well. She was passionate that he come and take a look at the one principal costume that I had, which was very simple—kind of arty-crafty. It was a marvelous outfit, actually. We were having the clothes made in a tiny shop in Puerto Vallarta. It was terribly hot and you didn't feel like taking all your clothes off and getting other clothes on. And I think Tennessee had said Yes, he would come, and sort of dived into the shop and took one look and you just felt he wished he wasn't there at all. And we said, "Hello. How are you?" again, and so on. He muttered something and shot out pretty quickly. I think we chatted for about five minutes, that was all, and about what, I really don't know, other than he thought the outfit was great. Dorothy did most of the talking.

MIKE: You were there at the same time, weren't you, Peter?

VIERTEL: Yes, I was. I remember he came in and made

some very complimentary remarks about Deborah, about her looks, and then buzzed off right away again.

MIKE: I think Tennessee was in Puerto Vallarta for about a week or two weeks, wasn't he?

KERR: About a week, I think, or ten days.

VIERTEL: I suppose he was there a week prior to our arrival and stayed about a week afterwards.

MIKE: Was he doing some rewrites on the script?

VIERTEL: I think he *said* he would, but then I believe he just fiddled around with one scene.

MIKE: That was the period when he wore a beard, wasn't it?

KERR: Yes, I remember. It was kind of scruffy, you know. It was startling. I remember it very well because he didn't look at all as I remembered him. It changed him enormously, didn't it?

VIERTEL: Wasn't he down in Mexico years earlier, when he had the idea for this play?

MIKE: I think he got the idea for the short story, which is not a precise basis for the play, during his first trip to Acapulco in 1940. The play didn't come until quite a bit later.

VIERTEL: But the play is based on the short story?

MIKE: I don't think it really is. He used the same title and minor aspects of the short story, and wrote an entirely different thing with it. The same way he did with the short story called *Three Players of a Summer Game*, which has a distant relation to *Cat on a Hot Tin Roof*. If you read the short story it is very minutely connected with the play. In fact, he's written another screenplay now called *Three*

Players of a Summer Game, which is taken more directly from the short story of that name.

KERR: He is a great man for titles, though, isn't he? *Night of the Iguana* is a marvelous title. *Summer and Smoke!* What a title! It's my favorite play of his. I really love it.

MIKE: It is a part you would have been beautiful in, too. You would have been very suitable for Miss Alma.

KERR: Yes. You know, I have only done the movie of the *Iguana.* I have never had a chance to do anything of his on the stage.

MIKE: When you were doing the film of *Iguana,* did you feel any autobiographical aspects in the character of Hannah Jelkes in common with Tennessee's own life, especially with his life with his Grandfather Dakin?

KERR: I would think so, yes. From what I know of him. You feel everything he writes about is very autobiographical. All his passions and feelings that he expresses in plays are obviously his own. Hannah represented his fight against the violence and brutality of the world. The period in which he wrote that play, the Germans represented brutality. I understand leaving that out of the film from a world point of view, but for me it was one of the strongest things in the play. This is what Hannah was against and yet had had to woo. She almost had to kind of prostitute herself to sell her drawings to the type of person who represented everything she really was against. And I am sure that expressed some feelings that were in Tennessee.

MIKE: Yes, it certainly expresses his feelings about letting his material pass on to a producer, especially a Hollywood producer!

KERR: Yes, that probably is the feeling to parallel, actually, personally, and you know him so much better than I do. I don't know.

VIERTEL: Well, actually he's been very lucky. He had a couple of very good ones, which is rare. *Streetcar Named Desire* was well done, and *Cat on a Hot Tin Roof*, as well as *Night of the Iguana*.

KERR: *Sweet Bird of Youth*.

MIKE: That was one of his favorite films of his work.

VIERTEL: So he's been very lucky. He really has no complaint against Hollywood, compared to most other writers.

MIKE: Of course, a writer's critical opinion of a film done from his own work is more severe. So just because Tennessee himself wouldn't think something of his is well done doesn't mean that other people wouldn't enjoy it.

VIERTEL: Yes, but he's the one that knows what he wants from it, and knows what he wanted to represent. So his opinion finally is the best opinion as far as that goes. But I think that on the whole he's had a pretty good shake compared to, for example, Hemingway, who never had one film really which was even close to what he wrote. Or Faulkner, who never had one that remotely resembled what he had written in the first place.

MIKE: How much do you think that has to do with the fact that a certain writer's material may be more easily interpreted by a screenwriter?

VIERTEL: I don't think that's the cause of it. Tennessee Williams was careful whom he sold his material to, and then, as he's a dramatist, the dialogue was all there and didn't need much adapting. A stage play is somewhat easier to adapt than a novel. Usually the writer who gets to adapt it is lazy or smart enough to just use scissors and a pot of paste! It's a little more difficult with a novel. Maybe that's why playwrights on the whole have been luckier than novelists with the movies. Even Eugene O'Neill has been quite fortunate. A couple of things of his have come off very well. Of course, Tennessee came at a later time, so his plays were bought for the screen when the screen was more adult.

KERR: I think that's very true. His movies, most of them, have been made at a time when, really, one can speak out.

VIERTEL: Not only speak out, but better people bought the material and made the films. Hemingway's books were always distorted and bastardized by the people who bought them. For instance, Howard Hawks made *To Have and Have Not*, and not one scene even resembled what the book was about.

MIKE: They were just buying Hemingway's name?

VIERTEL: That's right. He sold a book like *For Whom the Bell Tolls* to a man called Sam Wood, who was an opponent of Loyalist Spain. He wanted to make the book impartial.

KERR: But Ingrid Bergman was gorgeous!

VIERTEL: Yes, but it was a lousy picture, considering what a great book it was.

MIKE: Peter, you wrote the screenplay for *The Sun Also Rises*, didn't you?

VIERTEL: That was a bastardized version, as well.

MIKE: But didn't you have to do whatever studio heads or the producer would want in order to make a commercial film?

VIERTEL: Well, yes. In the case of *The Sun Also Rises*, there were scenes added, so the script was changed. And then we had to make concessions in casting. We never found the right Lady Brett, and the bullfighter was played by somebody who shouldn't have been playing that part. Still, there were moments that were good, but that's about all.

MIKE: Did you ever meet Hemingway and know him?

VIERTEL: Yes, I knew him very well. He wasn't happy with the picture.

MIKE: I don't think he liked any of his films, did he?

VIERTEL: The one he wanted made most of all was *Old Man and the Sea* and even that didn't work out very well, although the text was his. The picture he liked best was probably the first version of *A Farewell to Arms*, with Gary Cooper and Helen Hayes, which had good things in it and was, to an extent, true to the book. He also liked parts of *For Whom the Bell Tolls*. He liked Cooper's portrayal of the hero. But with Tennessee it's a different story. What Tennessee has to say, in my opinion, is much harder to sell to the public than what Hemingway had to say. Tennessee's message, as far as the general public goes, is one they have to reach for. Hemingway's was much easier to accept, especially because he more truly represented America. His feelings about physical bravery and *macho*-ism are very important to America. Tennessee represents the battle of the sensitive people against the brutalized people. And that's a difficult pill for the general public to swallow. But he's said what he had to say! And he said it in the theatre and he said it in the movies to some extent.

MIKE: Sometimes I think what Tennessee has to say is only really understood by the people who already feel the way he feels.

VIERTEL: I think that's true to an extent, but I think finally he reaches everybody. Because there's tremendous power in his writing. He really is a great playwright! He organizes the emotions of the people who see the thing and they're touched by it. Whether they're in agreement with what the writer says, they're being touched by it just the same.

MIKE: Like in *Streetcar*. Whether they identify with Stanley Kowalski or with Blanche DuBois, they still come out of the theatre with some sort of understanding of the play's message.

VIERTEL: In the theatre you have to understand everybody's point of view. Even if you sympathize with Stanley Kowalski, and if you're not put off by his brutishness, you can't help but be upset and impressed by the downfall of this tragic woman, Blanche. And if you are moved by it, that's half the battle.

MIKE: Deborah, when you met Tennessee in Puerto Vallarta during the filming of *The Night of the Iguana*, was there any particular aspect of his personality that impressed you or that you remember?

KERR: Well, I suppose probably the same thing that everybody notices: his intense shyness. And the feeling that he's about to say something to you and doesn't say it and you wish that he would, you know, whatever it might be. That was the impression I had of him. He appeared to be an extremely shy and sensitive person in just the few minutes he came in during my wardrobe fitting. You feel that he's about to say something that you'd love to hear, but he doesn't and dashes off.

MIKE: Did he work well with John Huston?

KERR: I think they got on very well. John is enigmatic, too. You never quite know him. Actually, I never really saw them working together.

MIKE: The reason I asked is that some of Tennessee's best work was done with Kazan, who is a very strong, domineering director, which I think Tennessee needs. And I guess John Huston is in the same category. It seems to me he would be a good director to discipline Tennessee to do re-writes and polishing on a script.

VIERTEL: Yes, except that in the case of *Night of the Iguana* the play had already been written. He had written a play and it was past history as far as he was concerned. You could feel that. They wanted him there to do some writing, but I don't think he did much. That's because he had done it, you know, and it was long past. Kazan always came in at the formative period of a play—when he had just written the play, and the play was being produced, and the creative process was still valid. The creative process with *The Night of the Iguana*, as far as Tennessee was concerned, was finished.

MIKE: Deborah, you have only played one Tennessee Williams part. Are there others that you find particularly suitable or interesting for yourself?

KERR: Yes. He is one of the few that write great parts for women. I love *Summer and Smoke,* as I said before. I think it's a marvelous part. I would have loved to play that. Who wouldn't want to play *Streetcar*?

VIERTEL: Yes, and it will be played again, obviously.

MIKE: You would certainly be right for that now.

KERR: Maybe it's time to revive it!

VIERTEL: I believe that all of Tennessee's plays will be redone in the next ten years.

MIKE: You would also be perfect for *Sweet Bird of Youth* now.

KERR: Well, yes. Unfortunately, I was working on another movie at the time it was filmed. I was offered it and I couldn't do it. Geraldine Page played it, and she was marvelous! She always is! That was seven years ago. Seven years makes a big difference. Now I would be great for it.

VIERTEL: It's casting against your type, though, *Sweet Bird of Youth*.

KERR: 'Tis a bit, yes.

VIERTEL: Certainly you're closer to *Streetcar* and in another ten years *Glass Menagerie*. Nobody wants to follow Laurette Taylor's performance . . . still, I believe they have redone it a couple of times, haven't they? *Glass Menagerie*?

MIKE: It's been done on television and it was revived in New York with Maureen Stapleton.

VIERTEL: Was it well revived?

MIKE: Yes, it was well received. Deborah, you're speaking in terms of theatre, not films, for revival?

KERR: Well, yes. Because they have all been done in films really, so there's not much reason to hope to redo *Glass Menagerie* again, unless . . .

VIERTEL: Who played it in the movie?

KERR: Gertrude Lawrence.

VIERTEL: Was she good in it?

KERR: Well . . . no.

MIKE: She was miscast.

KERR: And she—her specialty was a whole different world, wasn't it?

VIERTEL: Must have been very difficult—to follow in Laurette Taylor's shoes.

MIKE: I think it is interesting to remember how many British actresses have played Tennessee's parts.

KERR: The queen is Margaret Leighton! She's played practically all of his parts. It's funny. He sort of writes as if they were English, although they are usually Southern. But I guess that's almost the same thing.

ANAÏS NIN

Anaïs Nin had just returned from a month's stay in New York, where she had delivered the third volume of her Diary *to her publisher. We are neighbors in Los Angeles and for this conversation I casually visited her after her usual morning work session.*

In the dozen years I have known Anaïs, I have never been in her presence without experiencing a feeling of enlightenment from her intelligence, charm, and beauty. Of all the people I have met, she is the most perceptive, sensitive, and sincere. In the Los Angeles Times *review of her recent book,* The Novel of the Future, *literary critic Murray Gattis wrote, "Her thoughts are tiny bursts of light that illuminate intuition and imagination." True.*

The gentle and honest style of her Diary *reveals her natural talent for expressing her thoughts in a fluid and lucid matter-of-fact manner. There is no pedantry. Nor does the reader feel Anaïs is making any effort to be clever or cute with a play on words or ideas.*

She is completely feminine and lyrical in her surrealist style. This is at once evident in her titles, which for brilliance approach Tennessee's and Carson McCullers': A Spy in the House of Love, Under a Glass Bell, House of Incest, Seduction of the Minotaur, Children of the Albatross, *and* Cities of the Interior. *It is interesting that the movie makers are finally awakening to the potential of her novels as film material, as they are with Carson's.*

Anaïs Nin (*Photo by Marlis Schwieger*)

Los Angeles
December 7, 1968

NIN: My first memory of Tennessee Williams is in Provincetown in 1940, the summer of 1940, when Robert Duncan, the poet, who was then editor of a small magazine, brought him to visit me, saying that he had written some very beautiful short stories. Both Tennessee and I had a great deal of shyness with strangers, particularly, I think, in the early part of his life and the early part of mine. And that meeting didn't bring on any subsequent meetings. But I became interested in his work from the very beginning, went to all his plays, followed his career in the theatre. Every now and then we would meet at some public function or other, and Tennessee would always say something very lovely and then we would promise to meet again, and we didn't. I always need a great deal of demonstrativeness and warmth to come out, and probably he needed the same thing. I took his defense once: This I remember very well, when Maxwell Geismar wrote an article saying that Tennessee was writing outside the mainstream of American literature. This touched off a very strong article I wrote, which was never published, which I have in the *Diary*, saying how wrong could anyone be not to understand that the ecstasies and anxieties of every human being are part of the mainstream of literature, particularly when they were written by a poet. And a very sincere poet, a man who has experienced everything that he wrote about and whom I considered very close to D. H. Lawrence in his identification with women. The way he described women, I felt, was extremely sensitive, and extremely identified to women. So I admired him.

We had several meetings. One, I remember, in the house of a painter, a New Orleans painter called Olive Leonard. She was in New York and we met in her apartment. Tennessee came to see her. They were friends. And that was when I met Oliver Evans. Another time he came down to our apartment in New York. Another time I was invited to his place after the play *The Milk Train Doesn't Stop Here Anymore*. It was after the night that the play was opened. We went to his apartment. Another time we had a very amusing correspondence because I tried to interest him in Marguerite Young, who needed a grant to finish her enormous book, *Miss MacIntosh, My Darling*, which I admire a great deal. So I wrote to him. We exchanged very humorous letters because I said I thought he would be interested in this "oceanic unconscious" and Tennessee wrote back and said he preferred the "little condensed fragments of my unconscious" to this "oceanic unconscious." A very charming letter.

MIKE: You thought that Tennessee could arrange for her to get a grant, or to sponsor her himself?

NIN: Yes. Tennessee was sponsoring some writers at the time and I wrote to him about Marguerite Young, who really needed to be helped to finish this enormous book—a thousand-page book, which I consider on a par with *Ulysses*. So I wrote to Tennessee and we exchanged letters at that point.

MIKE: I didn't know that he had sponsored other writers.

NIN: He had set up a fund for writers.

MIKE: Was that the fund at Tulane University in New Orleans?

NIN: I don't know where it was. I wrote to him directly because I had heard about it. He had helped several friends —writers that I knew. My feeling for him was always that he was a great poet and that some of this poetry was lost occasionally in the staging and the film making. The atmosphere, for example, of the film of *The Roman Spring of Mrs. Stone* should have been very subtle and very suggestive, the way his writing was. His writing was always very subtle and it was symbolic, as a poet's would be, and being put on the stage, very often it was made too explicit.

MIKE: Do you think his short stories and his novella, *The Roman Spring of Mrs. Stone*, are representative of the kind of prose that you try to encourage other writers to write— the world of emotions as opposed to the world at large?

NIN: Yes. In fact I would have written about him in my book *The Novel of the Future*, but I didn't write about him because he demanded, or really deserved, a longer study And I didn't want to mention these things very casually. Certainly *The Roman Spring of Mrs. Stone* is what I call a poetic novel, and the stories, also. You know, I always felt he didn't need praise; he's had so much praise. So I took some of the writers that were less known, almost on purpose, because I feel Tennessee has received great recognition, don't you?

MIKE: Yes, of course. And I don't think he has ever written from a standpoint of sociological drama or prose. He is always writing from the individual standpoint, rather than that of society or social problems.

NIN: But I believe that the crisis we went through, which was called alienation, came from people's refusal to look inside of themselves. And Tennessee was doing just that! Looking into much deeper parts of a person's emotional life, psychic life, psychological life, at a time when the novel wasn't doing that.

MIKE: I think Tennessee is a person of extremes in his own life. Everything, every experience is so heightened, every emotional experience especially! When I first met him he seemed to be so very perceptive of other people, even though he was shy in expressing it to them directly sometimes. He embodied the idea you wrote about in *Seduction of the Minotaur* of a person who doesn't become static because he uses all his senses to relate to the world and continue making discoveries. Tennessee seemed to have a great capacity for observing and feeling, and sensitivity to people, places, and things. He is much more inward now.

NIN: I think what people do not often understand is his tremendous power of heightening, as you say, and dramatization, so that characters become almost mythological. They become larger than nature. And I think that the negative criticism came because people never understood that he was really making mythological symbolic characters. Are you also referring to my book on the novel? To my description of the people who are fluid? Are you thinking of him as he fitted into these, or just in general?

MIKE: I'm thinking also of your description. That enters into it also.

NIN: Yes. I would say he answers that definition. Absolutely. What I consider the person who is in touch with his own unconscious and other people's, and knows the drama that takes place underneath. Not the obvious ones. Because what I call realism is not reality. Tennessee was writing a great deal about that at one period. In the papers, you remember, when he was talking about his analysis in *The New York Times*. I remember reading articles about his subterranean life.

MIKE: Do you think a writer can have so much of the desired fantasy and ability to dream, which you write about, that his imagination is magnified to a point so extreme that his writing becomes very esoteric and he is the only person who can enjoy it? What the person is saying or trying to say, or dramatizing, reaches a smaller audience because it comes from too deep inside himself? Through an extreme ability to fantasize he actually stops experiencing real life and says, "Well, I don't have to do that," or "I don't have to go to that place, I can imagine what it's like." Or, "I don't want to go to see that play." "I don't want to go to that museum." "I don't want to go to that city, I can imagine what it's like." It could then make a full circle to where it's a danger, and you get back to something that is static and repetitive, and you don't go out and experience things, from a feeling that you have *already* experienced everything.

NIN: That's a danger. I think I see what you mean. It is a danger, but I don't know whether that's what happened to Tennessee, or whether his faculty for dreaming turned against him in the sense that the nightmare took over. This I'm not sure about. I have a feeling that the very thing that makes us sensitive to what is going on inside of us can make us prey to obsession! Then we become the victim of the nightmare rather than the one who is fulfilling or carrying out, using a dream as a blueprint of what is really happening to human beings.

MIKE: Yes, I think that is what has happened to Tennessee.

NIN: He did enter into this hell, you know. He did enter into the hell and produced marvelous things because he dared to.

MIKE: In *Sweet Bird of Youth* he says, "We each have our own private hell."

NIN: However, they're not private.

MIKE: Not for a writer, no.

NIN: They are not private. I think that all the poets have followed him and identified with him and have believed in his nightmares. The nightmares are just as real. They are just exaggerated states of consciousness. We have plenty to have nightmares about! But I think he has become haunted by them.

MIKE: I also think that almost everything he has written is his diary. If all his work were in one volume, it would be like the story of his own life, thinly disguised. I feel that very much. Rather than keeping a diary (which he did, however, for several years), his work itself is a very enlarged and symbolic retelling of his experiences, and beliefs and feelings.

NIN: You think he disliked the direct self-exposure? Or was he just fascinated by the transposition into poetry right away? I mean as soon as an experience came, he made fiction of it. He made a play, poetry, of it. So that he took it away from himself.

MIKE: He dramatizes his experiences, or fantasies and dreams, immediately. I think he would have feelings of guilt if he documented his life, like a proper diary does. Like yours, for instance. He would feel that a finger would be pointed at him, and that he would be thought of as a monster if he came right out and said, "This is I."

NIN: This is very interesting because actually people do that, too.

MIKE: Yes, I know. Christopher Isherwood nearly always writes in the first person singular, using his own name. And your style, of course, is just as honest.

NIN: And people do use that against you! Tennessee is right. You get two things: either genuine love because people do know you and you have exposed yourself; or else the hostility of people who take advantage of what you expose and wish to harm you. I think plenty of people harmed Tennessee, too. They give him both love and harmfulness, don't you think? It works both ways with the artist.

No matter what he does, whether he disguises himself or exposes himself, people always hold him responsible.

MIKE: When I say that Tennessee's works are like his diary, I don't mean that one of the characters in a play is patterned after him. I mean nearly all of the characters are a bit of him. It's astounding that when you really get to know him you recognize all these different characters inside him, summed up into the one severely complex character of his actual being. It's amazing, I think, to see the aspects of Stanley Kowalski in him as well as those of Blanche DuBois and Alma Winemiller, Valentine Xavier, or Alexandra del Lago, or Flora Goforth.

NIN: Well, you know how much of these many selves he distributed.

MIKE: You'd think, "How can a person have that many selves?"

NIN: Well, I think it was Huxley who said that genius is multiplicity of selves, which somehow or other the artist is able to maintain without blowing up, without falling apart.

MIKE: But then oftentimes I suppose they come into conflict with each other.

NIN: Oh, there are risks! There are many risks. Because the dreaming, particularly, is such a risk. Being a poet is such a risk. Because then you do enter the nightmare.

MIKE: But it's something you have no control over. You have no choice whether to take the risk or not. It just exists. You *are* that way.

NIN: Yes, you have to live on the level on which you experience things. If you are not a superficial person, you have to go right on doing what I always call my "archaeology of the soil or sea," you know, "bottom-of-the-sea type of life-existence." You choose the climate in which you can best function as a writer and as a poet. In life you are doomed to that.

MIKE: Do you think a person having an extremely strong imagination or sensitivity or awareness is complete enough within that extremity so that he doesn't need any type of drugs? You say in your book on the novel that if a person relates with all his senses to art he doesn't need drugs. Yet certain drugs, of course, heighten your senses!

NIN: Tennessee, with that imagination and that intuition, certainly had no need of drugs at all. I mean he was very open to experience and to the senses. I can see that in his work. In *Camino Real* he accepted the dreaming. He let himself be invaded by images. And that is what made the greatness of him.

MIKE: If a person has allowed that, and I am not talking about Tennessee in particular now, but if any artist—a painter, or a writer, a poet—has allowed all this to take place within himself, do you think that he can feel satiated by this having taken place in himself so that the experience is completed? Or would he feel that even if he were on what would be the highest level he was capable of, because of his genius he would still want to explore or discover something that he thought must be even a topper to that! Even if you went to heaven and lingered long enough to know the experience of being there, wouldn't you want to continue to some further place beyond even that? To an ultimate, if it could be acknowledged within yourself?

NIN: I can't answer that. Do you feel that Tennessee has reached a point where he feels that he knows everything? You said you were afraid of that.

MIKE: I think that, yes.

NIN: You don't think that it's fear of what he has gone into?

MIKE: Oh, yes. I think he certainly feels it's dangerous.

NIN: You see, if I use my feminine thing to say I identify now with what Tennessee is going through, I would say, well, I'm remembering the times when I was engulfed by experience, submerged by my reveries and my fantasies, you know, where the images sort of submerged me and I lost my control, which happens. But I have found a way to control this. You know, the rationale is like a marvelous race horse and sometimes it gets away from you. Whenever I have entered these hells, I have sought help, because I felt I needed to see clearly into these things so that they wouldn't become incubus, wouldn't take over. I don't know how much Tennessee did that, what I call going in and out of the subconscious world, getting out to look at it so that you cannot be drowned in it. That is what the drugs do. They *drown* you in it. But then you know that when they wear off, you are going to come back. You think you are going to come back to the same point. But when you create, you don't come back to the same point. You enter some other cycle. Every time you create you're really pushing into another cycle. So there is no peace.

It is interesting that you tell me Tennessee took all his many selves and really dramatized his multiple selves into so many characters. This was always a great concern with me. I think that's why I held on to what I call a human diary of a human reality of relationships, so that then I felt free to fictionalize, because I knew this was a kind of lie, a kind of illusion, that became something else. And I didn't want that transformation. I mention that in the *Diary*: that man, the great artist, the men artists, were always fictionalizing their own lives immediately, as it happened. In fact, Henry Miller used to say I shouldn't stop to record it. I should immediately start the fiction. Which is what Tennessee did. But I always felt that the danger of that was that your nightmares would take over and you wouldn't have anything to cling to that would bring you back into human life, that we would have to keep shifting our fantasies. We have to check with reality every day so as not to lose our footing.

MIKE: Yes. And by having your diary you can go back and refer to what happened years ago as it actually happened.

NIN: Right! Even the self I *was* is preserved. I can't lie any more about it! It's there!

MIKE: The real way it was. It guarantees you a contact with reality when you refer to it.

NIN: Your creations can become demonic, you know. It's like *The Sorcerer's Apprentice*. Your creations, if they come out of some things you fear—you're almost creating the demons. You are giving them life, and then they haunt you. For instance, I wrote about these women who had anxieties and fears, then they became so strong, in turn, I can't get rid of them.

I think almost every writer has a history of, somewhere or other, the bridge to the world breaking through traumatic happenings. And then he tries to reconstruct this bridge in terms of his own reality. That is, with his own sincerity, he tries to make a world where he can approach human beings again with a new kind of relationship that wouldn't have the traumatic element in it. I tried to do that, certainly, by my diary. When my father left, my bridge to the world broke. And I had to reconstruct that. Now with Tennessee I don't know his life well enough, you see, to know whether in living so much in his imagination and so much in the fictionalizing of his dreams, nightmares, fantasies, he dramatized *everything*, even the fear of death. I felt the fear of death in *Boom*. All his fears became dramas. They became people.

MIKE: He takes the ordeal of his death even further in *Two Scenes in the Bar of a Tokyo Hotel*. Although he told me that play was suggested by Jackson Pollock's death. Anyway, he is writing so much inside himself that—

NIN: That he embodied his fears. I mean he gave them life and a body and an identity.

MIKE: But it's still coming all from within instead of coming from any relation with actual events or people, so that there is in the viewer or the reader less of a connection in his ability to understand it or enjoy it, I believe.

NIN: Yes. Their ability to reach him then. To connect with him.

MIKE: Yes.

NIN: Or to respond.

MIKE: When the imagination or fantasy gets so extreme, then you have less of an audience, I think. Fewer people can identify with you. It's more difficult.

NIN: Yes, because what saves you, what saves the writer, is that when he does build this world of these many selves, and the people are able to relate to these different selves, and he loves them and he has friendships with them, they become relationships, don't they? And then in human life, he is not cut off at all. These people accept him. You see, when I saw Tennessee recently with you at the house he had rented here, I knew what his inner life was from the plays. And I could have communicated with him on that level. I could have said, "I understand that anxiety," or, "I understand this event," or, "I understand how you felt in Mexico when you wrote the *Iguana*."

MIKE: Nowadays even in his everyday life he uses dialogue that's in his plays. Especially in his recent plays. To a friend he'll repeat some particular line that he has just written as if it's not on the printed page but is coming from him at that moment.

NIN: Well, then he hasn't maintained that little separation that I think one has to maintain between one's fictional world. . . . You see, there was always a moment when somebody could ask me, "Anaïs, are you making this up or not?" And I was able to answer. That is what I always wanted. People close to me could always say, "Are you inventing?" And I could always tell the difference.

MIKE: Well, I wonder if Tennessee's using his dialogue in his everyday life is also an expression of his ego. That he likes a line so much that he wants to repeat it, and have other people hear it. As if he's patting himself on his back!

NIN: Do you think he's being his own audience?

MIKE: Yes!

NIN: I wonder about that. I wonder if it could also be that the boundary lines have been erased: that he is now part of his plays, and his plays are him, and he is in the plays.

MIKE: Exactly. It is best exemplified in his recent play called *The Two Character Play*. And the observation that he is his own audience also applies. All of these things are within him.

NIN: It could all be true.

MIKE: He loves to read his own work aloud. And he loves to read other people's poetry aloud. But he doesn't particularly like to be an audience to other people. He does not particularly like to listen to other writers read their work aloud. But he likes to demand that you are an audience to his reading his own work.

NIN: That's very dangerous. That makes for solitude. I have always said the only real cause of madness is solitude. I don't mean that he has to sit and listen to all the playwrights who would like to read their plays to him! But that is a part of relationship. And that saves you. You see, what saves one from the isolation that the artist can get into by being his own personage is his relation to others. And listening to another's play is part of that. It's terribly important: that human bridge, the fact that he should be able to listen to someone else's play. And he can select. He can be selective. But the point is that he can allow someone else into his world, and that he can see into somebody else's world. Because when the imagination is so strong in the artist, he can very well live in an invented world. Henry Miller is living all alone in an invented world, where the people are simply being invented as they come in. And that is a terrible loneliness. I think of insanity as loneliness. I don't even use the word "insanity." I say when we are alone we are really out of our minds.

Paul Newman and Rip Torn in the Broadway production of *Sweet Bird of Youth*. 1959. (*Photo courtesy Friedman-Abeles*)

RIP TORN

Rip Torn is an intense, energetic young man who has a great knowledge and experience to back up his talent as an actor and director. The letters RIP could never stand for Rest In Peace! His abundance of self-assurance and forceful temperament are the first things that strike new acquaintances. However, once you have an opportunity to know Rip you learn that he is a warm, friendly, and loyal person.

Like most theatre-trained actors, Rip is happier and more comfortable in New York. He and his wife, Geraldine Page, own a large brownstone house in the Chelsea district of Manhattan.

At the time of this interview they had leased an estate in Pacific Palisades as their temporary Los Angeles home. While Gerry worked on a film, Rip was back and forth between Hollywood and New York on various projects, but I caught him at home "between planes" late one night, and we sat at a kitchen table as he recalled some of his many memories of Tennessee.

TORN: Well, I had created a kind of minor scandal in college in an experimental theatre. A section of the University of Texas. This was before the movie of *Streetcar* came out and we did the scene where Stanley says to Stella, "We'll get those colored lights going." And that scene was pretty powerful at the time. I remember one of the faculty members got up and left, and somebody else put their hands over their eyes. And Katherine Grant, now Mrs. Bing Crosby, said to me some of the faculty members were upset that I had done Tennessee Williams. At that time he was tremendously avant garde. I think that when a true evaluation is made of his work—after all, even Shakespeare had to suffer in his time—the realization will be made in a historical context that he is a great artist. Especially in *Camino*, which is the forerunner of what they called the theatre of the absurd. I think, as an artist, his only flaw is that he has let criticism of his work worry him. He didn't write that way in the beginning. He wrote because he had to. He did say one thing a couple of years ago: that he found it increasingly easier to write and almost impossible to rewrite, reshape. He says these things. Of course I find it fascinating the way he writes. Most writers have always used a little bit of alcohol to carry out the day's work. I remember in Key West, Tennessee used to get up in the morning and have one or two glasses of orange juice and vodka and put on a rock 'n' roll record, very loud, and then shut himself off in his studio and work. Isolate himself.

MIKE: When you first went to New York you immediately got the job as understudy for the role of Brick in *Cat on a Hot Tin Roof*, didn't you?

TORN: Yes. Under the title of the published play is a fragment of a poem which Dylan Thomas wrote for his father,

"Do Not Go Gentle into That Good Night." And I talked to
Tennessee about this poem several years after I played in
Cat. He said that *Cat* was based on the relationship he had
with his own father, that he had never really made peace
with his father. His father had always bullied him and then,
of course, the father was rarely there. And Tennessee was
such a beautiful child, as you can see from pictures of him,
that women of the family made over him so much, and that
seemed to annoy the father, so he, being a large man, always
kind of mocked Tennessee. And the play, in the real sense,
was, I think, a poetic apology for both of them: father and
son, who couldn't get together. In the play they did. There
was a truth between them and I think that was the power of
the play. What we now call the generation gap. The son rebelling against society. Brick, instead of being a passive hero,
in the existential sense, refuses to have a child. Refuses to
give birth to a son in a society he thinks is full of hypocrisy.
The battle is between Big Daddy, who wants a grandson,
and Brick, who refuses. Of course, Tennessee loves children
but he has never had any. By the way, Arthur Miller thinks
Cat is one of Tennessee's greatest plays.

MIKE: Tennessee was at rehearsals constantly for *Cat*,
wasn't he?

TORN: Well, I didn't know him during that time. I came in
after the play was open. But I remember during the first
week of the run, the dirty joke about the elephant had to
be taken out. That story, which now on stage would be appreciated, at that time was a scandal. He said the police
would close him down and he was upset about that. Because
he said this is what Big Daddy would do. He would come
in and say, "Brick, I'm going to tell you a dirty joke." And
that was the bond between these two men. If it was going
to chase everybody else out of the room, that was all right
with Big Daddy. It was a beautiful dramatic device. But

I really didn't know Tennessee yet, though we were at parties and so on, and he saw me at understudy rehearsals. Then I read for *Orpheus Descending* and I got a note from the casting agent saying, "You're wrong for the role." So they cast Bob Loggia but something happened with the interpretation and they got rid of Bob and put in Cliff Robertson. But the play didn't last. So a year later Tennessee rewrote it or something and they were doing it down at the Coconut Grove and I read again for Tennessee and the director. And Tennessee said, "Oh, that was marvelous. He's perfect. Isn't he just perfect?" I turned around and looked at him. And he is so perceptive and sensitive. He caught the glint in my eye and he said, "Oh, you were wrong last year, but you're perfect this year." So I played the role in Florida. And recently I was down there to see Gerry in *The Little Foxes* and the people still remembered it. They said it was one of their most successful productions. I did it with Maureen Stapleton. I remember Bill Inge was down there and Tennessee was very upset because *Picnic* was going to be done just before *Orpheus Descending*. And I said, "Why are you upset?" And Tennessee whispered, "It's the same myth." I said, "Well, that figures. Painters borrow from each other, so do musicians, and so do playwrights." In *Orpheus Descending* the virile young man comes to town and the local ladies are taken by him and in the end he is destroyed. In the original, *Battle of Angels*, he was not an entertainer. He was a writer, and his name was Val. And in Bill Inge's play, the similar character was named Hal. And he comes to a Midwestern town because Bill has an uncanny ear for the rhythm of Midwestern speech the way Tennessee does for the more poetic Southern speech. But at the end, Hal is not destroyed. He runs off romantically on a freight train with the girl. That's a retelling, in a way, of *Summer and Smoke*. It's very clear Inge has not copied Tennessee, but he has been inspired by him. Bill Inge would be the first to admit that, because he became a playwright after seeing *The Glass Menagerie*. Anyway, during this incident in Florida, Tennessee was very jealous of Bill Inge and I said, "Why? I admire Bill. Why would you be jealous of him?" He said, "He gets more money than me."

People have always scorned Tennessee for his concern with money. But the thing to remember is that Tennessee did live in relative poverty when he was young, and he was an early prototype hippie. He was always all over the country. He lived on the street and in almost any kind of job. I, many times, wished that it would have been possible for him to drop his affluence and get back closer to the people he once was so close to.

I remember when we were doing *Sweet Bird*, it was my twenty-eighth birthday and he had a little party for me. At least he bought some champagne. And he made a funny toast which was prophetic. He said, "Here's to Rip, poor baby. He has but two more poetic years left. Then he is consigned to playing villains." Of course I let out a string of obscenities. But what used to be the villains are now heroic parts.

One of the funniest things I remember about Tennessee is at the first reading of *Sweet Bird of Youth*. He laughed all the way through it, which he is apt to do. His laughter does not really connote a conventional idea of what people might be laughing at. He might be laughing with great pain. So he laughed and all the actors were cutting their eyes to each other, saying, "Gee, he really digs it." And at the end he turned around to Kazan and said, "Forget it, baby, it will never go." So he is eternally pessimistic.

MIKE: But he is somewhat of a ham actor himself.

TORN: Yes, he is an actor. He loves to act. I have always, when I worked on his material and if he was around, asked him to read a certain passage out loud and I would get clues from him. He writes for the actor.

MIKE: How do you think the pressure of always having to produce a success has affected Tennessee?

TORN: Well, I think that's the wrong focus for him. I think it's the wrong focus for anyone. I think it was Thomas Wolfe who, in talking about success in America, said we build up gods, golden people, and then almost the next year we have to destroy them. That seems to be some kind of need. When was the *Time* cover story on him?

MIKE: March, 1962.

TORN: Well, they usually give you that kind of cover story when *Time* thinks you're past your peak. I mean at least for athletes it's true. If you're a champion runner and you get a *Time* cover story, you're going to break your toe! So I think Tennessee stubbed his toe shortly after that. But I know he continues to write every day while his health holds. His bouts with alcohol are probably one of the greatest advertisements for pot!

MIKE: I'm glad some good is coming out of it.

TORN: [*pouring whiskey*] As I take another sip. He should take his future plays and go back to the community theatre: these small professional or amateur theatres away from the commercial mishmash of Broadway. Most of his early plays were done that way. *Summer and Smoke* was first done at Margo Jones's theatre in Dallas. Even *Sweet Bird* was first done down in Miami, Florida. It would be the best thing possible for Tennessee now. And I'm not so concerned with acting in one of his plays now as directing some.

MIKE: When you were rehearsing *Sweet Bird of Youth*, was Tennessee giving any of the actors any rewrites?

TORN: Yes, and quite a few of them affected the part I was playing, Tom Junior.

MIKE: You played Tom Junior on Broadway, but on the national tour you played Chance Wayne. It must have been interesting from an acting standpoint to play two such contrasting roles in the same play.

TORN: Especially Tom Junior. That character was like an early George Wallace. An ominous but magnetic kind of character. Full of strengths and weaknesses. Of course my coming from the South and playing that part, a strange thing happened. Black people would climb up the three flights to my dressing room to see me and talk to me because they had never seen a Southern white man portrayed that way—one that would actually be a prototype of someone who would torment them. They had always seen this glossed over and never concretely there. I remember that was when I first met James Baldwin, because he was Kazan's assistant and a friend of Tennessee's. He was very curious how I had arrived at my characterization. That I didn't scream at Chance when I said I was going to kill him. That I just smiled instead. But then I played the role of Chance.

MIKE: You probably identified more with Chance than with Tom Junior.

TORN: Well, I think every actor, when trying to get work, has to hustle. That was what Chance was: a very unsuccessful hustler for his biggest ambitions. I thought in some ways possibly I understood Chance better than Paul Newman did. I was actually from the South. And, also, Paul was already a successful actor while I was very hungry and struggling. So I understood the gauchery and desperation of the character. So as Chance Wayne's luck would have it, on opening night in Los Angeles, which was to have been for me my big splash in Hollywood, a typical Chance Wayne

idea that "Now I'm going to make it tonight," the prop man
was drunk. He didn't put out the fur coat, which was the
key prop for that first scene. The lights failed and they only
had one spotlight. You have never seen such a crowded little
circle of light because everybody that was playing a minor
role in it was just like me. They were all there to be "discovered." So when we played one certain scene, there must have
been ten people crowded right around me getting in the
light just to be seen! And then when they turned on the
music cue, they hadn't tested it, and it picked up some four-
square revival-meeting music from a nearby church instead
of the Heavenly Bells theme. And then in the middle of one
of Gerry's big speeches, there was a meeting going on for
Konrad Adenauer next door in the Biltmore Hotel and about
thirty police motorcycles gunned their motors and roared
off into the night. And so it was an incredible opening night!

MIKE: Do you think Tennessee has ever intentionally been
political in his plays?

TORN: No, I don't think so. But in the sense that true politics is the care and preservation of man, I think Tennessee
is political, because he writes the truth. I think that by writing the truth it becomes political. He never wrote any big
diatribes, but for instance in *Battle of Angels* the writer who
is finally killed for being different, for not conforming—and
not conforming is a type of politics, not conforming is a
political act, is it not?—he turns around to the old black
medicine man and says, "What are you doing here, brother?"
And the old man says, "I'se been dispossessed." And the
writer says, "Well, we are both dispossessed." In that sense
Tennessee is political. But not belonging to a political party
or anything.

MIKE: He has a social conscience.

TORN: The conscience of the true artist.

MIKE: In terms of the individual rather than the world.

TORN: No, the world being men. In caring for men and women. He wrote an early play which was inspired by the maltreatment of prisoners who were locked in the prison when it caught fire and they were all burned alive. I think he is appreciated by people who are politically conscious more than he appreciates people who are politically conscious. In Godard's film *La Chinoise*, the young revolutionary writes upon a blackboard the names of people he considers have advanced the cause of freedom and equality. And one of them is Tennessee's. And as he reads and goes on, he erases various names but he never erases Tennessee's. But I doubt if Tennessee is aware of the effect he has had. He'd laugh if you told him about it. And I have heard writers, who are political writers, scorn Tennessee and say, "Why doesn't he ever write a real play of social significance?" when all his plays are of social significance.

MIKE: On a human level rather than on an intellectual level.

TORN: His plays have lives all their own. But he has a great intellect. I mean when he is feeling well and in good form, you can't bullshit him. He picks up. And he's greatly read. He knows other people's work. I have never really heard him say a malicious or cruel thing about a fellow writer, a fellow artist. He has always spoken about people with appreciation, which, I think, is a superb tribute to him. He is the true artist. He is the greatest dramatic poet writing in the English language. There is no doubt of it. I can't think of someone greater.

MIKE: Do you think his plays could be directed better by someone reared in the South?

TORN: No, I don't think it has to do with a regional kind of thing. I just think I feel close to him and his work for reasons other than our both being Southern. We had a terrible argument over politics. At that time I was more conservative. But since that time I have become more aware of the world and I am not as conservative as I was. Anyway, after the argument and we had mutually apologized, I told him I felt that we were like blood kin. That's because he had a sister, and I had a sister, and we were both very close to our sisters as children growing up. His father was gone, as a salesman; and my father was gone into the service. And I was closer to my grandfather and grandmother, as Tennessee was with his. And I stayed a lot with them. There were certain parallels and it gave me a certain understanding of the plays of Tennessee. I think it used to be only Southerners who were aware of the closeness of violence to the veneer of good manners and civilization. But I think that is all changed since the assassination of John Kennedy. Years ago people thought Tennessee exaggerated the incipient violence in our country. And that was the thing that frightened Tennessee and he felt compelled to write about it. And that's why, as I said before, black people came and talked to me. And a writer like Gore Vidal, who came from the South, sought me out, even though I was playing a minor role in *Sweet Bird*, to tell me, "I knew somebody just like that." What I was able to do was to flesh out, to bring alive, something that Tennessee had written which I think I would not have been able to bring into live form had I not had an understanding of it. I was lucky in the beginning of my career, before I became more aware of the world and more able through education to play other roles, that Tennessee's plays were there. That there was a poet-playwright whose work I instinctively identified with. So in my youth, as an artist, his work gave me a platform to speak from. And so I have always appreciated that, although I once told him that playwrights have the terrible flaw, out of enthusiasm, of promising parts and promising roles to whatever actor they happen to be at a party with, drinking with, or visiting with. Gerry and I visited him many times. I like to fish and we would go down to Key West. But, you know, one thing about him: We never could get him out on a boat to fish!

MIKE: I finally got him to go deep-sea fishing in the fall of '67.

TORN: Well, you're the first.

MIKE: But every time a fish took the bait, Tennessee would turn the rod and reel over to me. He didn't want to put his drink down!

TORN: No, it's not his game.

MIKE: But he enjoyed sitting in the sun and being on the boat and thinking about Ernest Hemingway.

TORN: There is a wonderful article by Kenneth Tynan about his taking Tennessee to meet Hemingway in Cuba and Hemingway sending them both to meet Castro. Tennessee was so wicked, though! They were sitting in the Capitol Building, waiting to meet Castro. Tennessee, of course, knew what Castro represented, so he looked at one of the guards and whispered to Kenneth, "Do you think we can send him out to get us a few tacos?" You know, he may not be that kind of mean-witty about other writers, but he would have to be full of fun to make a remark like that. He liked Castro.

MIKE: He said that when Castro shook his hand he said, "Mr. Williams, I admire your play *Cat on a Hot Tin Roof.*" Castro thought of himself as being a cat on a hot tin roof!

TORN: Probably, because Castro is a pretty artistic man.

MIKE: What did you think about Tennessee's manner of living in Key West? Do you think it is his favorite place and is a proper retreat for him?

TORN: Well, I think he liked it better before Frank Merlo died. He knew Frank before he was a success. He had met him in Key West. Frank was a Sicilian, and had a great sense of honor. And if he ever heard at a party anyone make any kind of remark about Tennessee, he was there like white on rice, although he must have been only five six, to defend his friend. And I think that was a comfort to Tennessee. When they lived at Key West they had a very good home life and it was a refuge. I think the main reason he went there, he once said, was that it was the only place he found in the continental United States where it was warm enough for him to swim every day. He loves to swim in the sea. He has been very much of a family man all of his life. He is very close still to his mother, his brother, and one of his reasons for always being concerned with money was to have enough to take care of everybody in his family. To take care of his sister, Rose, particularly. I think he always was afraid that he wouldn't be able to do that. I always twitted him, maybe foolishly, on the fact that he didn't ever find a woman that he really could make it with in the full sense of the word. Groove with. Because many women have found him to be very manly, very attractive, and have asked me about him. And I think that his writing always shows that he understands and appreciates women, although he has sometimes been labeled in print by a few writers and critics in his later age as being a homosexual writer. He never was, never is. He is a writer of mankind. And I don't think there is any writer ever that, without sentimentalizing, has written about women with greater appreciation. I remember one of the saddest things that happened was after the opening of *Period of Adjustment*. I think it was Dorothy Kilgallen who made some kind of snotty remark that the two men seemed more interested in each other than in their wives. And Tennessee said, "Well, I guess all they are going to say about me is that I'm a dirty old queen." Which is a sad commentary.

Not on Tennessee, but on society. A man must, in great portion, be known by his work. Tennessee has always been a great and masterful worker. He has worked no matter how sick he has been. He has never been a really well man. A consummate hypochondriac, but he's actually had the excuse at different times.

MIKE: I've seen him when he would have difficulty walking and you'd think he was low on energy, and five minutes later he would dive into the swimming pool and swim twenty laps! More than I could swim.

TORN: As long as he can swim, he can stay alive, so that's why he stays in Key West.

Geraldine Page and Paul Newman in the Broadway production of *Sweet Bird of Youth.* 1959. (*Photo courtesy Friedman-Abeles*)

GERALDINE PAGE

Geraldine Page long ago won my vote as the First Lady of the Theatre, with all due credit and respect to the other very talented ladies. A fond memory of mine is being with Tennessee on one of the many times he went to see Gerry's performance as Miss Alma Winemiller in the off-Broadway production of Summer and Smoke. *A star was born beginning with the opening night of that play some fifteen years ago, and since then Gerry has been considered one of the most extraordinary interpreters of Tennessee's stage women. Her unforgettable portrayal of the Princess née Alexandra del Lago in the stage and film versions of* Sweet Bird of Youth *won great acclaim for her.*

Geraldine is more active in the theatre than in cinema. Her acting style is so special and unique that film parts are rare. Good starring roles should be written especially with her talent in mind. Yet she is a highly versatile actress, and has proven this over and over. And she is equally at home in heavy drama or comedy. One need only compare her roles in the film You're a Big Boy Now *and the television play by Truman Capote* A Christmas Memory.

When Gerry combines her talent with that of her husband, Rip Torn, they form a particularly outstanding duo.

The future will undoubtedly give us many treats from the Torn-Page team.

The film Gerry was starring in had completed shooting, but she was "looping" some of her speeches in a recording studio at M-G-M when I arrived there to do my own recording with her.

PAGE: Well, that's when we were doing *Summer and Smoke* at the Circle in the Square, and it was the most embarrassing thing the night that he and Frank saw *Summer and Smoke.* You remember how the old Circle was, with the bar on the landing, well, I was waiting down by the bar to make my entrance for the second act, right after intermission. Most of the audience was back in, but there were two people going up the staircase ahead of me in the dark, and I was so annoyed that they weren't in their seats. I just got around them in time to make my entrance. And afterwards I said to the stage manager, "Who were those two nuts in the way when I was trying to make my entrance?" And he said, "That was Mr. Williams." He came backstage afterwards and that's when I met him. I was so astonished I thought I would just collapse.

MIKE: I am sure he was just as thrilled, because you were the first actress to bring that part alive in the way he had envisioned it.

PAGE: We did the best version of it. We did an earlier version, which was a longer version. The fact that we did the long version and we did it at its own pace and didn't worry about getting people home on the commuter trains— some missed their trains but they had a good time—I think that contributed greatly to the fact that it was so effective.

MIKE: I think the intimate staging of a smaller theatre, the center staging, helped *Summer and Smoke,* don't you?

PAGE: Yes. Some day I would like to see how it feels to play it in a large theatre. But of course those intimate stages are great. I miss the propinquity.

MIKE: In doing film work, do you feel an intimacy, also, because of the camera's ability to be so close?

PAGE: I'm gradually getting so it doesn't frighten me, so that I can enjoy it more. It takes a while to get over the strangeness of having a camera almost in your face. I've gotten so now that my nearsightedness helps me a little to forget about the camera! The camera's so scary.

MIKE: Do you know if José already knew Tennessee when he directed *Summer and Smoke?*

PAGE: No, he didn't.

MIKE: How long did it run down there?

PAGE: Oh, it ran nearly two years. Three of us had played Alma in that production before it closed: me, Betty Miller, and Ann Weller.

MIKE: When you did the film of *Summer and Smoke,* did you think the screenplay was close enough to what Tennessee wrote?

PAGE: Well, my trouble is I'm a fan of Tennessee's. I like the way he wrote it. Of course now, if this is for publication, then all the people who worked on the script are going to get their feelings hurt, but I liked the way Tennessee wrote it, and I even have a preference for the version we did at the Circle that starts at the Fourth of July band concert and has the great scene between Alma and old Doctor John that weaves the exposition more integrally and emotionally into the main body of the drama. I'm convinced it's more effective.

MIKE: It would have been good if he had written the screenplay himself.

PAGE: I think so. Why didn't he? Is it too painful? He hates to go back over things? He is lazy, or what? I don't know.

MIKE: I think mainly it's that he doesn't want to go back to work on something he considers he's already finished. And also he considers the theatre his medium. But he's slowly coming around in his attitude, because he feels so protective about his work he doesn't want other people to adapt it.

PAGE: Oh, good. I'm glad, because whatever cinematic mistakes he feels he might make, his mistakes would be marvelous.

MIKE: But on the other hand, Tennessee recently told me that he thought the screenplay of *Sweet Bird of Youth* was an improvement on the play.

PAGE: Oh, did he!

MIKE: At least he thought the film itself was more enjoyable than seeing the play.

PAGE: Well, I do know that the second act particularly was very difficult on the stage, and those events took more naturally to film. But over the years, after hearing him say things about different things, I'm never terribly surprised at things he says, because he has great enthusiasm for what he has been exposed to at the moment, you know, and he is very appreciative of everybody's efforts in all directions. And so I have learned to take a lot of his praises of things with a trifle grain of salt.

MIKE: Yes, because the next day he may say something with an opposing attitude.

PAGE: It's a kind of terrible thing to say, I don't know whether I want to see it written down that I told it, but when he saw *Summer and Smoke* he told me it was the best performance of one of his female parts since Laurette Taylor. In the first flush of glory I quoted him to someone I wanted to impress, and she said, "Oh, he tells that to everybody, for Christ's sake!"

MIKE: In your case I don't think it was just a temporary enthusiasm though, because he still will say that your portrayal of Miss Alma was one of the best performances of his work. But I know well what you mean by his temporary enthusiasm on other occasions!

Gerry, after you had such a success off-Broadway in *Summer and Smoke* and it made you a star, then you went on to Broadway to do *The Immoralist*, didn't you?

PAGE: No, the first one was *Midsummer*, then came *The Immoralist*, and then *The Rainmaker*. Then I replaced Margaret Leighton in *Separate Tables*, and then came *Sweet Bird of Youth*.

MIKE: What other of Tennessee's plays have you done?

PAGE: I had the good fortune to do *Streetcar* in stock many long years ago. For five days I got my hands on it! That's beautiful!

MIKE: Which part have you enjoyed more? Miss Alma, Blanche DuBois, or the Princess?

PAGE: Well, for personal enjoyment, I enjoyed playing Miss Alma most. The other two are such great challenges, and I love the struggle of playing them, but I do have to struggle in the playing of them, whereas Miss Alma, I feel, fits me like a glove, and it doesn't take as much effort.

MIKE: Do you think the Princess in *Sweet Bird* was patterned after any actresses in particular?

PAGE: Oh, yes, I did. But when I said who, everybody said, "Oh, no, no, no." Especially Tennessee said No. It seems so very much like Bankhead to me, which he denied vociferously.

MIKE: It could be a combination—

PAGE: I'm sure it is.

MIKE: —of Tallulah Bankhead, and perhaps Rita Hayworth.

PAGE: Yes, of actresses and other people who aren't actresses.

MIKE: Plus, very much, Tennessee and his own experiences.

PAGE: When we were working on the play, Kazan gave me a collection of photographs of silent-film stars and asked me which one I thought my Princess might have been, and they seemed to fall into four categories. They polarized around Mary Pickford, Theda Bara, Clara Bow, and Garbo. I thought at first the most appropriate one for me the Mary Pickford ones, that it would be an interesting thing to see how the struggle had hardened someone whose whole life had been dedicated to selling sweetness and light, but I had to realize it was laziness, because it would be less work but really wouldn't be what I objectively thought she had been—that there would be more of the steaminess of Theda, plus the energy and sassiness of Clara. The remoteness of the Garbo quality I thought would be something that the Princess might admire and try to assume, but it wouldn't be indigenous to her nature, so I was stuck. But there was one face that I couldn't fit into any one category, and it belonged to Norma Talmadge. She seemed to have an air of great vulnerability, as of someone who would greet everything and everyone with a spontaneous open-heartedness, and I was very touched by it. I felt that the shocks and hurts that would fall full force on a heart like that could turn someone into a complicated, volatile phenomenon like the Princess, and that was my choice. I had never seen a film of hers and knew nothing about her life. Her name, of course, was familiar to me, so I was startled when Rose Hecht came backstage and said, "Oh, my dear, you reminded me so of poor dear Norma!" She had known her, you see. . . .

MIKE: Gerry, when you and Rip have visited Tennessee in Key West, how have you enjoyed yourselves?

PAGE: Well, Rip loves that climate because he's from Texas. But I grew up in Chicago! And it's so exotic a setting for me that I feel estranged there. The humidity is very weird. It's like another planet. It's very foreign to me, that environment, but it's fascinating. I always feel strange there and out of my element, you know. The water is so blue it looks like people spilled ink in it.

MIKE: You went deep-sea fishing, didn't you?

PAGE: Yes, and it was so funny because Rip was trying to corner Tennessee into going one time, and he finally consented. He was going to get up and go, and then he ratted out the last minute. He wouldn't get up in the morning. He said it was too early, and he wanted to work, anyway. He locked himself in his little workroom.

MIKE: I know there isn't much to do in Key West, except to work.

PAGE: We went out a few times, but we used to sit up fairly late and talk, I remember. But the heaviness of the weather and that indolence of the climate, I was never very full of gumption.

MIKE: When you were doing *Sweet Bird of Youth* in New York, was Tennessee at rehearsals most of the time?

PAGE: He was. And I remember when we were out of town in Philadelphia with that last act. They were so unhappy with me in that last act. Evidently Kazan had given up. He didn't know what else to tell me. And they called me one day for a rehearsal up in that mezzanine foyer where we rehearsed in the theatre, just he and Tennessee. And I thought, "I wonder what's going to happen?" The atmosphere was so kind of strained. Finally Tennessee started talking to me. He used such wonderful direction. He really ought to direct sometime. He has fantastic directorial gifts, but he's probably so polite that maybe he has trouble forcing his opinions on people. But I don't know why he doesn't do it more because the things he told me were fantastic. He was telling me that that big speech in the third act has to top in dramatic intensity the second-act curtain, which is a logical thing to say. But the second-act curtain was so powerful! I told him nothing short of an atomic bomb would top his second-act curtain. And with his Southern charm, he said, "Oh, yes, honey, you can do it. You can do it." And I thought, "Well, I'm already bursting every blood vessel in the attempt. I don't know what more they want from me." And he was saying that the language, particularly in that speech, was heightened language and that unless it had a vast emotional current underneath to carry it, it would just sound pretentious. And so when I went to play it that evening, I thought, "What are they trying to do? Are they trying to kill me? I'm doing my utmost and they want more. So I'll show them; I will. I'll go out and I'll do more and it will probably kill me and I'll lie on the stage a corpse and they'll be sorry they bothered me." Of course the speeches are like arias and my poor lungs were already bursting with those long beautiful lines. They took such tremendous doing. And then I launched into that big speech and after the second sentence, I felt I had really come to the end of my lung capacity, my strength. But just to show them, I pushed harder. I went further. And then a weird thing happened. It was like a door opening. And then I had endless room and an endless new supply of energy! But I thought I was going to burst going past that point. But once I got past it, I then had a whole second wind and was able to sail on through to the end of the speech. And then went over and sat on the trunk, you know for that little coda at the end, and suddenly my scalp broke into sweat, so that I got drenched with perspiration from my scalp, sitting on the trunk. And I was thinking to myself, "Well, there it is. I have a hemorrhage or something. I've burst a blood vessel, and now they'll be sorry." But of course nothing happened. I just broke into a sweat. Afterwards I came off panting and staggering off stage, and Tennessee came backstage and I looked at him like, "Well? WELL? Did I do it?" And he said, "Well, that was a little better."

MIKE: Were you able to repeat that experience in other performances?

PAGE: Well, it took so much will power to have the courage to force myself past that point, but I did try. But I really couldn't do that every performance or I would have really literally exhausted myself. But after I had done it a couple of times, I at least got the feel of it and the sound of it, so I didn't have to literally do that every time. I could fulfill the lines technically better, so that the whole playing of the third act came up enormously from that experience. And as often as I had the strength and will power to do it, I did it. But I could not do that eight times a week. I just couldn't. Even with the best role in the world.

MIKE: When you put that role on film, did you strive for that experience in that scene?

PAGE: Oh, well, it was a totally different character in the film. Totally different character. It was a totally different lady and it didn't have any of that grand passion in it. They didn't want it. It was much more of a light-comedy performance in the film.

MIKE: And certainly a tour-de-force performance.

PAGE: But it didn't have the deep dramatic colors that the
stage performances had. I missed seeing them, of course.
But the people who didn't see the stage play were perfectly
delighted with the Princess that was in the film. She's such
a great character, so much color to her, that even if you
just sort of skim through it, it's still a fascinating part. I
enjoy it myself, watching the film. I enjoy the character that
she is. But my heart belongs to the lady who was on the
stage because that was, to me, much more heroic. Big-size.
And the palette was more vivid and the canvas was larger
on the stage. So that I keep inwardly comparing the two
and finding the character in the film less interesting to me
than the other one was. But still, the character itself is so
fantastic that even done on a smaller scale, it's still fantastic.
It sticks out, you know.

MIKE: I'll never forget seeing the first screening of the
film at the M-G-M studio. Everybody who worked on the
film was there, as well as Hedda Hopper, Louella Parsons,
and a few other people like that. And after your telephone
scene in which you're speaking with Walter Winchell and
you find out your comeback film has been a success, everybody in the audience applauded and almost broke up the
screening.

PAGE: Well, you know, what's marvelous about that particular scene in the film is that contrary to the practices I
have observed in most film making, and that I have participated in, Mr. Brooks took a good deal of time with that
scene. Ordinarily they would give you two shots at it. They
don't bother to wait until you really get it. They have to
press on. But the patience he had with that particular scene
was marvelous. And I remember that I was having such
difficulty with it. It wasn't right, and it wasn't right, and I
was sort of lying across the bed with the phone, hanging on
to it in a complete state of demoralization. And Brooks came

over to me and very quietly said, "Now, there's no rush. Take it easy. There's plenty of time." And he started talking away to kind of calm me down so I wouldn't get too discouraged. And as he was talking to me, it was the weirdest thing, I could feel the scene coming on. I could feel it gathering, and he's talking away to me, and I said, "Will you get out of here and let me act?" And he caught what I meant right away and just backed up and said very quietly to the cameraman to roll and that's the time I did it that's used in the film. But ordinarily nobody takes the time to try and capture it when it really takes off, you know, and that was marvelous. Which reminds me of an incident during the filming of *Summer and Smoke* which was funny. I felt so passionately about all the different interpretive points that I had had on the stage in that role. And I kept trying to sneak them in somehow into the film and was blocked at every corner with that. They said, "Oh, no, we can't have that in the film." And Peter Glenville got so weary of me, always interjecting and asking to do this, and asking to do that. Then we got to the scene in the park where Nellie brings the present, the handkerchief, and she tells me that Dr. John said she was an angel. To me, having played it for a year on the stage, that is the turning point. That is when the tables turn. Progress has been in one direction, and that is the point in which she turns around and goes the other way. I thought it was so important, that my whole interpretation of it turned on my next speech, which was when Miss Alma goes over to the statue in the fountain and says, "This is the only angel in Glorious Hill. And her body is stone and her blood is mineral water." And Peter explained to me that in the film you don't need to say all that. He cut that line! I said, "You cannot cut the pivot. I'll rebel. You can't! You can't! You can't!" But he said, "In film, you see, we're close; we see in your eyes. We don't need all those words. On the stage they are quite usable, but we don't need them in the film." I said, "But Peter, but Peter . . ."

and by this time he was so far ahead of schedule that he felt generous about it and he said, "I'll tell you what. To prove my point we'll film it your way and we'll film it my way, and you will see why I cut the line. That it is not necessary." So I said all right. So it was my way first. But of course, the fountain was different in the movie. At the Circle in the Square the fountain was the center pillar in the theatre and I was standing right next to it and I could just turn around where I was standing and hit my fist against it right where I was and say, "This is the only angel . . ." Well, in the film there was the statue and there was a big moat around it and then a wall! I was about five feet away from the statue. But, stubborn as I am, I came at the cue and I walked around over to the statue and said the line. And halfway through it I thought, "Oh, he's right. This is like *La Bohème*. It's hammy and awful, and he's right." Well, we finished that take, and I said, "Oh, Peter, you're right. We'll do it your way." And then we filmed it his way. And he gave me the cue and I walked up to the camera and looked in, and then walked away. And I went back to New York after the film was over and explained to everybody how I learned about film techniques, you know, that really in films you don't need so many of the words because you can convey things without them. Then, when we came back out here, we went over to Mr. Wallis's house for a screening of it. It came to that point and they had used the take where I had said the line. I leaped up in the middle of the gathering and said, "You used it, you used it! You needed it! I was right!" It was so embarrassing, but I was so pleased. But I won that argument. But then I felt terrible because I thought if only I had been more hysterical and insistent, I might have won a few other battles! It's fine for me to tell you a story like that, but because of Peter I can't really have that kind of story . . .

MIKE: Oh, things like that happen frequently, though, don't you think, in filming. Peter probably realized you were right and left it in there, and was probably grateful in the long run.

PAGE: Oh, I hope so. I remember when we were doing *Sweet Bird* in New York, and Tennessee was in Key West and sending rewrites up from there. He rewrote a speech for me and he wrote me a letter with it and he said to throw out those awful other lines and put these in instead. And I wrote him back and bawled him out and said, "I'll say whichever one of your lines you want me to say, but don't talk that way about any of the lines you write. They're all beautiful, and if you prefer some over others, all right, but don't disparage any of them. You can't talk that way about that kind of writing." I would read over everything that went out. I wanted to keep all of the new stuff and say all the old stuff. It's so hard to let loose of any of it. It's sheer, pure gold.

MIKE: Hume Cronyn told me that when they were doing *Streetcar Named Desire*—he was, of course, not connected with the production, but watching his wife out of town—he thought the play was too long, and I guess everybody felt it was too long. And he went to Tennessee and said, "Don't you think you should cut out about twelve or fifteen minutes and the play will be tighter?" And Tennessee said, "I'll give you the permission to do that." And so Hume Cronyn very seriously went to his hotel room and worked all night and came back the next day and said, "Tennessee, I've found there's no place at all you can cut."

PAGE: Well, you know, people will always ask in interviews about what I think about his work and everything, comparisons with other writers, and I always think that his work is closely related to Chekhov's and to Shakespeare's. Ben Jonson complained about Shakespeare that he went on and on and he should have blotted a lot of those lines and he kept going on. The thing is that people who worry about neatness don't write as good plays. The greatest plays of the world will probably always remain Shakespeare's. And he wrote like there was no stopping. And it's better to let them go, let them write their hearts out, because what you get is so good it doesn't matter if they don't worry about the style so much. Not that I don't like the other kind of plays too! Like I think Miller and Hellman, people like that, are more like Ibsen and the Greek playwrights and they are just as great in their own way. I don't think everybody should write the same way. I think it is perfectly marvelous that Tennessee is comparatively formless and shapeless That's great! So rich and overflowing.

MIKE: He can also write like the Greeks in his using the themes of the downfall of aristocracy and lofty characters.

PAGE: Yes, but that's included. It's not with him, I don't feel, as spare, as stark, as straight as the Greek things. Like Chekhov, you know. He gives so much of the drama out of the surface noise of life. I mean in a lot of the Chekhov plays, people are sitting around talking about tea or going fishing or things that are not to do with the central drama, but to do with the way human beings express themselves and convey these things. And Tennessee uses that too. And his ear is so fantastic for colloquial speech, and he uses that. I just finished working in *The Little Foxes*, you know, and in Hellman's plays the things you say as the character are almost always directly right into the center of the play, which reminds me more of the Greek plays. But if you start working on the Shakespeare things and the Tennessee things, you've got your feet right in the deep all the time, while your head may be up in the poetry, and your hands busy handling around the props. You're right in the thick of things. It's not to say that I think either Chekhov, Shakespeare, or Tennessee is fluffy compared to the Greeks at all. It's just that it's a wider lens.

MIKE: Of course you've played Chekhov and Tennessee Williams. Have you compared, as an actress, their ability to write tragicomedy?

PAGE: Well, I love that business. I don't think anybody has the art of mixing the comedy and the tragic in the alarming proximity that Tennessee hits almost in every play. It is incredible. And very few of the people have the nerve to do that.

MIKE: That's his main comparison to Chekhov, I believe. The ability to do that, which is true genius.

PAGE: But, you see, Tennessee's plays are more playable, generally, than Chekhov's. Chekhov's are so hard to do right, and if you don't do them right you can put people to sleep with them. But with Tennessee's plays, like Shakespeare's plays, even when you do them badly or ineptly, there's so much vivid life going on that the worth of them still comes through. I mean everybody knows that Shakespeare's plays are marvelous. I think most of the people don't know that Chekhov's plays are marvelous, because they never saw a good production! Actors understand, because even if they aren't able to fulfill it in working on it they know it's there. But in Tennessee's plays everybody knows that his plays are marvelous. Even the ones that they get all upset about at the time and say, "Oh! Isn't that awful! That wicked man! How can he write such a decadent thing?" But they wouldn't miss one for the world.

MIKE: Do you have any preference of Tennessee's plays? Which one would you place first?

PAGE: I still think that the version we did of *Summer and Smoke* was one of the most perfect things, both in form and content and everything else. But that's maybe my personal bias towards the part. My natural empathy goes faster to Miss Alma than some of the other characters he has written. I love *Sweet Bird* in spite of what some people call its flaws. They were all upset because the second act was different from the first act and the third act, but I thought that was marvelous. That's as though he used a very fine brush with lots of detail for the first act and then took poster colors and a big brush to the second act, and then went back to the fine color for the third act. I think that most people have been used to having those done in the same vein and were shook up by that. But I don't think it was necessarily bad. It was like when Picasso started some of his things. Everybody said, "Ack! What's that?" Then many years later they said, "Oh, I see." I think the mixture of styles in *Sweet Bird* upset some people but I don't think that is necessarily bad. And the other hilarious thing was at the time that we did it. Everybody said, "Where did he ever dream up that character of Boss Finley?" I don't think anybody who is in arms' spread of a television set today could think that he dreamed that up somewhere. It's been forced on all our consciences that there are such people. It was not a figment of a mad playwright. That's life, exact as he put it down. Not any exaggeration or bias of any kind. His plays are going to be done regularly for at least five hundred years or more. They are just so true.

MIKE: What parts of Tennessee's would you like to play that you haven't played?

PAGE: Oh, Blanche I would like to try again someday. And I also have very strong opinions about Stella. I would like to play Stella sometime. I also someday would like to try both of the ladies in *The Night of the Iguana*. I enjoyed *Period of Adjustment*. I missed seeing the stage play, but the film of it I thought was delicious. It was marvelous.

MIKE: And in *Camino Real*?

PAGE: Oh, luscious! What a magnificent play that is! That is one of the most difficult of his to do.

MIKE: I think it's an American classic.

PAGE: Brilliant, brilliant, brilliant play. And the one-acts! Oh, those beautiful, beautiful one-acts.

MIKE: Tennessee more than once has, when your name has come up, said, "Oh, she's a tigress!"

PAGE: He only says that since *Sweet Bird*. He denies it now, but when Kazan wanted to cast me for the Princess he thought he had lost his mind entirely.

MIKE: Tennessee still saw you as Miss Alma, probably.

PAGE: Yes, and he never thought Miss Alma was a tigress. Or that I was when I was playing it. That is only since *Sweet Bird*.

MIKE: He looks on the Princess as a tigress, and really thinks of Blanche DuBois as a tigress. And also there is Maggie the Cat.

PAGE: And you know what's interesting about Alma? What's interesting about Alma is that underneath her extreme femininity and delicacy is a will of steel. And her stubbornness. The way she held out so long for what she thought was right. These are very strong elements in Alma. Tennessee's characters are so full of facets. The Princess, when she is vulnerable, is so soft and so helpless in a way. And Blanche, in spite of trying to be a fighter, in her core is terribly soft. That's why she gets defeated in the end. So that is why his characters are so lifelike. Why they are so valid on the stage, because they are not all just all one color. Because none of us are in life. Most of us like to think we are all sweet. That we are all this, and we are all that. But we are everything all mixed up together. We're all assortments of different things. And he gets these colors in each of his characters!

MIKE: I think Tennessee himself has so many colors in his own personality it is hard to sever him from his characters. His life is in his characters, and he is that complex, I believe.

PAGE: Oh, yes.

MIKE: As you say, you never know from day to day what enthusiasm he may have, and it may be contradicted the next day or altered in some way. He is very much a man who relates to the moment, I think. Whoever is with him at the moment can become his favorite person and whatever he is doing at the moment is most important.

PAGE: This is part of the way his powers of concentration work and that's probably why he is so observant and gets so much written down of what he sees and hears around him. Whatever is there to observe at the moment he listens to and watches with such concentration! It's a very funny experience when you work on a piece of his. You get the feeling that you know him so well because you feel very close to him while you are working on his work. Then when you see him, you're so full of wanting to convey and discuss with him some of the intricacies of the part, and his shyness removes him from you and you get the impression, out of frustration really, "Oh, I don't think he's read his plays even. He doesn't know anything about them." It's hard for him to let down his defenses and really level with you about things. And he gets embarrassed and says things and you think, "How could he say that after having written that?" Some people have the facility, whoever they meet or whoever they are talking with, to just drop everything and open up immediately, but not anyone as shy and complex as he is.

And it is so frustrating. You want to shake him and knock him on his head and say, "Open up and let me in to talk to you." That "you" that's way back in there, inside, that does the writing. But I imagine the number of people who have been able to really share that part of his work with him on a conversational level are very few.

MIKE: I think so, because he never intellectualizes his work or feels obligated to interpret it himself. He would never explain what he means by some image or symbol.

PAGE: And that's so wise, because whatever he'd say wouldn't cover it anyway. The only way that he can say it is the way he does say it. On the page. When he writes it. Also I think that he is a terribly instinctive writer. It's theory on my part, but when he writes, it's sort of like Zen. It just comes out. And even afterwards when he reads it himself he might not be that consciously, intellectually aware of what-all is in it, and he knows that, and therefore doesn't try to chat about it.

MIKE: I think that is one reason he doesn't like to rewrite. Because whatever he has put down has come spontaneously from the heart and from emotion.

PAGE: And you know what else you find when you work on his things? That the poet in him selects images. Even the props are described with such poetic reverberations that if you change them, you rob things. Like when I was doing *Streetcar* in that little bitty stock company for the five days. I had a line of Blanche's about that "heart-shaped box that I keep my jewelry in." And I thought I would die when I didn't have a heart-shaped box, because it's important. It's essential! It conveys all sorts of thinking. He made that choice for it to be heart-shaped because it is so expressive. And these tiny details must be very religiously attended to.

MIKE: That particular image relates later to Blanche's line, "How could anyone think of me as being a destitute woman when I have all these treasures locked in my heart?"

PAGE: Yes, that reverberated back and forth through the play. Oh, it's marvelous! And in *Sweet Bird* the Princess' name was originally Ariadne, when I first read it. At the end she left, but left Chance a thread to follow. In Greek mythology Ariadne gives Theseus the thread that leads him out of the maze, the labyrinth.

MIKE: And Theseus deserts Ariadne, the way Chance Wayne deserts the Princess.

PAGE: I don't know how conscious of that myth Tennessee was when he named the princess Ariadne, but I felt disappointed in the final play when he didn't let it remain her name. Because I thought her leaving him a way out of it was related to the myth, through the name. I find these images in his work, and I feel they are being violated whenever they are changed, because the initial impulse with which he writes has an identity.

MIKE: And nobody should tamper with it. Not even Tennessee.

PAGE: I don't think they ought to.

MIKE: Like the myth Tennessee uses in *Orpheus Descending* by naming the lead male character Val Xavier; Val for Valentine, or love, and Xavier for the savior, so that the character becomes the savior of love.

PAGE: What a gift! What a gift! He's so precious. I hope he lasts three hundred years and keeps writing every minute. You know, around the time of *Summer and Smoke* or a little bit after, they did a ballet of *Streetcar*.

MIKE: Yes, I saw that. Valerie Bettis did the choreography.

PAGE: I was so thrilled because Tennessee invited me to go with him to see that. So he and Frank and . . . what's the name of the lady who wrote *In the Summer House*?

MIKE: Jane Bowles.

PAGE: Jane Bowles and her husband, Paul, were with us. We went to the opening night of that ballet and we sat, like in the second row. And he was so thrilled with it. And at the end he leapt up yelling, "Brava! Brava!" and I was thinking, "Isn't that funny! He doesn't know how to pronounce 'bravo.'" I found out later you are supposed to say "brava" when it's a lady. And he was so enthusiastic, but then when the curtain calls were finally over and the people started to get up to leave, the people in front of him turned around and started asking him what he thought of it. Right away. They knew it was him and they wanted to talk to him. Just strangers. Turned around and asked him. Then they started telling him what was wrong with it from their point of view. They wanted to show how much they appreciated him and the original play by talking about what they had seen. And then we got up and walked slowly up the aisle and it took a long time to get all the way out to the street with the crowd. By the time the people got through talking to him he began to wonder if he had enjoyed it. I wanted to knock them all on their heads and tell them to leave him alone. It was so peculiar. But then, of course, we went backstage and by the time we got back around backstage and we were meeting the artists, his enthusiasm had come back again. But they had shaken him.

MIKE: I know he has always had to cope with people in the audience purposely coming up to him to make some dig or some kind of snotty remark. I have seen that happen over and over again. People feel a compulsion to come up and put him down sometimes. I can't really hit on what is the motivation for it.

PAGE: Oh, but if you read any history at all, that's been human behavior since the beginning of time. Any time anybody does something and people don't understand how they did it, it frightens them and they feel hostile and they want to cut the stranger down to size so they will feel better about themselves. It's always that disturbing thing that there is one strange person like a Martian in their midst. They don't know what makes them tick or how they can do what they have done.

MIKE: They feel uncomfortable, so they want to eliminate what makes them feel uncomfortable.

PAGE: Yes, and we see that all around us in different forms, you know. I think it was in *Reflections in a Golden Eye,* one of Carson's books . . . maybe it was *The Heart Is a Lonely Hunter.* It was a marvelous little incident that was subsidiary to the story. There's this little boy, and down the street lives a little girl who is terribly pretty. And it drives the little boy crazy that she is so pretty, and he doesn't know what to do about it. Well, one time she comes out in a party dress and she is running around the sidewalk. He can't stand it. He goes and gets the shotgun and shoots her! When I think about all of the assassinations, I think there's some human law, unfortunate human law, that's related in there. Other people get so upset when somebody does something so marvelous that they can't understand how the person did it.

Tennessee Williams, Shelley Winters, and William Tate at the open-ing of *Camino Real* at the Mark Taper Forum of the Los Angeles Music Center. August, 1968. (*Photo by Rothschild*)

SHELLEY WINTERS

Shelley Winters is a three-ring circus! She's a clown, a lady on a tightrope, a lion tamer, a side-show barker—you name it! Sometimes she's as sweet as cotton candy, and at other times her temper can be so explosive you would think she'd just been shot out of a cannon. But Shelley is also a realist, and you can be sure she knows what's going on during and between acts. She is a down-to-earth person, natural, friendly, and genuine.

Shelley calls her large, roomy Central Park West apartment in New York City home, but she also maintains a house in Beverly Hills in which she has lived since her ex-husband, Vittorio Gassman, bought it for her.

The afternoon I went over to get this interview she was recovering from the flu and was stretched out on a couch in the living room. As the interview progressed, she became more and more animated, until finally she was pacing the floor, full of the famous Winters energy. In fact, she wound up my visit by cooking dinner for me and her actor friend Richard Tate. That's Shelley! Unpredictable, hospitable, warm, and, certainly, domineering.

WINTERS: We'll make it like a cocktail party since we are all having sherry and Hong Kong flu! I met Tennessee Williams out here at the same time I met Dylan Thomas. They both knew the same people: Christopher Isherwood, Ivan Moffat, Thomas Mann. Salka Viertel had a salon out at the beach where everyone would gather.

MIKE: Oh, yes, in Santa Monica Canyon.

WINTERS: I knew who Tennessee Williams was. I didn't know who Dylan Thomas was. And they all thought that was a big joke. But where in Brooklyn or Hollywood, you know, being a starlet, would I have heard who Dylan Thomas was? Oh! I'll tell where I *actually* met Tennessee, although it was just backstage. It was a very funny story. I was in the process of becoming a starlet at Universal. They sent me all over America. Oh, God knows what picture that was! Maybe it was *Ma and Pa Kettle,* which I wasn't in, or *South Sea Sinner,* with Liberace, which I was in. I don't know what the hell movie it was! The guy who became head of Universal's publicity and exploitation in New York, Charlie Seminelli, was, at the time, an office boy in Chicago. And I had to change trains in Chicago to get to Minneapolis. They were sending me around, you know, in the process of making me a star. I had done one picture, *A Double Life.* In Chicago I saw this ad at the train station of *The Glass Menagerie,* and I knew Tony Ross from hanging around Walgreen's drugstore basement in New York. I didn't know anybody else connected with it. I just saw the sign saying *The Glass Menagerie* and I recognized Tony Ross's name and I said to Charlie, "Listen, we're going to the theatre tonight." And he flew into a rage and said, "Listen, you little bitch, I've got to get you on a train and have you in Minneapolis tomorrow for a press conference or I'll lose my job." And I said, "Shut up, we're going to see my friend Tony Ross in a play." He said that I couldn't go. And I said, "You'll either take me to the theatre to see this play or I won't go to Minneapolis *at all.*" So he had no choice and he changed the train tickets, and shivering, we went to see this play, *The Glass Menagerie,* which had just opened in Chicago. I didn't know who Laurette Taylor was or anything. I prefer to be up on the stage with the actors, but if I don't have a choice, I'm in the first row. So I watched Laurette Taylor act. I thought she actually changed her clothes and make-up and became a young girl in one scene. I'll never forget the performance that I saw! That and *Death of a Salesman* were the best things I ever saw. And Kim Stanley playing Cherie. So, anyway, I went backstage afterwards and Tony Ross introduced me to this little skinny playwright and I said, "How do you do?" and I remember he was from St. Louis and I was from St. Louis and we talked about beer or something. But I was so entranced with Laurette Taylor, although her name didn't mean anything to me, and Tony said, "Shelley, would you like to meet her?" And we all went tripping into her dressing room. And Tennessee introduced us. He said, "Shelley Winters, this is Laurette Taylor." And I looked at her and said, "Do you have an agent? You know, you really should be in Hollywood. You know that part where you change the clothes and become the young girl?" And Tennessee said, "She doesn't change her clothes." And I said, "Would you be quiet, please, whoever you are?" *Then he was scared to open his mouth!* It was his first play. Laurette Taylor took it as a sort of compliment. But I couldn't believe this transformation happened before my eyes! Just with the words. Because I knew nothing about *any kind* of acting, much less method acting. She suddenly became a young girl! She had a filmy, raggedy chiffon dress. It was an incredible thing.

She suddenly became a young girl. She blushed. Her face became flushed. And it was an incredible thing. I thought it was some kind of trick. But that meeting backstage was really the first time I met Tennessee and I sort of ignored him because of my awe of Laurette Taylor. I thought the play was so marvelous, but I think I thought the actors made up the lines themselves! It all seemed too real. And I had been so moved by it, especially because I was born in St. Louis.

It was at the meeting at Salka's, though, that I began to know Tennessee. I was going through my seven years at Universal and Tennessee used to drag me to see plays downtown and operas and stuff. I didn't quite understand, if I was going to be a movie star, why I had to go to concerts. I didn't see what the connection was. I was busy putting on four pairs of eyelashes! He was very, very sweet, very nice to me. And I became great friends with him and Marguerite Lamkin and Dylan Thomas at Salka's and Charlie Chaplin's houses. I remember Tennessee driving around Hollywood. He drove very badly. And either he or maybe Ivan Moffat had a car they called the Green Hornet. We used to go to a restaurant on Sunset called The Players where all the actors went. They would get too drunk to drive. Tennessee can drink but Dylan Thomas would get rigid! Rigor mortis would set in. So I would drive. I didn't have a license, I only had a learner's permit, but Marguerite would give me instructions. When we would go out we would start drinking about five o'clock and then have dinner. And to get downtown to the Biltmore Theatre you had to drive all the way down Sunset. There were no freeways. We used to go to the Pickwick Book Store on Hollywood Boulevard. It used to be open late at night. And Tennessee would give me lists of books to buy. I remember once the car broke down and we rode a trolleycar from Hollywood all the way to Santa Monica, drinking gin. We fooled around in Santa Monica and killed a bottle of gin. I remember I had a crush on Tennessee.

When Maureen Stapleton was doing *The Rose Tattoo* at the Biltmore, she was staying in my apartment with me. I almost got Maureen to have her nose operated on. She had all kinds of contracts offered to her and she could have been a big movie star. But she's got this kind of pudgy nose. A famous plastic surgeon here was going to fix it but at the last minute she ran away. She thought she was going to betray her ethnic background! It was a little before Barbra Streisand's time!

My whole impression of Tennessee was that the man and the playwright are two separate human beings. One is someone I have fun with and kid with, and then I'm very in awe of the great famous playwright, who seems like someone I don't know. I can't sort of put the two people together. Do you ever have that experience?

MIKE: Yes, when I first met him. I thought, "How could this little man have written those plays!"

WINTERS: I had a lot of fun with him. There used to be an Actors Laboratory here and we used to go to that and go all around to the places in town. This was before the freeways!

MIKE: Why was Tennessee out here for so long at that time?

WINTERS: I don't know. He was out here for a long period. *The Rose Tattoo* was here. Then it went to San Francisco and then came back. And then Tennessee was here while they were filming *Streetcar*. That's right! Marlon was doing *Streetcar* at Warner's and I was doing some crazy picture at Warner's. Oh, yes, the remake of *High Sierra*. They called it *I Died a Thousand Times*. When I saw it, I did! Jack Palance had the lead, and Lee Marvin was in it. I knew Marlon from New York. A very funny thing happened. He was building up this legend, you know, *enfant terrible*. I visited the set of *Streetcar*. Tennessee was there and Kazan, of course. And Marlon said he wanted to talk to me about something and I stepped into his dressing room, one of those wooden dressing rooms on the set. He slammed the door, put the lock on, and he started to shake the dressing room and said, "For God's sake, scream. Don't you want to help me build up a reputation? Scream!" So I said, "All right." So I was screaming away and he was shaking the dressing room and everyone on the set was running around. Everybody got upset but Tennessee. He knew it was an act. Gadge was saying, "Marlon, cut that out! What are you doing? She's a minor! Leave her alone!" But Tennessee knew it was a joke.

Let me see, I served my seven years at Universal and I used to fly back and forth to New York and attend the Actors Studio, and often Tennessee would be there and I would go to parties with him or people would give him parties. You know, it was a very strange thing. But I feel the turning point of Tennessee's life was a play called *High Point Is Built on a Cavern*, which was later called *Period of Adjustment*. And he was beginning to be a very political writer. Because if you really read the first draft of that play, there are two couples discussing potency but meanwhile the house is sinking and the walls were cracking. And the actors pay no attention to the house sinking. They just discuss who can do what to whom. I don't know who produced or directed that but Tennessee, contrary to most of the young new writers, is very susceptible to criticism and tries too hard to cooperate with the producer and director. He won't stick to his ideas and only a very bright guy, like Kazan, knows how to guide him into the path that is not just stylish but long-lasting. I think Tennessee is a very long-lasting playwright. I think hundreds of years from now they will be reading his plays. I think that play, although it wasn't a failure if it had been produced properly, was the turning point for Tennessee to begin to try to examine our society, not from a physiological or sociological standpoint, but from a political one. I was very sorry to see that that production was so bad, when I believed the play was so good, and the political aspects were kind of pooh-poohed. And the film, even though an ex-husband of mine, Tony Franciosa, was in it, still didn't fulfill the original play. I would like to do that play off-Broadway some time. The first script, before anybody monkeyed with it, was absolutely extraordinary. Tennessee was way ahead of everybody. He had taken a kind of attitude toward himself in society, which certainly wasn't true in the beginning of his writing. I've got some early plays of Tennessee's that he wrote when he was working in a shoe factory in St. Louis. I don't know how I came by them. They weren't very good but, come to think of it, they were very political, you know, unionish, WPA and the like. You know, he was a young writer and these plays were very surrealistic. They were, you know, Brechtian, and his impulses were to examine the social phenomena. Tennessee came to Broadway during the results of McCarthyism, when almost the only things they felt safe to write about were aberration and sex. Whether they were conscious of it or not. The natural inheritors of Clifford Odets and Lillian Hellman and Arthur Miller were across the ocean—John Osborne and Pinter. *Look Back in Anger*, if you really examine that play, could have been written by Tennessee. I don't say Osborne copied Tennessee. Osborne's a big talent, and all writers inherit from one another, but even his style of language and his imagery was confined that way. I think that Tennessee Williams—the poet and the playwright—will get his second wind. I still think he is very young man, you know, if you compare him to Somerset Maugham and George Bernard Shaw. And I hope, because I love him dearly, that he will examine the totality of his work, which is enormous, the ideas he has communicated. Ibsen and Shakespeare—the playwrights who have lived long—have been the ones who have communicated enormous ideas. And that's what Tennessee has done. Not only the words. And I think he will get a second wind sometime soon and will re-examine this world that is falling apart around us and write about it.

You know, Tennessee and I have a very funny relationship. We seem to meet each other in times of national disasters. Very strange thing! The night J. F. Kennedy was assassinated we were together, and it was just so appalling. One of the people with us that night was a political writer named Barbara Propst Solomon. She had just written a piece in the November issue of *The Nation* examining the atmosphere in Dallas in which she almost predicts that Kennedy would be assassinated if he went there. For some odd reason, we all just pretended it hadn't happened. We just couldn't deal with it. Tennessee had invited us to dinner in an Italian restaurant, and he had his dog with him. Then we went over to Downey's. On the way I bought a record player and a record about Lincoln's funeral, *The Lonesome Train*. We played the record there, and I was trying to keep up with Tennessee's drinking, which is thoroughly impossible. We were drinking gin martinis or whatever, and suddenly, sitting there, I went into hysteria listening to the thing about Lincoln. And the last thing I remember is Tennessee carrying me with one arm, and the Victrola, the record, and the dog under his other, staggering out of Downey's. I think we were asked to leave. That was the only time I was ever eighty-sixed! And I somehow got home.

Another time out here we were together when there was a disaster. I don't think it was when Roosevelt died. No, I think it was Hiroshima. We went downtown to a place where Nat King Cole was singing and spent the evening together drinking and forgetting.

A lighter thing I recall was when I was in *Night of the Iguana*. I had no desire to go into that. Bette Davis, whom

I replaced, had already gotten the reviews. I had seen the play in the Studio with Patrick O'Neal and Rosemary Murphy and they were extraordinary! And they did the play at the Coconut Grove. You know, there is a kind of honor among members of the Studio about taking each other's roles. I don't know what happened, but Bette wanted to leave the New York company. She had gotten good reviews, and the play had gotten good reviews. Tennessee called me up and, you know how he talks, he said, "Darling, come on and do this part please." And they were expecting theatre parties and so on. Groups that were coming expecting to see a "movie star." I didn't want them sitting there comparing me to Bette Davis. And I hadn't seen the play. And I was a little sore at not having been given the part in the first place! But Viola Rubber, the producer, talked to me about it and I went to see the play and I thought it was one of Tennessee's most beautiful. Not especially my role, which was exciting, but certainly Margaret Leighton's role and certainly Pat's. I agreed to go into it and I stayed in that play through the winter and summer. Tennessee got the New York Drama Critics Award. He's had the Pulitzer Prize a couple of times too, hasn't he?

MIKE: Yes, for *A Streetcar Named Desire* and *Cat on a Hot Tin Roof.*

WINTERS: Not for *The Glass Menagerie?* I've got to do *The Glass Menagerie* some day, in four or five years. I'm working up to it! I have an autographed picture from Laurette Taylor. She gave it to me that night I met her in her dressing room in Chicago.

MIKE: Didn't Tennessee come to the theatre a lot during the Broadway run of *Night of the Iguana?*

WINTERS: Yes. There was a long period in the second act when Maggie and Pat had a long scene, and one night Tennessee said, "You know, there's forty-five minutes when you're off stage and I have got a watch, so let's go across the street to Harold's Bar and have a drink." And I said, "Well, I don't know." But I told the assistant stage manager and he said all right. But he was a kid, you know. I really didn't know that you weren't supposed to leave the theatre during the performance. I went across the street with Tennessee and we had a drink. Then suddenly, in storms somebody—I don't remember if it was Chuck Bowden or the stage manager. Anyway, we had only been about twenty minutes and I had had one drink. A brandy. And they shouted, "You mustn't leave the theatre during the perform-ance! Get back over there!" I went back and we had plenty of time. So then after the performance, in front of the entire company, the stage manager *and Tennessee* bawled me out! And Tennessee had invited me! He had done eight, nine plays, so he knew better than I.

MIKE: Maybe he was teasing you.

WINTERS: But he has really great roles for actresses, and he writes very important, moving plays.

MIKE: Weren't you at a reception in the White House once with Tennessee and other artists?

WINTERS: Yes, and all the bigwigs were there—Robert Kennedy, Adlai Stevenson . . . I remember we had to line up alphabetically to march into the room where they had the reception. It seems to me it had something to do with Omar Bradley. Anyway, I was next to Tennessee because it was Williams then Winters, alphabetically. Over a period of twenty-odd years I have found myself next to him at various functions.

MIKE: Tennessee told me that at that reception you and he were already in the line and Thornton Wilder came up looking for his place, and he playfully but pointedly said,

"I think I belong in front of you, Tennessee." And Tennessee gamely replied, "If you do, it's the first time!"

WINTERS: Yes, I remember that! I don't think we let him in. That's right. I remember the line because you stand in a long reception line before you march in and sit on gold chairs. I remember that, but I don't remember what the function was for. That's odd!

I'll tell you about Tennessee looking at my apartment to buy. The apartment I am staying in now was for rent for about $450.00 a month. It has the best view of New York there is, and I tried very hard to get him to buy it, since he wasn't happy where he was. It had a marvelous room for writing, this great view, and everything, and I just couldn't understand why he didn't take it. I think maybe he likes little places. Remember that small, damp apartment he had on the East Side at one time? Each room was about eight by ten feet and in a very unsafe type brownstone. One time he had a cold or something and I brought him some food, I don't remember what, a corned beef sandwich or something constructive like that. And he wouldn't get out of bed. He was supposed to go someplace, but he said, "There are some days when I come out the door and I look at the sunset, and if it's a certain shade of red, I go back inside and get back into bed."

MIKE: That's poetic, whatever it means.

WINTERS: It means, to him there are just some days that he can't function and the vibrations in the air are scary.

I would like to visit Tennessee in Key West sometime. I have never done that. You know, I long to do *The Rose Tattoo*. I have married Italians, but I've never done that play. My daughter is about old enough to do it now with me.

MIKE: Is Vittoria going to be an actress?

WINTERS: No, no. She isn't. She's very good in math and science and things like that.

MIKE: What other plays besides *Iguana* have you done?

WINTERS: Oh, I did *Streetcar* out here. At the Circle Theatre. Richard Boone directed it and Dennis Weaver played Stanley Kowalski. And he was marvelous! It's a very dangerous play to do in the round in a small theatre. One night we had somebody from the audience get so excited he got up and took the scissors out of Dennis's hand. The audience used to get so involved in the play. This was before it became an intentional reaction. For instance, when you go to New York, go to the Fillmore East. The *audience* takes their clothes off! In this intimate theatre where we did *Streetcar*, it was very dangerous. The audience would get so involved in the play, Stanley's brutalization of Blanche, that they would talk. They would be absolutely stunned by it. I played Blanche and Stella. I was marvelous as Blanche, except I had a slight Brooklyn accent at that time which made an interesting characterization.

Then I did *Sweet Bird of Youth*, in which I thought I was atrocious. I had a whole other idea about doing it. I was very preoccupied with an aspect of the role which was bad for me and I did not have a good or strong director and I played the obvious strength of the woman, that she would survive regardless of what she says or does. There is something indestructible about her, like there is about Gloria Swanson and Joan Crawford. You know that if Joan Crawford is not a movie star, then she's going to run Pepsi-Cola, and if that fails, she's going to run Greece! In a certain kind of way they are—you know what I mean?

MIKE: Nobody stops them.

WINTERS: That's right. If there's a blank wall here, they go around it or through it or they go someplace else. So, even though the pathos comes over, this anguish and loneliness and everything, there is this strength in them. And I was busy not imitating Gerry Page instead of creating my own role. And it was an impossible theatre to do it in. You know, we did it when Martin Luther King was shot, was killed. You know, that's another one of Tennessee's political plays. Like we had the bartender played by a black actor. You played the bartender in New York, didn't you?

MIKE: No, I was the dialogue director on the film.

WINTERS: Anyway, there were many Negroes as the townspeople in our production, and we were doing it up in San Carlos, I don't know the name of the theatre, but five or six or seven thousand seats, and the day Martin Luther King was shot the place was three-quarters full and we sort of had a meeting whether we should go on performing or not. And the Negro kids, you know, the black kids, wanted us to, because in the play there was a parade, and the whole idea that in allowing the castration of a Negro, you had better be damned careful you're not castrated too. And we tried to make that the emphasis. And we did. And we raised money and the producer gave a certain percentage of the box office to the Southern Christian Leadership Conference. It's very interesting that in the last few decades the powerful writers have come out of the South. You know, Carson McCullers, William Faulkner—

MIKE: Truman Capote, Harper Lee, Flannery O'Connor.

WINTERS: —They've all come from the South. You know, the period before that was sort of New York and New England.

There have been times when I hated Tennessee—mostly because he didn't give me a role I wanted to do! And there are times I love him, as a man, you know, his kind of sweetness and fun and his sensitivity and appreciation of agonies that I've gone through. Of course, there are times I become very angry with him, like at the performance of *Camino Real* in Los Angeles. Opening night was dreadful. You know, it's an interesting play, but opening nights frighten him, so he got drunk. In summer stock I have done other of his plays. I've done scenes from *Sweet Bird of Youth* at the Studio and *Rose Tattoo, Orpheus Descending*, and the other play, *Cat on a Hot Tin Roof*, which is also a political play. He thinks he is not a political writer, but he was the precursor of the political writers that the kids all rave about now. Playing his plays stretches you, just as doing Shakespeare's does if you don't have good speech. If you play Shakespeare you have to speak well, and if you play Tennessee Williams you have to act well. If you get at the reality of human beings, whatever they are, if you get at the reality no matter how strange they seem, when you find the thing underneath the words, you have to become a deeper and better actress. I'm very grateful to Tennessee.

ESTELLE PARSONS

Estelle Parsons, as far as the public is concerned, became a star overnight. She won the Academy Award for Best Supporting Actress of 1967 for her first film, Bonnie and Clyde. *When this award was given she was starring on Broadway in Tennessee's play* The Seven Descents of Myrtle. *It is interesting that Estelle has achieved such success as an actress when her main talent is in musical comedy. She has a fine, powerful singing voice, which is yet to be exposed to her large following of fans.*

As Myrtle in Tennessee's last-produced Broadway play, Estelle won high praise from the critics. I was the dialogue coach on the production, and although many problems were encountered which one wouldn't even come across in an amateur theatre, Estelle proved a hard-working professional.

More recently, Estelle was starring in a new play by Murray Schisgal called A Way of Life, *but rewrites prevented its Broadway opening. I visited her after one of the New York previews of this play and she invited me to her apartment to discuss Tennessee and her work.*

Estelle Parsons and Brian Bedford in the Broadway production of *The Seven Descents of Myrtle*. 1968. (*Photo by Martha Swope*)

MIKE: Had you known Tennessee before you played Myrtle?

PARSONS: No, never. He wasn't even at the readings. Audrey Wood was there.

MIKE: Yes, that's right. Tennessee was at his home in Key West at that time. I was there with him for ten weeks while he worked on the film script *One Arm.*

PARSONS: So the first time I met him was when we had that first rehearsal reading of the play at the theatre, sitting around the table.

MIKE: What was your general impression of him from what you had heard and from his plays that you had seen?

PARSONS: It's embarrassing. I don't think I've seen any of the plays. I was not in New York when they did *Glass Menagerie,* or *Streetcar.* I remember being here when they did *Orpheus Descending,* but I was working on television on an early-morning show and I never was able to get to the theatre. Oh! I did see *Camino Real.* I covered that for my television program, *The Today Show,* and I remember thinking that was an extraordinary piece of work. It was about the only piece of theatre I had seen in New York that I thought was really extraordinary and real theatre. I thought about that play for days, but that was the only thing I had ever seen of his. I've never seen any of the others till this day, in stock or anything.

MIKE: So you had never even played in any of Tennessee's work before?

PARSONS: No, I was an absolute ignorant, except for some of the one-acts, which I did when I took classes from Lee

Strasberg at the Actors Studio. I did *Hello from Bertha*.
I played Big Bertha, and I loved it. I remember when I did
it Lee said, "Gee, you're extraordinary in that part, but it's
so far removed from you." I didn't know quite what he
meant till a few years later when I looked back on it. I was
very young and surely not any kind of fading, dying whore
in the South. It must have been rather bizarre, but I took
very much to the material and to the flamboyant quality.
There are destructive things but also a lovable quality so
basic to everything he writes.

MIKE: The character of Myrtle was as far removed from
you as Bertha, I suppose.

PARSONS: Yes, almost.

MIKE: Having done Bertha and understanding that character must have helped you with Myrtle.

PARSONS: It did, except I didn't find in the play version of
Myrtle so much of the flamboyant quality and so much
largeness of character. I found more from the short story,
The Kingdom of Earth. In the play I couldn't find all the
qualities that I found in the story. I remember in Philadelphia Tennessee first told me that I must read the short story.
That bouncy thing that Myrtle had, somehow, wasn't fitted
into the play. Or at least Tennessee didn't fit it into the
production we had.

MIKE: Since I worked with the play I can say that more
rewrites should have come out of rehearsals and the out-of-
town tryout.

PARSONS: Well, maybe. I think also there was a terrible
error in casting. I don't think anyone would mind my saying
that. And that was in Harry Guardino playing the part of
Chicken. I personally think that should have been played
by a Negro. At the very least a half-Negro. Someone who

at least looked Negro, because the story came out of relationship between a Negro man and poor white trash and
how when two kinds of opposites are thrown together, of
necessity they make their own adjustments. I think it was
quite a beautiful thing the way these two people ultimately
found their humanity and went beyond their color. Harry,
as they all say, is a lovely Italian man and plays that beautifully, but was a little bit out of order when he tried to
play a Southern man with Negro blood. I think it's absolutely essential that the character give the audience the
effect of a Negro meeting a piece of poor Southern white
trash. Out of that some other colors might have come for
her and for him. And a lot of playfulness, because we always
think of those Southern Negroes as having a very comic,
playful vein along with their sorrow. I think that would have
brought out a lot of colors in Myrtle that we were unable
to get in our production.

MIKE: I believe in the film version they are planning to use
a Negro actor. However, I don't think Tennessee ever intended Chicken to be played by a Negro. An octoroon perhaps, but not a darker person. It would change his concept,
so that the story would automatically put the accent on
black and white relationships. I agree that would make it
more dramatic, perhaps even give it a better plot. It would
certainly be more commercial, controversial, and sensational,
as well as a highly fantasized depiction of life in the South.
That approach is likely to make a good film. But it would
not be Tennessee Williams. When reading Tennessee, one
must be aware of how each play fits into the overall framework of his literature and how his themes evolve and progress from play to play.
    In *The Glass Menagerie* Laura represents the delicate,
sensitive, gracious, and romantic aspects of life—soft qualities which do not prepare a person for the harshness of the

world we live in. So the last line in the play is: "Blow out
your candles, Laura, for nowadays the world is lit by light-
ning." This outlook is intensified in *A Streetcar Named
Desire* when Blanche, who represents the same soft qualities
of Laura, is driven insane by Stanley, who represents the
crude and vulgar and brutal elements in man—man's hard
side. Finally, in *Kingdom of Earth* this outlook reaches its
conclusion. The character of Lot, although a man, represents
the soft side of man's nature. Chicken represents the hard
side. At the end of the play the effete, but not homosexual, Lot dresses in his mother's clothes when he is dying.
Tennessee told me that when he has Lot die, he is killing
off all the wispy, willowy women he has written about, that
he wasn't going to write that kind of woman anymore. Well,
when Lot dies, Chicken, who represents all that is coarse
and vulgar and hard, inherits the land—symbolically inherits this earth. He vindictively shouts, "Chicken is king!"
Tennessee's viewpoint is the opposite of the biblical dictum
that the meek shall inherit the earth. He has come to believe
in the survival of the hardest. In his own life he sympathizes
and identifies wtih Laura, Blanche, and Lot, and is sharing
their destiny! To know Tennessee's work one must always
refer to the pages that only he himself has written and not
rely on any other medium except the stage.

While working with Tennessee, what impressions of
him did you get?

PARSONS: Well, I felt right away what a very emotional
and passionate man he seems to be. I have never taken to
his material; I suppose because I'm from New England and
the fact that I haven't seen anything except *Camino Real*.
But, naturally, I was taken with him immediately. I'm sure
everybody is, because he seems to be so honest and interesting and humble and so passionate in his nature. Not like a
lot of writers, who are not so passionate. His personality has
more of a theatrical quality, doesn't it?

MIKE: Yes. I remember during that first rehearsal how Tennessee sat there and giggled so often as he heard the cast read his play aloud for the first time.

PARSONS: Yes, that bothered me a great deal, how much he laughed at things!

MIKE: But it showed how pleased he was with your characterization from that very first reading.

PARSONS: Really! That's very nice but I remember feeling that maybe he was laughing out of some nervousness of his own. Sometimes it would be nice to hear him laugh and other times I would wonder what he was laughing at, because he has such a big laugh you couldn't miss it. I felt that he seemed very naked, and I suppose naturally that goes without saying that a playwright is naked when his play is read. But you seem to really feel it from Tennessee. You feel things from him and that's very unusual, because you meet few people even in the theatre who are not awfully well covered up in social circumstances. But Tennessee doesn't seem to be. He just puts his heart right out on the line the whole time. Whether you're in one of those crazy psychedelic places like that Electric Circus in Philadelphia, or whether you're working on the material, he always seems to have his heart right out there ready to offer to anybody and ready to offer to the situation. Extraordinary. Really extraordinary. I suppose it must be terribly difficult to live that way. He must be hurt an awful lot of the time.

MIKE: To be that exposed—

PARSONS: Yes.

MIKE: —because it makes you vulnerable, doesn't it?

PARSONS: Oh, tremendously so, I would think.

MIKE: I know he wasn't at the rehearsals for *Myrtle* as often as any of us would have liked him to be, but did you ever have a chance during the pre-production to discuss the character with him? Did you get any "notes" from him personally?

PARSONS: Not really. I had met Kazan shortly before I was going to do *Myrtle*. I had never met him before and I sent him a letter saying that I hoped he had seen my work in *Bonnie and Clyde* and that I'd like very much to meet him and work for him some day if that might be possible. I had a very nice note back saying that he'd be in New York and I should come to meet him, which I did. He said, "Well, I know you're going to do Tennessee's next play." And I said, "Yes. Of course, I'm scared to death." And he said, "Well, I'll give you some very good advice and don't forget it: Get with Tennessee every hour of the day and night. Whenever you can sneak out to be by Tennessee's side you be there, because he knows more about his work than anyone and he'll tell you." So I did try to do that.

MIKE: I know that in Philadelphia you were with him more often those two weeks.

PARSONS: Yes, but he never talked an awful lot about the play. He said small things, little points and little things that I could perhaps read differently or do differently, but as far as the over-all work he seemed to be a little hesitant about offering advice or suggestions, which I knew he must have somewhere, because every once in a while some little thing would slip out. But he seemed not too willing to talk about the character or the play.

MIKE: I wonder if it meant that he didn't feel he needed to.

PARSONS: Gee, I don't know. It would be nice to think that, but I don't know. Of course there were so many things going on—the title problem and then the problems with the play. Maybe we didn't give him a chance to get too many words

in! We were all too busy giving advice to him about what
he should be doing.

MIKE: That's true. What was your opinion of their changing the title from *Kingdom of Earth* to *The Seven Descents
of Myrtle*?

PARSONS: Well, of course, I liked *Kingdom of Earth* best.
I thought it said what was to be said. I thought it was a
glorious title and I was very sorry that they changed it,
because all the new title did was have people counting how
many times she went up and down the staircase, really. Then
they'd come back and say, "Well, you didn't go down seven
times." "There weren't seven descents." *Kingdom of Earth*
was such a beautiful, beautiful title and said the whole thing
so well that I felt the other title threw the whole thing out
of focus.

MIKE: Also, when some people heard the title spoken they
thought it was *Seventy Cents of Myrtle*.

PARSONS: That's right!

MIKE: It was unfortunate. I remember also in Philadelphia
after rehearsal when we'd be out having drinks or something
to eat, Tennessee would often make the comment that he
felt actors and actresses didn't like him.

PARSONS: Yes.

MIKE: He seemed to have a hangup about that.

PARSONS: I remember that, yes.

MIKE: One didn't know how seriously to take him, or what
he meant by that.

PARSONS: Yes, I remember trying to assure him that that
wasn't so at all, that they liked him. He kept saying that
they didn't like playwrights. And I kept saying that's not

true, they always love playwrights, which I think they do. It's the directors that get in the way, not the playwrights! Tennessee very often feels that people don't like him, don't you think? It goes along with the fact that he's so vulnerable and gives of himself so much. Very few people have the capacity to give back, in return, as much as he gives.

MIKE: Have you seen him since the play was done?

PARSONS: No, I never did see him again. Never did. But I had a telegram from him when I won the Academy Award.

MIKE: Estelle, when you went into *The Seven Descents of Myrtle* you had already filmed both *Bonnie and Clyde* and *Rachel, Rachel,* hadn't you?

PARSONS: Yes. I remember I thought when I read *Myrtle* what a wonderful movie it would be. It seemed to me much more a movie than a play. It seemed to me it would fit more in that medium, because the flood was such an important thing. The elements had never been so important in other things that Tennessee had written. The elements—I mean the natural elements, the weather—seemed to be the principal character in that play, and of course it's very difficult to do that on stage, isn't it? Particularly with Tennessee's work, though Shakespeare did that in *King Lear* a lot and it worked. But somehow it didn't work in our production. Perhaps the sets were much too naturalistic. I kept thinking, "What a wonderful movie this will make when people see that water rising!"

MIKE: Well, I thought it was strange, since you did win the Academy Award last year, and you're very much on the tongues of the younger generation and you had played Myrtle on the stage, why they didn't want you or why you didn't want to do Myrtle in the film. To me it seems like the natural sequence of events—

PARSONS: Yes.

MIKE: —that you should do it.

PARSONS: But, I don't know. They seldom put someone in
a movie that's done the play. They did speak to me when
I was in Hollywood for the Academy Awards, at the Warner
Brothers party. They had bought the material. We were still
playing in New York at that time. But they spoke to me
about doing it in a production in California with another
director. They wanted to see it again with a different cast
and different director and see what they really had. They
said they had no idea what sort of property they bought,
and would I do it again. I said, well, yes, I would do it
again with other people if they wanted to. And that was the
last I heard of it! But I actually never felt I was right for
that part. I felt it really required a woman like Marilyn
Monroe or Elizabeth Taylor. I'm thinking of someone more
soft and round in actual type than I am and more sensual
in a way. Not that I can't play sensual parts, because I'm
always getting them, Heaven knows, and emotional things!
But I felt that they had a certain pathetic quality along with
physicality that I don't think I have at all. When I look back
at the pictures taken during *The Seven Descents* it seems to
me that I have a much too intelligent look and a much too
straightforward personality to really portray that character.
Visual aspects are more important than anything else in the
movies. On stage you can act characters you might not be
just right for, but in the movies the visual, physical element
is so important! It sort of reminds me a little bit of what
Uta Hagen must have been like playing Blanche DuBois.
I remember when we were in Philadelphia Tennessee said
that he had seen her play Blanche, and she had been foolish
enough to ask him who was the best Blanche DuBois,
because she did get rave reviews for doing it, and everybody
thought it was astounding and he said, "Well, of course,

Jessica Tandy was the perfect Blanche DuBois." She was so crestfallen and he said, "After I said it, I felt so bad, but she asked me! What could I do?" I sort of felt a little that way about playing Myrtle. I had much too straightforward a quality to play that poor little pathetic girl. There's nothing very pathetic about me. In another production it might have been different, because I did feel very strongly something that Dan Isaac brought out in his *New York Times* story about Tennessee which makes sense. Dan felt that the play and Tennessee's later works had now a vertical quality where it wasn't so much the story line, but it was characters. The exploration of characters more than a story line. I felt that was very true with this play. I felt that they were fascinating characters and no matter what they were involved in or going through, their behavior would be extremely fascinating. Unfortunately, in our production somehow they tried to make it into a story-line production and when you try to play the story line you got what Walter Kerr described as my "shrieking." I guess it became all monotony. It just became one scurrying through the story line, which was a very monotonous thing of the flood coming and their fear of it. Whereas if it had been played out in character behavior, in relationships, I think it might have been extraordinarily fascinating. We didn't have a chance to do that.

MIKE: Of the many parts Tennessee has written, in his one-act plays as well as his major works, which ones are appealing to you as an actress?

PARSONS: I liked *The Lady of Larkspur Lotion,* the woman who runs the house in that. I've done that in classes.

MIKE: I can see you as Serafina in *The Rose Tattoo.*

PARSONS: Yes, and I like the part of Maggie that Barbara Bel Geddes played in *Cat on a Hot Tin Roof,* but I think my favorite part is the Princess in *Sweet Bird of Youth.* I'd like to play that sometime. That really excites me. But I do adore the short plays and stories, because they have such bouncy life. Kids in the classes at Actors Studio were always doing Tennessee's plays. Seven or eight years ago I did *Baby Doll* there, just after the film. Tennessee Williams was always one of the big favorites. I'm sure he still is. Other actors are always calling me up to do auditions or work on scenes of Tennessee's. I must say I never initiate it myself. I guess, being from New England, my mind doesn't exactly run to Southern characters.

MIKE: Did Tennessee attend the Actors Studio as an observer while you were there?

PARSONS: I never saw him there. Actually, I got admitted the year after Kazan left. Tennessee was often there when Kazan was, but the Studio kind of had a different complexion after he was gone.

MIKE: Are you still active with the Studio?

PARSONS: Not very much any more. I don't have the time or the inclination now. When I want to do a particular part I go right to the regional theatre and do it. You know, find some theatre that would want me to do some part in a real production, instead of just workshop things. I guess that happens because I've got more confidence in my work. I used to love to do things at the Studio when I wasn't quite sure what I could do. Now, since I've won the Academy Award, I feel a lot more confident about what I can do, and I prefer to do a complete production, with all those levels, instead of something under workshop conditions.

MIKE: Does your primary interest remain the legitimate theatre instead of films?

PARSONS: I like doing films better, actually. And I'm much better suited to them, obviously, because I've only done two and I'm much more successful than I've been during all my years on the stage. Of course you reach such a wider audience. I find I drive myself to keep working on the stage, but I only do the movies I think are really good. I've turned down loads of film roles because I thought there was no point in doing them. Whereas I'll try an awful lot of things on the stage just to be working on the stage. I somehow feel that it's very necessary to do that.

MIKE: Obviously what lies ahead for you is to move back and forth between Hollywood and the stage, which is the ideal situation, I suppose. I think too many people who began on the stage have remained in Hollywood and forsaken the theatre. Knowing you as well as I do, I don't think that will ever be your case.

PARSONS: But it's funny what happens to you after you do the movies. You're treated so well. And you don't have that business of having to prove yourself to an audience. When you act for the camera you don't really know whether you're good or bad. It's over and you don't think about it. I notice since I've been in the movies I have a great block about learning lines. I have a great resentment about having to go out to prove myself night after night, which I'm sure is why I drive myself to do it. Every day you have to re-evaluate your talent and what you're giving to the audience and what you're getting from them. But you don't have any of that rugged road to travel when you're in the movies. You can sit back and think that you really are as great as everybody says you are. Boy! When you're working on the stage you've got to prove it!

MIKE: You still have the rugged road in films in other areas. Like seeing to it that your part is well written.

PARSONS: Yes, but the fight there is before you start the filming. You've got to see that you've got the good part in the good script with the good people.

MIKE: But even during filming there's a certain amount of influence necessary to handle the way your part is treated by director, cameraman, et cetera. And there are rewrites during the shooting.

PARSONS: That comes when you first read it, too. Then you can figure out what part is essential. Lots of times you read a movie script and there'll be a big part and a pretty good one, but you realize that if something's got to go then that'll go. It doesn't really have to be there. I think the trick is to pick a part that has certain essential elements that have to remain in the film. And then you're pretty safe.

MIKE: I've heard young people say that they went to see *Bonnie and Clyde* several times mainly to see you in it.

PARSONS: Oh, gosh, that's nice!

MIKE: I felt in *Rachel, Rachel* your part could have been better written to explain clearly that you were playing a "closet" lesbian. I felt they were too busy building up Joanne's part, giving too much time to her characterization, so that not enough attention was given to the development of other characters.

PARSONS: Yes. Actually the screenplay was kind of written that way. And Paul kind of fell in love with working with Joanne and making the film center on her, which he readily admits now.

MIKE: I find very little fault with the film. I think it's a beautiful film and I really enjoyed it, but I would like to have seen your part more explicit.

PARSONS: Well, it was to be actually that she was not a lesbian. The point was that this came out as a bit of a shock to her, too.

MIKE: Well, the part would have been more interesting if that idea had been explored so that the audience got that.

PARSONS: Yes, but it was left very vague and I think Paul was a little afraid of it. But right from the beginning he kept saying, "This just kind of happens. She isn't really a lesbian. This just kind of happens." And he wanted it to have that quality.

MIKE: It's a good quality to have as long as the audience gets it.

PARSONS: Yeah, people are always saying, "Oh, I've got a question to ask you." They've been arguing about it around the country, whether she was or wasn't a lesbian. I suppose she could have gone either way, the way the film actually turned out. You just didn't know whether it was something she suppressed, which I feel must have been true. She must have known she was, but suppressed it. That was why she chose to live alone and have few friends in the town.

MIKE: What was the character's name?

PARSONS: Cala.

MIKE: Cala. Maybe they should make another film on her story!

PARSONS: Wouldn't that be nice!

MIKE: *Cala, Cala!*

PARSONS: I was thinking the other day, as the film turned out she seemed to be such an interesting person.

MIKE: I really think there's a whole story waiting!

PARSONS: Yeah. She was really much more interesting than Joanne's character, as a basic character. She really was.

MIKE: When Tennessee was out in Los Angeles this fall for the opening of *Camino Real*, we were driving along a street in Westwood Village and the marquee on the theatre said *Rachel, Rachel* and Tennessee said, "Oh, Estelle's in that. Let's stop. Let's see if we can go see it now." And we did.

PARSONS: Terrific.

MIKE: And nearly every time you'd come on the screen, he'd say, so that practically everyone in the theatre could hear him, "Oh, there she is. That's Estelle, that's Estelle."

PARSONS: How did he like it?

MIKE: Very much. He liked the technique of the film, going back to the childhood sequences.

PARSONS: I don't know too much about movies, on the one hand, and on the other hand, I suppose I know more than I think I know. But the guy who wrote it, Stewart Stern, wrote *Rebel Without a Cause.* He writes what must be pure movie technique, because you can't do anything with them. You can't act them. You simply stand there and say what he has written, and that makes the impact. It's the most interesting thing, and if you try to act them you are really in great trouble—they're not actable. You can only stand and say the line, which is just what the camera wants. You know that old story that Michael J. Pollard told, which we were always talking about during *Bonnie and Clyde*: They put together film, a very funny sequence, and then a close-up of Gary Cooper. And then a very sad sequence, followed by another close-up of Gary Cooper. And Gary Cooper had to do absolutely nothing; the point was made by the film. Stewart really writes that way. I noticed so much in Joanne's work that she would simply be there saying the lines with nothing behind them, with nothing of what we call acting on the stage—you know, no emotionalism behind them. And Paul would direct her by saying, "Pinch your lips together now in this. Pinch your lips together now in this." And his direction—I won't say all of it, but almost all of it—seemed to be purely physical, like eyes closed or opened, or the lips pinched or the face strained or some kind of physical or visual image. It was a very interesting experience.

As you know, Paul Newman just won the New York Film Critics award and so did Joanne. And I felt so badly that Stewart didn't win because everybody was so faithful to the script. Paul really filmed what Stewart had written and Joanne really played what Stewart had written, which is not the case in many movies, which you probably know. Most movies go through a lot of stages and rewrites and God knows what before they finally come out. But that whole experience was very faithful to the screen writing. It's very interesting what happens to you in this country. You start out wanting to be a success in the theatre. And, well, say you get to be a success. Then it's like you play only leading roles and your agent says, "You know we got two thousand for you for this play. You can't take another play with a smaller offer of five hundred." Even if you like the role you have to keep the price up. That happens in plays. Then, in the movies it's the same thing. You can't be a star in the movies and then say, "Gee, I love this role and all these people. I want to be in this movie." The agent tells you that you can't do it because you command so many thousands a week and you have to play leading roles. I think that's why the actors in our country don't develop. They seem to develop right into oblivion, or worse! You know, drinking or God knows what kind of destructiveness, because there's no feeling that you can work in theatre at what you want to work at. You have to be a star if you're successful and good. You no longer play roles just because you find them exciting to play. It's silly that actors have gone along with this. I guess that's what happens when you become a star when you're young. I didn't even start in the business till I was about thirty. So I can look at my agent and say to him, "Hah, hah, hah, there's a one-scene part I want to play and I'm going to play it!" And I'll take what that part is worth—five hundred dollars. Then if people want me or need my talents for a starring role next season, they'll pay me two or three thousand or whatever I'm worth for that part. But we become so limited we don't give and take. The British have a better attitude. Even Vanessa Redgrave, I read in the paper, was up in Birmingham, England, or some little rep company, doing a brand-new play. I recently came back from doing a world première of a play in Cincinnati and people were treating me like some kind of goddess because I deigned to work in Cincinnati in a brand-new play after I had won the Academy Award. The whole syndrome is too topsy-turvy in this country. It's not conducive to the development of an art form or an artist.

MIKE: Unfortunately, it has been made into a commercial enterprise.

PARSONS: Yes. And you can't put all the blame on the agents or say people do it to you, because, obviously, every artist, or would-be artist, makes the final decision. You know, people say to me, "Your agent won't let you do that." And I say, "I make the decisions. My agent handles the contracts." So you can't blame it on the commercial forces. Naturally, they want what they want but they have to be battled as they are in every other field.

MIKE: You told me that you were not very interested in the New York theatre of the fifties. Can you explain that more?

PARSONS: Well, the best example of it was *A Hatful of Rain*. I felt that the whole play, the behavior and everything in it, was so naturalistic that all you had to do was walk along the streets and sections of New York to see people like that, see their behavior. To see it in real people is so much more interesting than what actors can do with it. I don't feel that the theatre is interesting when merely holding up a mirror to life. I find life infinitely more interesting than anything any actor can give me—or almost any actor. I'd have to exclude someone like Marlon Brando, of course. But if I go to the theatre I'd much rather see something really theatrical. Real in theatrical terms, like Tennessee or Shakespeare or Edward Albee, rather than just see what I've already seen on a street corner on the way to the theatre. I don't think the theatre is as interesting as life if it tries to copy life. I think life will win all the time. Like I think nature will always win over art. You know, it's my personal taste. I love to see theatre in its own reality. Really blossoming.

MIKE: So you feel the theatre is most interesting when it has more fantasy or more pageantry?

PARSONS: Yeah, when it's really theatrical. When it's something that doesn't happen in real life. When it's a take-off from real life.

MIKE: Yes, a very heightened experience of life.

PARSONS: Yeah, an extension of it, that's what art should be. So that after you look at it, you come out and then you look at everything in the world with new color and a new frame of reference.

MIKE: I think Tennessee has been highly successful in doing that.

PARSONS: Yes, extremely theatrical. That's why I loved those one-act plays so much. They're rooted in a natural realism, but then they just go off from there. You can fly with them!

MIKE: I think one reason Tennessee recently became a Roman Catholic is that he likes life as well as art to be as theatrical as one can make it. As long as fantasy or theatricality doesn't take over completely. And the pomp and circumstance of the Church is appealing to him.

PARSONS: I don't blame him. I think if I were religious I would prefer to be a Catholic, too. To go the whole way. Or it seems like going the whole way!

Maureen Stapleton and Don Murray in the Broadway production of *The Rose Tattoo*. 1951. (*Photo by George Karger, Pix Incorporated*)

Maureen Stapleton and Cliff Robertson in the Broadway production of *Orpheus Descending*. 1957. (*Photo courtesy Friedman-Abeles*)

MAUREEN STAPLETON

Maureen Stapleton has starred in more of Tennessee's plays than any other actress. She created the role of Serafina in The Rose Tattoo, *played the original Baby Doll in* 27 Wagons Full of Cotton *when that one-act play was done on Broadway as part of an evening called* All in One, *starred as Lady in* Orpheus Descending, *then starred in a revival of* The Rose Tattoo *at the New York City Center. In 1965 she played Amanda in the Broadway revival of* The Glass Menagerie.

During all these years Maureen has remained a close friend to Tennessee. She was an exceptionally close friend to Tennessee's secretary-companion, Frank Merlo, partly because of their Italian background.

At the time of this interview, "Mo" was nearing the end of a year's run as star of the Neil Simon comedy Plaza Suite. *I visited her in her dressing room after the performance one night to make this brief tape. Perhaps at some other time, place, or occasion she would have really opened up and drawn upon her wealth of experiences with Tennessee, because she is one of the people most qualified to speak on the subject of Tennessee Williams.*

MIKE: The first Broadway play you did was *The Rose Tattoo,* wasn't it?

STAPLETON: Yes. In 1950–51. We played almost a year in New York, and then we toured.

MIKE: Did you know Tennessee before that?

STAPLETON: No. I had been a fan and admirer, but I had never known him.

MIKE: But you became close friends during the play.

STAPLETON: I became an even more ardent fan. Eli and I had to read a lot of times for the parts because they were taking a chance in casting two totally unknown people. I think we read five times or more. When my agent finally called to say I had got the part it was an anticlimax. I was sort of sure I had the part at the last reading, but they seemed to want more assurance I could handle it. I said, "I don't know, I'd like to, and I hope so, but I can't promise." Tennessee jumped up and said, "I don't care if she turns into a dead mule opening night!" That to me was extraordinary. It meant he was willing to take all the consequences. I remember when we did *27 Wagons Full of Cotton* in Louisiana. Felice and I got down to New Orleans before Tennessee. There was a set ready at Tulane University. The set is supposed to be the porch of a Mississippi farmhouse. But that set was so powerful and grand that it would be the only thing left if the atom bomb fell! When I saw it, I thought that it was for something else. When Tennessee came to the theatre and saw it he said, "What is that?" Someone said, "It's your set." Tennessee calmly said, "Who is responsible for this disaster?" They all started passing the buck. Tennessee was wonderful. He stayed there until four o'clock in the morning telling them how to do the set. He never got mad about it.

MIKE: Did you work on any of Tennessee's plays at the Actors Studio?

STAPLETON: Sometimes. I went to the Studio when it started in 1947. I went very steadily for about ten years. But I had two children, and life went on, and I thought I had had it, and I just stopped going.

MIKE: You starred on Broadway in *Orpheus Descending,* but Anna Magnani starred in the film. How did you feel about that?

STAPLETON: Well, I had already been through that with *The Rose Tattoo.* I did the play, Anna did the film. I would like to have played in the films, but I'm not sentimental about work. I understood. If I were a producer I would have hired Anna, too! I wouldn't find it easy to take that kind of rejection in my personal life, but in my work I'm not sentimental. I can only do the best I can and I only have myself to compete with.

MIKE: Your parts in *Rose Tattoo* and *Orpheus Descending* have many similarities, but Amanda in *Glass Menagerie* must have been quite a switch for you.

STAPLETON: Not really. Only the aging. Tennessee writes great acting parts. It's infinite what you can do with them. There's always something more to find in a part. Nobody writes like that.

MIKE: I know you have met Tennessee's mother. Did you draw any of your characterization from her when you played Amanda?

STAPLETON: No. That part is any mother. It's just "Mother." Tennessee's wellsprings are so deep that he gives you enough to act without your having to go outside the part to find values. I remember when they were going to do the first production of *Sweet Bird of Youth* down in Florida, they called me to play the young girl. I was younger and more trim then! But I read the play and I fell in love with the part of the Princess. So I called Tennessee in Florida and told him how much I loved the play and I said, "I've decided to try to tell the truth from now on in my life. I don't want to play the young girl. I want to play the older woman, the Princess." And he said, "We've already got somebody for that." But before he said that he said, "Oh, yes. I decided to tell the truth in 1946. I was sitting on a bus and I decided to always tell the truth." It just absolutely knocked me out. If there is such a thing as too much honesty, he has it. He's ruthless with himself. More than one should be. He has such difficult standards for himself. I'm still a fan! You get that, don't you? I can't remove myself from a certain awe I have for him. Sometimes when we are together I can only tell him when I get half loaded things I want to say. Then I can bust through and say serious things in a funny way. "Ah, fuck off. You're not dying and you know it. We're all dying. You'll outlive us all."

MIKE: How do you think Tennessee has held up under the pressures of success?

STAPLETON: I think he has borne up in an incredible way. Nobody makes me feel about their life or their work as he does. I always think people should say, "Hallelujah!" every time he writes anything. He was so successful that that vague sort of "they" started to knock him down. You know, if you don't walk on the water every time, they take pot shots at you.

MIKE: Maureen, you're the first close friend of Tennessee's I've spoken with since he became a Roman Catholic recently. I personally think it's a very good thing.

STAPLETON: I was very happy about it, because anything that helps him is good. I mean that *really* helps him, not half-ass helps him. It always shook me up to hear him talk about desperation. I think the Church will do him good. He's not a casual man about anything.

MIKE: I was concerned over his reason for becoming a Catholic. He was quoted as saying, "I wanted my goodness back." I never thought he lost his goodness. He has always been on the side of the angels.

STAPLETON: Always. But because of whatever private devils he has that pursue him, he evidently needs a form he can trust. He's very hard on himself, but now he can say he has his goodness back. And I believe it. He has his goodness back.

Anne Jackson and Tod Andrews
in the original Broadway production of *Summer and Smoke*. 1948.
(*Photo by Eileen Darby, Graphic
House, Inc.*)

Eli Wallach and Barbara Baxley
in the New York production of
Camino Real. 1953.

Eli Wallach, Tennessee Williams, Elia Kazan, Jo Van Fleet, and
Joseph Anthony. First rehearsal of *Camino Real*. January, 1953.
(*Photo by Talbot*)

ANNE JACKSON
AND ELI WALLACH

Anne Jackson and Eli Wallach are a well-matched team on and off the stage. They own a beautifully decorated apartment on Riverside Drive overlooking the Hudson and the Palisades, and are completely oriented to New York life. They are constantly attending art galleries, the theatre, and various exhibits. Their artistic life is reflected in their children, who show a great deal of talent in sculpture, painting, and the making of amateur movies.

Eli created the roles of Alvaro Mangiacavallo in The Rose Tattoo *and Kilroy in* Camino Real. *He also starred in the film of* Baby Doll, *playing Vicarro.*

Anne was in the original Broadway production of Summer and Smoke, *in which she played Nellie.*

When not starring in a Broadway play, they both keep a very busy schedule with frequent film roles, which take them on location to various parts of the world. Eli had just returned from Czechoslovakia when I interviewed them.

New York City
February 5, 1969

WALLACH: Our theatrical careers were sustained and given life by Tennessee over a long period of time. The first time Anne and I met was when we were doing a one-act play of Tennessee's called *This Property Is Condemned* at the Equity Library Theatre. I was too old for the part, because he's a fourteen- or fifteen-year-old boy and I had just come out of doing my five-year stint in the Army. But anyway, we did the play, met, fell in love, got married. Tennessee has had a big part in our lives and our careers in the theatre. After that, we made a movie of it for two hundred dollars. A silent movie. And then Anne went into his play *Summer and Smoke*. The original Broadway production with Tod Andrews and Margaret Phillips that Margo Jones did. We both were in the Actors Studio from the beginning and we worked on scenes from Tennessee's one-act plays. Joshua Logan was a guest director at the Studio, and he directed me in *The Strangest Kind of Romance*. And as an exercise in fantasy, Kazan worked with me on a scene from *Ten Blocks on the Camino Real*. He showed it to Tennessee and he loved it. And out of that I was picked to do *The Rose Tattoo* with Maureen. Danny Mann directed that Broadway production. Then we did *Camino Real* on Broadway, and eventually wound up doing the film *Baby Doll*. Meanwhile, I'll turn it over to Anne.

JACKSON: Well, when I came into the theatre the only great playwright—living playwright—that my generation knew about was Tennessee. He was, really and truly, my first introduction to a modern playwright and modern theatre. At the Neighborhood Playhouse, which I attended, they had done *The Lady of Larkspur Lotion*, *This Property Is Condemned*, and other of his one-act plays. And it remained in my mind as a dream that I would do more of his works somewhere, some day. I was in love with Tennessee Williams and I didn't know there was anything else except him and Chekhov. Not only in my life and Eli's but in the lives of all of the young people of the theatre twenty years ago he was one of the greatest influences. I think he still is and will be in the future. I don't think there is any doubt in anybody's mind about that. I worked on *Glass Menagerie* for ten years until I finally had an opportunity to do it in stock with Eli. I had done it three times at the Studio and never once could find a way to play Laura that pleased me. What you can find in his parts is endless. But Eli and I finally did a stock tour of it, with Jo Van Fleet playing Amanda and Bob Gehringer as the Gentleman Caller. The style of *Menagerie* and *Streetcar* stimulated a whole wave of new actors and playwrights. Tennessee's lyric style was a departure from the naturalistic acting and writing of the Group Theatre. The writers of today are certainly influenced by Tennessee: Edward Albee. *Camino Real* certainly came before anybody in this country knew about Ionesco or Beckett.

WALLACH: When we were working on *Menagerie*, Tennessee came to watch a rehearsal, and it stimulated *him* with ideas! There was a little change he made in the scene between Laura and the Gentleman Caller. Something to do with the little glass animals. That was years after it had been done on Broadway!

JACKSON: You know, every important actor of the last twenty years has done his plays. Paul Newman was already a star in Hollywood when he came back to do *Sweet Bird of Youth*, which was a very good thing for his career, in my opinion. But it is also a very brave thing for an actor to do.

MIKE: Did Marlon Brando ever come back to Broadway after *Streetcar* and his film success?

WALLACH: Once. He came back to do Shaw's *Arms and the Man*. I keep thinking of the interesting little incidences that occur when you work with Tennessee. For example, in *The Rose Tattoo,* for weeks we tried to find an ending. We couldn't find an ending! Tennessee finally came in one day and said, "I want Mangiacavallo to leave his shirt in the room when he runs up the hill. Then Serafina passes a bloodstained shirt up the hill." You see, Tennessee is able to pick out touching and poetic things which could be real and couldn't be real: Blanche singing "It's Only a Paper Moon" in *Streetcar* when she's in the bath. By the lyrics of a song he is making a comment on the whole scene and on our lives. It's that kind of extracting that Tennessee did!

JACKSON: I get very up-tight when any actor or any theatre person talks of Tennessee in the past tense. I truly do. Recently, yes, he has written some plays that were difficult to get on or did not get hurrahs and kudos from the critics. But he is a genius, in my opinion. He is still our greatest living playwright. I'm sure that he's ruminating. I'm sure he will continue to come up with more theatrical work. He may not necessarily do it on Broadway. We don't have a Broadway at the moment. But I am positive Tennessee will continue to do work of the standard that we've been talking about. He loves the theatre. It is not only his own plays he preens over. When I was in Ann Arbor doing Jane Bowles' play, *In the Summer House,* Tennessee came to see that play three or four times. He's one of the most interested parties on other people's work and his own, isn't he, Eli? He came to see Eli and I in *Luv* and talk to us about it. He's a constructive human being in the theatre.

WALLACH: I don't expect a playwright to get up to the

plate and make a home run each time. We've just had five years playing in Murray Schisgal's work. He's had three or four successes in a row and now his new one isn't going to open. That doesn't mean he's washed up as a playwright or as a creative person. I feel that in this country the creative writer comes to a kind of gap or moat. A time gap, generation gap, or economic gap. Something happens where the well dries up for a time. Now, the geniuses can leap over that gap and not be crushed, and create again. I'm sure Tennessee will come forward again and all his denigrators will be shamed by the work he will put out.

JACKSON: This country seems to spawn more than others. You suddenly see your life in terms of tens. We say the thirties were Shirley Temple or Betty Boop, or whatever. And the forties were the war pictures, and so on. We have a tendency to put aside everything: cars, houses, furniture. Replace things with new things. We don't hold on to anything, so it is little wonder we hold on to our playwrights or our actors or our directors for any length of time.

MIKE: I think whatever Tennessee has written that has not been acclaimed a success will still have its day. For instance, it took *Camino Real* over ten years to be praised as highly as it recently has been. His work is durable.

JACKSON: He is fortunate that way. That it's on the printed page and will endure! Not that he's fortunate, but that generations to come are fortunate.

WALLACH: *Baby Doll* is one of those durable works you were talking about, Mike. You see, during its time it was thrown out of some movie houses. It was never shown on television. Now, in light of what's happening today, people say, "Why? What was all the fuss about?" And *Camino* will be revived time and time again because it contains certain insights that Tennessee had. I want to tell you an incident. Some studio was having a screening in a small room at their New York office of one of Tennessee's films. And Tennessee's friend Frank asked Anne and me if we would like to go with them to see it. So we all had dinner together and then we arrived at this little theatre on the ninth floor of a building. A woman came out with a pad and very officiously said to Tennessee, "All right, where are you from?" She meant *The New York Times, Saturday Evening Post,* or some other publication. But Tennessee said, "I'm from Mississippi." She said, "Oh, smart? Well, you're not getting in!" He was crushed and he turned around to go back down the elevator and Frank said, "Wait a minute, Tennessee. Where're you going?" And the woman said, "Are you Tennessee Williams?" He said, "Yes." She said, "Why didn't you tell me who you were?" He said, "You didn't ask me who I was. You asked me where I was from." That's Tennessee. I think one of the biggest struggles Tennessee has is that even with his insights, he fears the cruelty of people. He, in the market place, in the commercial arena, is bruised.

JACKSON: Oh, and he can bruise. He hurt me terribly not so long ago. He has pain and he can inflict pain. But he can do that. He can be downright mean at times.

MIKE: Both of you have been very close to him and know him well.

JACKSON: Eli has been around him more than I.

WALLACH: You know, Tennessee swims nearly every day of his life. Ever since he had a slight heart attack when he was young. I think Kilroy's character in *Camino* stems from that. I'll never forget opening night of *Camino* in New Haven. Kazan, Tennessee, and I went to the Yale swimming pool for a dip, prior to the opening, to release *my* tensions.

The three of us swimming in there bare-ass naked was amusing. He likes his daily swim and a warm climate for it. I remember when we were on location in Mississippi for *Baby Doll* it was in November and very cold. So Tennessee just left. He went to Key West, where it was warm.

MIKE: Returning to *Baby Doll*, Karl Malden said much of that film was done as an expansion of Tennessee's writing, in an improvisational manner.

WALLACH: Yes, but that was in the action and direction. Not in the words. One of the great things about Tennessee's writing is his selection of words. If you don't say them exactly you lose his rhythms. He has a marvelous ear. He'll listen to you and say, "That's not what I wrote." So you must be very particular in playing what he writes. Within what he wrote for *Baby Doll*, yes, we did improvisations in trying to find ways of doing things to bring the characters to full life. In *Camino*, for example, Kazan would say to me, "Now you go out on stage and make friends. I can't tell you how to do it." Then he tells all the rest of the people on the stage, "Don't have anything to do with this boy. He smells, he's been on a ship, he's a leper. Spurn him." So I go on stage and the game starts and the conflict starts within the framework of what Tennessee had written. I would say to Tennessee or Kazan, "My God, you've got me leaping out of a box in the audience, running up and down the aisle, saying speeches like, 'Where's the nearest exit?' 'Where's the nearest Greyhound bus depot?'" It was too much to do, so Tennessee would cut and snip and make it easier so long as he maintained what he had intended: a man in flight, running. I think Tennessee loved that production of *Camino*. It was done under extreme pressure, with no money. They didn't even put up pictures in front of the theatre, or posters! And when the closing was announced the police had to come to keep order, because we couldn't have gone on, the place was so jammed. We put that show together in twenty-one days prior to opening in New Haven, although we had worked on scenes from it at the Studio. After opening night one critic said, "Tennessee Williams is our greatest playwright and this is his worst play." Tennessee took that play and went back South and rewrote the whole thing. In the recent production on the West Coast the hippies latched on to it because they see in it—

JACKSON: —the comic strips. It's the most marvelous play ever written. What a concept to show man's passage through this ugly world as a comic strip.

WALLACH: Actually, I always thought of it as Alice in Wonderland, you know, going through the mirror into that strange world. I'd like to do that play again. I'd like to play Kilroy again, even at my age now, at the National Theatre of England.

JACKSON: A lot of the old cast could be rounded up. But it would have to be a Kazan production, and Tennessee would have to be there.

WALLACH: I'd like that. Now I'm going to tell you a story that happened with *The Rose Tattoo* in 1951. We were playing in Chicago because Tennessee thought that Claudia Cassidy had helped *The Glass Menagerie* immensely with her encouragement. So we took *The Rose Tattoo* there to open it. It was a tough play for that old lady to swallow, but she took it! There was a furniture convention in town. One night I was downstairs in my dressing room getting dressed. My character, Alvaro, didn't come on until about a quarter of ten, and a man came down who was very drunk. He said, "I love this play. I've seen this play every night for the whole damn week, and I love it. I like you and I like Maureen. But you're not the only one with a rose on your chest." I said, "What do you mean?" He said, "I have a rose on my chest, too." I thought, "My God, did he go out and get himself tattooed?" I just painted my rose on between acts. When it was real hot it would run! But this drunk man ripped open his shirt and he had a real rose stuck on with tape! Finally, they had to come and throw him out of the theatre and he said, "I'll see you in New York on opening night!" By God, he did come to New York, and Maureen and I hid in the dressing room and we didn't want to come out. Tennessee would be around all the time. He hardly ever had his shoes laced, and he never knew what time it was. I'll never forget once when he was introduced at some luncheon he stood up and his fly was unzipped. He zipped it up and sat down quickly! He has a marvelous, infectious laugh! Does he still smoke through a cigarette holder?

MIKE: He's stopped smoking. When Frank Merlo died in January of 1963 of lung cancer, Tennessee gave up cigarettes.

WALLACH: Frank was a lovely guy.

MIKE: Everybody seems to have thought highly of him. He was beneficial to Tennessee in his work, also.

JACKSON: He was a very good human being. He was loyal to people.

WALLACH: He was very bright. He had a marvelous sense of what Tennessee was striving for and was very good for him. I'd love to do a play of Tennessee's now. So would Anne. I've often been approached about directing. I've had two experiences at directing, both of them tied to Tennessee. I directed the Canadian company of *The Rose Tattoo* in Niagara Falls with Maureen and me and Canadian actors. That was a pleasant experience, having just done it on the road. The other one I did as an exercise at the Actors Studio.

I directed *Hello from Bertha.* I took Margaret Phillips, who was always playing these ethereal ladies like Miss Alma in *Summer and Smoke,* and I made her the madam of a whorehouse, the landlady. And Maureen played Bertha in bed and Anne had a part in it. Before it began I went out to explain to the audience why I had picked this play. I said, "I picked this play because I'm interested in prostitution." And I got a laugh, which was like blood to me, and I wouldn't get off. I kept making remarks about my work in the Army with venereal diseases and how I was fascinated with prostitution. I went on for twelve or fifteen minutes and then I said, "And now the play!" And Josh Logan said, "To hell with the play. Keep on with the sex lecture." Then the curtain went up and none of the actors did what I asked them to do. It was such a trauma that I haven't directed since.

JACKSON: I like the story, Eli, about the night Tennessee did the poetry reading.

WALLACH: Oh, yes. A few years back we were going to do a reading at the poetry center at the YMHA at Lexington and Ninety-second. Barbara Baxley and I read scenes of the gypsy's daughter and Kilroy, and Tennessee read all the other parts in *Camino Real.* He reads beautifully. He was drinking what I thought was a glass of water, but it turned out to be straight vodka. He began to read lower and lower and people said, "Louder!" and without changing a beat he got louder. Then at one point he stopped reading from *Camino* and said, "I think I'll recite a poem now." I thought, "Well, all right." And the title of the poem was "Two People Who Scarcely Know Each Other Find Themselves in Bed Together for the First Time." Do you know that poem?

MIKE: Yes. It's now called "Life Story" and is in the volume called *In the Winter of Cities,* which William S. Gray edited.

JACKSON: They light a cigarette in bed and burn up together!

WALLACH: That's the end of the poem and Tennessee read it beautifully.

Mildred Dunnock

MILDRED DUNNOCK

Mildred Dunnock has created some of Tennessee's most memorable characters: Big Mama in Cat on a Hot Tin Roof, *Aunt Rose Comfort in* Baby Doll, *Aunt Nonnie in* Sweet Bird of Youth, *and the Bitch of Capri in* The Milk Train Doesn't Stop Here Anymore.

One of Millie's most distinguished performances was as Linda Loman in Arthur Miller's masterful play Death of a Salesman. *She had the rare distinction of starring in the Broadway, film, and television productions of that play.*

I visited Millie in New Haven, Connecticut, where she was teaching acting at the Yale School of Drama, and performing with the Repertory Theatre, which was presenting a delightfully entertaining show called Story Theatre. *We sat in her dressing room before the performance to chat about Tennessee.*

DUNNOCK: I remember first meeting Tennessee when there
was a reading for *Camino Real.* I think it was held at the
Actors Studio. Of course, I had heard of him. As a matter
of fact, in summer stock I had done the play *You Touched
Me* with Ruth Ford. At the reading of *Camino Real,* I must
admit, I was dying to play the role of Camille. I didn't get
it, though. Later I tried again for the role in *Cat on a Hot
Tin Roof.* I knew that Gadge was going to direct that too.
I had worked with him. I also knew that Tennessee wrote
the best women's parts in the whole world. I was born in
Baltimore, Maryland, which isn't very far South, but I've
always thought of myself as Southern. I like Southern people and I find Southern women especially articulate, expan-
sive, free. It's very rare that you find a playwright that's
particularly interested in women. In most plays there are
dozens of men's roles and very few women's roles. And Tennessee understands the women that he writes about. So I
was dying to be in that play. I asked the producer if there
was anything for me and he said there wasn't. I said, "Well,
if there's any chance of my reading, I'd like to read." I don't
know whether anybody remembers the original script of
Cat on a Hot Tin Roof but Big Mama was described as a
short, squat woman with big feet, looking like a boxer dog
or a Japanese wrestler. Well! That's kind of a hard description to live up to! Women spend their lives trying *not* to
look like that, particularly actresses.

MIKE: Too bad Elsa Maxwell wasn't an actress!

DUNNOCK: Yes, she would have been very good! But, at
any rate, for one reason or another, there just wasn't anybody of that description. I kept nagging away asking for a
chance to read for her. And so I read for it. I got the part.

I had a friend in college whose mother had a strange, husky, whiskey voice. It was just one of those rasping voices. And when I started to read for the part I guess I felt, "I've got to compensate for not having big feet or looking like a Japanese wrestler." And so those descriptive words somehow or other gave me a picture of the grotesquerie which I found in my voice.

I did do Big Mama and I adored her. She had an element of women in her that I feel is so real: that capacity, that desire, to pull down the curtain on things that they don't want to see. She knew all about Brick, and she knew all about Big Daddy. But she never wanted to look at its harsh reality.

MIKE: Southern women are often like that.

DUNNOCK: Oh, I think so!

MIKE: I think Tennessee's mother is like that. I know my mother is like that!

DUNNOCK: Well, I think a great many women are like that and that's what appealed to me about Big Mama. She was the brunt of all of Big Daddy's jokes and hideosities but she never chose to see them, so that she never became annihilated by them. She had guts of her own, which matched those of Big Daddy. Tennessee does that. It's his art, his great talent, that creates his women so that they never lose their character. Later I played the part of Aunt Rose Comfort in the film *Baby Doll*. Oh, that was a wonderful experience! I loved that old woman. I remember I went up one day to Tennessee in Greenville, Mississippi, and said, "Oh, please, Tennessee, won't you do something more with Aunt Rose? She just drifts away." He said, "Honey, I'm so sick of that old woman! You know more about her than I do anyhow, so do anything you want to do with her." He knew I wasn't going to do anything with her that he hadn't done himself. You know, he was wonderful on that picture. He came down to Greenville and moseyed around and was there to help us. I loved doing that picture. Did you like that picture?

MIKE: There's a lot about it I liked, but certain things about it I didn't like. I thought it gave a phony impression of the South. Many people who don't know the South took it as the way things really are. Tennessee is an extremely powerful dramatist and he takes poetic license quite often. Northerners tend to believe what he writes about the South and its people is a literal picture. Just as wrongly, Europeans take his work as the prime depiction of American culture.

DUNNOCK: Well, I think *Baby Doll* is a sophisticated picture. If people do take it on its face value, then it is a disaster.

Well, I loved my old woman. I'll never forget that "greens" scene with Karl Malden and Eli Wallach! I like old women, you see. And I think Tennessee likes old women just the way Tallulah used to like old women. I think Southern people have that marvelous empathy with the young and with the old, a knowledge of life without talking about it.

MIKE: A sort of respect and admiration for your elders even if you don't agree with them.

DUNNOCK: When I was making *Sweet Bird of Youth* I said to Richard Brooks, the director—he had also directed *Cat*— "Why in the world did you cut the most beautiful speech in the world that Tennessee ever wrote for anybody?" He said, "What speech?" So I quoted the speech and he said, "Well, you know, film is a visual medium and the theatre is an auditory one." But I have the answer to anybody who criticizes Tennessee. I always quote Big Mama's speech, and I'm sure you don't remember it because you didn't play the part, but it's a wonderful speech in which she says to Brick, "Time goes by so fast. Nothin' can outrun it. Death commences too early—almost before you're half-acquainted with life—you meet with the other. . . . You know, we just got to love each other an' stay together, all of us, just as close as we can." I think that's a fantastic speech! Who could say that but Tennessee? I don't think anybody in the world could say, "Time goes by so fast. Nothin' can outrun it." It's just a special thing. You know, when I went down to Greenville to do the movie of *Baby Doll*, I took the train because I'd never been through that section of the country and I wanted to see it. I got off in Memphis, where you have to move from one railroad track to another railroad track to go South. It was very early in the morning and I went over and got myself a newspaper. And I got myself some breakfast at the counter. While I was sitting there listening to the talk of the men I opened the paper and it described a football game in the Rose Bowl, and I swear it was just as though Tennessee had written up this account! You know, the place is part of his blood. It's part of him. It's his skin. He writes that way about the South and about its people.

Another great experience was in Spoleto, where we did *The Milk Train Doesn't Stop Here Anymore.* I still feel that play has not been done yet. I feel it was a terribly, terribly exciting play, in which Tennessee wrote about something that was happening to him. Something so important, and so exciting, and so different from anything else that had ever happened to him. We did it in Spoleto and anything that one does in Spoleto is a glorious experience. Tennessee was there. It's an ideal world because you're not in a commercial world. You're in some never-never land where anything is possible. Then we came to New York. I'm not sure why it wasn't successful. I have my ideas on the subject. Everybody has his ideas, but I thought it was a most extraordinary play. And, of course, I was so excited to be

given a chance to play a bitch! You know, nobody ever sees
me as anything except a long-faced, dour person, and the
Bitch of Capri was just delicious. Wonderfully dressed, too.
And such a pleasure working with Hermione Baddeley. My
experiences with Tennessee have always been sporadic. I
was in Key West once on a vacation and Tennessee was
there at the same time. He was darling to my husband and
me. And warm. I admire him extravagantly. He's just, to
my way of thinking, the best. He's a great poet, a great
writer, and great creator of women's roles, and one of the
most compassionate people and writers. Tennessee has a
strange personal quality which makes you want to over-
protect him, which gives you a sense that he is incapable of
dealing with the mundane things of the world. I don't know
what that springs from. I'm not inclined to go to people or
take care of them. I'm not a strong egoist. I'm not made up
of star material and I have to pipe very hard to maintain my
own ego, but with Tennessee you are automatically drawn
toward him. I remember when we were on the road with
Cat in Philadelphia prior to the New York opening. There
was a lot of publicity work to be done, but no one available
to do it! Burl Ives was making a new venture, making a step
into a new world, because he had always been a personal
performer rather than an actor integrated into a play. He
was very shaky about the whole thing. Needlessly, but he
was. Barbara Bel Geddes was the other star of the play with
Ben Gazzara. They had heavy roles. A lot was demanded
of them. Well, a great many broadcasts were done early in
the morning. By "early in the morning" I mean morning
shows at nine o'clock or ten o'clock. As you know, Tennessee
likes to talk and tells a marvelous story. He was willing to
do publicity. I was corralled into going with him in the
morning. We would meet and I would make sure that he
had his grapefruit juice and that he had his three cups of
coffee, and then we would go! Tennessee was great fun to

go to these places with. He'd have fun and he'd make me feel wonderful and warm with him. I think this desire to protect him, which I'm sure is one of the worst things that could happen to him, springs from the fact that the artist finds in his writing such sensitivity, such awareness of other people. We sense and feel that it must come from his own sensitivity and his own needs, so we are constantly drawn toward wanting to protect him. Then constantly drawing back for fear that we will become so enmeshed in his personal problems that our own selves will disappear. Is that not possible? So I have never gotten too deeply involved with Tennessee, much as I would like to, for that very simple reason. But one is very able to become completely involved in the characters which Tennessee creates. That is so satisfying that you're eternally grateful to him.

MIKE: You and Tennessee had a mutual friend that you both were very close to, Tallulah Bankhead.

DUNNOCK: Oh, yes! Wonderful woman! Tallulah seemed to me to be, in a kind of curious way, the epitome of certain aspects of Southern women. I always felt that she should play *Glass Menagerie* in films. You know, I feel that Southern women should always play these parts. I get very upset when they're given to English actresses. I think that they are as peculiar as a Lancaster part would be to a Lancaster person. I felt always that Tallulah definitely should have played that particular part of Amanda. But for a person like Tallulah to move out of stardom into a great character role was very, very hard. Tallulah was always way up there in some kind of never-never land of stardom; much of it had to do with her own personal magnetism and her own personal aura. But, oh, what an actress she was! I played with her in *The Little Foxes,* not in the original production but in a later production. I also played with her in *Foolish Notion.* She was such a performer, and such a giver. If she

had had a great director she could have done anything in
the world, anything. People who saw her play Blanche
DuBois say it was brilliant. Of course, Blanche was done
well by so many different actresses. I didn't see her in that
second production of *Milk Train.* I wish I had. But Tallulah
had many aspects of the Southern woman. She had that love
of children. That love of old people. She also had a kind of
brilliance. A mind that was as sharp as a razor. Also, a kind
of lustiness. She, it seems to me, would have been marvelous
for *Milk Train.* Just absolutely marvelous. Then you've got
to get the rest of the cast. I hate to think of her not being
around! It's very upsetting. I miss her terribly. I just miss
the feeling that she's alive, you know, because she was such
an alive person. I remember Herman Shumlin asked me to
come in and see him about touring in *The Little Foxes.*
People had told me that you had to stay up all night and
play bridge with Tallulah—you had to. I was afraid of her.
I was really afraid of her. And then, when I got to do a
show with her, I found her the most understanding person
in the world. We played together one summer during the
war. I had a daughter who was nine years old at that point
and she had come home from camp. I asked Tallulah if we
could come over and swim and she said, "Yes, bring her
over." This was in the country and it was wartime. I took
her over and a colored man said to me, "Miss Bankhead says
come down to the pool alone before you bring your little
girl." So I went down to the pool. Tallulah was in there
stark naked with half a dozen people and she said, "Darling,
do I have to put my clothes on for that baby of yours?"
And I said, "Of course not." So I called Linda down and
she took one look at all these suitless people and said, "Oh!
Mommy, can I take off my suit too?" But Tallulah had that
kind of awareness of other people's conventions. She had
that sense of "I won't offend. If Millie doesn't want her
child to see me in the pool naked, I won't offend her."

MIKE: There's too little of that kind of consideration for other people nowadays.

DUNNOCK: I think Tennessee has all of this, in those fantastic roles that he writes.

MIKE: I was with Tennessee the last time he saw Tallulah. It was at a dinner party in the summer of 1965. After eating, we watched some color slides a mutual friend of theirs had taken on a trip to India. And at the end of the evening Tallulah embraced Tennessee to say goodbye. They were both happily drunk and Tallulah said, "Tennessee, you and I are the only constantly High Episcopalians I know."

DUNNOCK: The word "Episcopalian" reminds me of another occasion, just before the out-of-town opening here in New Haven of *Milk Train*. It was a very curious, strange thing that happened. His relative, Sidney Lanier, who was an Episcopalian priest, came down the aisle at the end of rehearsal when we were being given our notes. Tennessee saw him coming and suddenly rushed across the stage to him, laughingly and jokingly, yet seriously, and said, "Bless me, Father! Bless me!" And then, right there, as Tennessee knelt, Sidney Lanier put his hand on his head and gave him a blessing. It was a curious, curious thing.

INDEX